UNHOLY UNION:
A Memoir of Clergy Sexual Abuse Within the Salvation Army

UNHOLY UNION

A Memoir of Clergy Sexual
Abuse Within the Salvation Army

BUNNY STEVENS

WORDS @ WORK INK

Copyright © 2014 by Bunny Stevens

Cover and interior design by Michelle George
Edited by Kate Hanna

Scripture quotations marked (ASV) are taken from the American Standard Version.

Scripture quotations marked (NIV) are taken from the Holy Bible, New International Version®, NIV®. Copyright © 1973, 1978, 1984, 2011 by Biblica, Inc.™ Used by permission of Zondervan. All rights reserved worldwide. www.zondervan.com The "NIV" and "New International Version" are trademarks registered in the United States Patent and Trademark Office by Biblica, Inc.™

Except for where noted, all italics in book quotations have been added by Bunny Stevens.

All rights reserved. No part of this book may be reproduced or transmitted in any form or by any means whatsoever, including photocopying, recording or by any information storage and retrieval system, without written permission from the publisher and/or author.

    Stevens, Bunny.
      Unholy union : a memoir of clergy sexual abuse within
    the Salvation Army / by Bunny Stevens.
      pages cm
      Includes bibliographical references.
      LCCN 2013923594
      ISBN 978-0-9911201-0-9 (pbk.)

      1. Stevens, Bunny. 2. Sexual abuse victims--United States--Biography. 3. Sexual misconduct by clergy. 4. Salvation Army--Clergy--Biography. 5. Adult child sexual abuse victims--United States--Biography. 6. Multiple personality--Patients--United States--Biography. I. Title.

    RC560.S44S74 2014   362.883'092
                              QBI14-600007

Paperback ISBN-13 978-0-9911201-0-9 | ISBN-10 0-9911201-0-8
Kindle   ISBN-13 978-0-9911201-1-6 | ISBN-10 0-9911201-1-6
ePub   ISBN-13 978-0-9911201-2-3 | ISBN-10 0-9911201-2-4

Printed in the U.S.A.

1 3 5 7 9 10 8 6 4 2

PRAISE FOR UNHOLY UNION

Highly recommended, compelling and heart-wrenching, *Unholy Union* is the shocking story of spiritual, emotional and physical abuse in the hands of Salvation Army ministers, and ultimate victory. Bunny Stevens has, indeed, survived, thrived and "made it." God bless her for her bravery, spunk and willingness to speak—and courage to live in joy—when all her early training told her silence to the abuse was expected ... at any cost.
In reading *Unholy Union*, I cried, raged, shook my head in astonishment, and wondered where other characters are now. What happened to others whose innocence was ripped from them by those in authority, who preyed on their flock rather than shepherd, love unconditionally and humbly serve them as Christ calls?

I firmly believe that *Unholy Union* is essential reading for those who have left, or are seeking to leave, toxic religion that, far from loving God and neighbor, abuses human beings and is abhorrent to the God. A must read.

The Reverend Denise Mosher, Chapel by the Sea Presbyterian Church, Lincoln City, OR

A page turning tragedy. *Unholy Union: A Memoir of Clergy Sexual Abuse Within the Salvation Army* is about a specific organization and specific men who used their power to take sexual advantage of a specific vulnerable woman. But it is sad as hell how familiar this story is, how men and women charged with the nurture and trust of a family and flock abuse and break trust, and misrepresent and distort God. But it is not just the individual men who are dangerous. Not that we are not all vulnerable to "sin" no matter where we are, but I think Bunny's story reveals the danger of closed systems, of organizations where leaders are allowed to be infallible stars rather than human, and where checks and balances are lacking. Belief systems where some are "all good" while the rest are "lost" seem to catch vulnerable people who have a strong need to find a home where they are "in" and "saved." But they also set up "children" and "fathers" for a "fall." There has been some claim that such clergy abuse is a recent phenomenon, due to the infiltration of "liberal values" into culture and faith communities. But we can be sure that the only thing new is the feminist and Liberation Theology's understanding that the victim claim her voice and speak the truth, despite what the patriarchs and their systems demand. Also clear from this testimony is that early childhood trauma and sexual abuse creates deep wounds that require time and talent from not just any therapist. Hurrah for Bunny and her therapist for digging deep, having patience, and speaking truth.

Reverend Max Lynn, St. John's Presbyterian Church, Berkeley

It happens in Pakistan, Japan, India, the Middle East, Africa and yes, in the United States of America. The systematic subjugation and sexual exploitation of women continues unabated. Sometimes it's in the name of God, sometimes in the name of nothing more than narcissistic self-gratification. Bunny Stevens' *Unholy Union* offers an intensely personal insight into one woman's experience with men she knew and trusted. Every day around the world 200,000 daughters are born, and they are all at risk for this kind of degradation and abuse.

Kevin Renner, author, *In Search of Fatherhood: Stories from Women Around the World*

Bunny Stevens, in *Unholy Union*, has shown us, with great honesty, sensitivity and feeling, how lasting damage results when authority figures we are taught to trust use that trust to sexually exploit the vulnerability of both children and adults. The reader can walk in her shoes as she endures these exceedingly painful violations, but we are also inspired by her having found the strength to speak out against these wrongs as part of her healing journey.

Peter Rutter MD, Psychiatrist, Jungian Analyst, author of *Sex in the Forbidden Zone: When Men in Power—Therapists, Doctors, Clergy, Teachers, and Others— Betray Women's Trust*

For Douglas—You were my first
For Jason—You were my biggest
For the two of you together—because you are the
finest thing I've ever done.

For Claire Imeson
Because you always answer your phone.
Which means you are either a very good friend or you're crazy.
Or a perfect combination of the two!

For Dennis U. Evans, M.D.
From all of us:
Kevin, Curtis, Phyllis Ann, Claudia,
Josie, Bunny Too, Delia, Charlotte,
Star, Rose, Phillip and the babies.
And from Bunny.
Because you extended yourself.
You figured it out.
You stayed the course.
You loved us.

For Laurie de Vera
Child of my heart.

Table of Contents

Accomplices xiii
A Few Words Before We Begin xv
Chapter 1: Silent No More 1

PART I
A CHILDHOOD

Chapter 2: In the Beginning, There Was Daddy 5
Chapter 3: And Then There Was Aunt Dolores 9
Chapter 4: Of Brothers, Big and Small 15
Chapter 5: On Our Own in a Pretty House 22
Chapter 6: The Watcher 27
Chapter 7: Too Young and Not Ready 34
Chapter 8: A Bigger Move This Time 37
Chapter 9: Thanks to Mr. Froehlicher and Miss Buehler ... 40
Chapter 10: Captain and Mrs. Irby of the Salvation Army ... 42
Chapter 11: Pete Copes … Or Doesn't 46
Chapter 12: The Dog Bite 49
Chapter 13: High School Years 52
Chapter 14: Preparing for Ministry 60
Chapter 15: Community College and Boys 65
Chapter 16: A Further Word About Dissociative Identity Disorder 69

PART II
BETRAYAL

Chapter 17: John 75
Chapter 18: John's Family 79
Chapter 19: Sex in the Forbidden Zone 86
Chapter 20: Did it Really Happen? 94
Chapter 21: Please, God, Make Him Stop 97
Chapter 22: What About Peggy? 100
Chapter 23: Rich Love 103
Chapter 24: Together More and More 107
Chapter 25: In a Secret Place 113
Chapter 26: During Worship 116
Chapter 27: Getting Away 119
Chapter 28: Finally, I'm a Cadet at Training School 123
Chapter 29: Mind, Body, and Soul in Action for Good 126
Chapter 30: A Growing Suspicion 130
Chapter 31: It All Comes Tumbling Down 132
Chapter 32: Punishment Sure and Swift 138
Chapter 33: The Salvation Army's Reaction to Reported
        Clergy Sexual Abuse 147
Chapter 34: Joining the Upton Family in Phoenix 151
Chapter 35: Intimate Knowledge 158
Chapter 36: Who Was Lincoln Upton? 163
Chapter 37: My Complicity 166
Chapter 38: What About Mother? 169
Chapter 39: The Uptons Leave for Portland 172
Chapter 40: Auntie Rita of the Morality Police 175
Chapter 41: The Emotional Toll 181
Chapter 42: Help Located at an Address Near Me 184
Chapter 43: Captain and Mrs. Riley 190
Chapter 44: Another Victim 194
Chapter 45: The Lieutenant Commissioner Comes Calling ... 198
Chapter 46: Considering Change 201
Chapter 47: The Last Time I Saw Linc 205
Chapter 48: Going Back to Salinas 208

PART III
HEALING

Chapter 49: Salinas Again 213
Chapter 50: The Past Comes Calling 217
Chapter 51: Voices From Out of the Past 221
Chapter 52: Two Beautiful Boys 224
Chapter 53: Did You Know You Were My Hero? 232
Chapter 54: A Beginning 236
Chapter 55: Boundaries 240
Chapter 56: Finally, a Diagnosis That Makes Sense 244
Chapter 57: Everyone's Invited 248
Chapter 58: Object Constancy 253
Chapter 59: Transference Issues 262
Chapter 60: Without a Price to Pay 266
Chapter 61: Drawing on Both Sides of the Brain 269
Chapter 62: Exorcising John 278
Chapter 63: And Then Linc 287
Chapter 64: Naming Names at Last … 291

PART IV
SEEKING JUSTICE

Chapter 65: Remember Me? 299
The Last Chapter 359
Photos 361
Author Bio 367

Accomplices

I WOULD VENTURE TO SAY THAT LITTLE OF VALUE IS ACCOMPLISHED IN A vacuum. There are always those who add to, question, challenge, encourage, caution, listen, advise and then get out of the way. Some of these people in my life are mentioned in the dedicatory page. Many are a part of the narrative itself. And then there are a few others:

<u>June Silva</u>. A friendship that started with four pregnancies (two for you and two for me!) over an exhausting 18 month period. Your Anthony and Chad. My Douglas and Jason. Camping, church, amusement parks, milking goats, growing organic vegetables way before it was chic, and even making time for the occasional girls' weekend getaway. In addition to all that, you always believed I could do anything I set my mind to. You've humored me and encouraged me and stood by when I jumped off yet another proverbial cliff. You've never said, "Enough already!" What a friend you've been.

<u>Barb Elliott</u>. I remember when I first saw you at church soon after I moved to the Oregon Coast. I thought, "She's beautiful and smart and talented and involved in everything. I'm sure she has all the friends she needs." So I hung back. When I finally got brave enough to make friendly overtures, I found out that you are beautiful and smart and talented and involved in everything and you had just enough room for one more friend. We eat and drink and talk and savor. You were my first reader. You're the reason the manuscript

was not shredded when I could see no value in it. You believed in its value long before I did.

<u>Kevin Renner</u>. After I read your column in *The Oregonian*, I emailed you—never actually expecting a response. After all, you were a published author. Who was I? Your response was immediate. You agreed to read sample chapters. And then you met with me and encouraged me to pursue publication. You made introductions and referrals. You've stayed in touch. You've done everything you said you would do. You are the real deal, Kevin: a helping hand with an open heart.

<u>Books by the Sea</u>. We've read and discussed and talked and debated and occasionally we've agreed to disagree. All the things a good book club should do. And then you listened to my first timid, mumbled declaration that I was pursuing publication of my own book. You looked at me with admiration. Your faces gave me the courage to begin to own my story in a way that has enabled me to go public with it. What a group.

<u>Chris Cournoyer</u>. A true believer.

<u>Kate Hanna, Editor,</u> and <u>Michelle George, Designer:</u> I've always wondered why authors invariably feel they must acknowledge their editors. And now I know why. My amazing editor took a multitude of squiggles and ambiguities and grammar faux pas, tossed them aside, and polished what remained into a product worthy of the word "Book." And then she handed that product to my equally amazing designer, who lovingly and gently massaged and tweaked until the end result was worthy of the descriptor "Beautiful Book." I went into this process knowing that publishing is akin to giving birth. Thank you, Kate and Michelle. This is one beautiful baby.

A Few Words Before We Begin

THE STORY YOU ARE ABOUT TO READ IS BOTH A MEMOIR—A RECORD OF events based on the writer's personal knowledge—and a documentary—events presented in a nonfiction but dramatic form. It is a memoir because it happened to me—all of it. Every sentence is based on my firsthand, personal knowledge. It is a documentary because it is nonfiction and because the dramatic events I recount to you are supported by others—witnesses to the drama.

As you will soon learn, I was sexually victimized by my father while little more than a toddler. If you have seen the very troubling—and yet compelling—movie *Precious*, you know the core issue in my story. Because my mother discovered my father and me in the midst of one of the incidents you will soon read about, he left, never to return. Paradoxically, from that moment, my mother—who had never been loving or nurturing—blamed me for the loss of her husband and saw me as the sexual predator a baby could never be. Innocent, so very innocent in every meaning of the word, and yet blamed and despised. That was the setup for what came later.

When I was a teen, I found a place of safety, of release—a place where I imagined I had regained what had been taken from me. I felt seen, valued, capable. I felt whole. I found this place within the local corps of the Salvation Army. You will read about the place this organization held in my family's life—it was our church, our recreation, our community. From an early age, I aspired to full-time service to God as an ordained officer in the Salvation Army. From ages 12 to 17, I attended church at the Salvation Army on my own.

My mother's life was so far from what she had imagined it might be, she was so caught up in ferocious disappointment, that she gave up any idea of a higher power to whom she was responsible. She was lost in blaming, confused violence, and isolation. My two brothers were no longer interested in church. It became mine alone. I thrived. It was a total escape from the tragic, predictable chaos of home.

My corps officers (ordained clergy) during those years were Captain and Mrs. Carl Irby. You will meet them too. They were everything to me—the loving parents I never had, the spiritual leaders who introduced me to a God who was not punishing or vindictive, and the teachers who challenged me to grow and mature in my knowledge of the Bible and then be the youth leader who mentored the younger ones. I was the perfect candidate for all of it.

What I discovered with the Irbys was that I was bright, articulate, and a natural leader. They saw in me all the ingredients necessary to fulfill my dream to be like them—to be an ordained Salvation Army officer.

Later, I would experience the dark side of the Salvation Army—a side riddled with predators who victimized the innocent and vulnerable in their care. Not one, but two ordained Salvation Army officers sexually used me over a period of time. Manipulated, blindsided, and then threatened with violence, I was caught in the sticky web of their debauchery, greed, egoism, and deceit. The Salvation Army's response, when the sexual activity became known, was to reenact what my mother had done 17 years earlier. They blamed me. I was seen as no longer "good" and unworthy to serve in their organization. I was expelled with the order to "tell no one." It is important you understand that I was as innocent when I was 20 years old as I had been when I was three.

In reading my story of trauma and betrayal, you will need to understand the psychiatric syndrome Dissociative Identity Disorder (DID). Formerly known as Multiple Personality Disorder, DID is a defense mechanism by which a child is able to absent herself from her own body to escape a reality that would be too horrific for her to be fully present for. I began dissociating when my father was sexual with me. Because of my mother's ongoing violence to me and my brothers—especially my younger brother—dissociation became a way of coping with my own trauma and of distancing myself from the violence she visited on my younger brother when I could do nothing to protect him.

One of the ramifications of dissociation is "switching." When differentiated parts of the psyche take on a life of their own—with their own memories, their own interests, their own histories, and their own specialties within the personality system—they can and do demand their own time "out" in control of the host body. This was aptly portrayed in the iconic movie *Three Faces of Eve*. I have dealt with this all my life. Interestingly, when confronted by someone who obviously knows me but of whom I have no knowledge or memory, it has been universally positive. A common comment has been, "Bunny, I will never forget what you did for me." So it seems that even when I was not aware of it, I was doing good.

But what part does Dissociative Identity Disorder play in my being vulnerable to sexual predation by two Salvation Army officers? DID has the disadvantage of setting the sufferer up to be "blindsided." Because there may be no organized, congruent memory of past victimization, the person with DID does not see danger signs, there is no early warning system, and she can easily be victimized again. There is also the fact that, as is true in my case, there can be split-off child parts within the host personality. These child "alters" are stuck in a state of innocence and naiveté that makes them extremely vulnerable to predation by anyone they see as an authority figure. Again, as in my case, they may be willing to do anything required to avoid physical or psychological repercussions brought about by disobedience.

At appropriate points throughout the telling of my story, I will refer to the book *Diagnosis and Treatment of Multiple Personality Disorder* by Frank W. Putnam, M.D. I will use these references for the sake of clarity only. I purchased this book shortly after I was diagnosed with DID. I put it aside and did not read it. At that time, I was afraid of what I might find out about the disorder and the long-term prognosis for healing.

And so, when I originally wrote my story in 1992, I did not

include any information on DID. I hoped I could tell the story without it. In revisiting the whole issue after the recent completion of my therapy, I found that I must include this information in the story. DID is such an integral part of who I was when these betrayals took place. When I decided that I had to include the information on my dissociative disorder, I looked at Dr. Putnam's book for the first time and found that the information therein illuminates the struggles begun within my family of origin—incest and violence—the relative calm when the stressors were reduced during my junior and senior high schools years, and then the volatile re-eruption of dissociation as a coping mechanism when clergy reenacted the sexual betrayal originated by my father.

Dr. Putnam's book did not inform the writing of this book, but I believe it definitely has enriched it. When added to my subjective experiential retelling, Dr. Putnam's objective, scientific lens provides clarity and validation. It is in this light that I include references when appropriate.

Since my father was lost to me at a time when, for good or for evil, he was the parent to whom I was bonded, I was set up for a lifetime of trying to identify a man on whom I could fulfill all my unrealized hopes of a good father.

You will come to know that throughout my childhood, my mother was totally without functioning boundaries—she stated that she "owned us," that we were hers to do with as she pleased, and we learned that absolute submission to authority was imperative to survival. We obeyed without question. When we missed a beat, we were beaten. So I had no idea that I could say no to anyone in any position of authority over me.

A basic teaching in the Salvation Army as I was growing up reinforced my mother's position on obedience. As children and young people, we were enlisted as Junior Soldiers in our corps. We signed a pledge that we would obey our corps officers without question. Because of the military model on which the organization is based, we were taught that unquestioned obedience was part of being a soldier in God's army. We were told that our officers were over us in the Lord, and obeying them was a part of obeying God.

My DID, the early loss of the father whom I loved but who was sexual with me, my mother's violence and projected blame, my lack of knowledge that I had any right to my own body, and the Salvation Army's own teachings on obedience fashioned the perfect storm of vulnerability to sexual predation.

This is why I can say that I was as innocent at 20 as I was at three. I was innocent of the knowledge of sex—I had a healthy interest in the opposite sex and had many boyfriends by this time, but I was the proverbial "good" girl—I had made up my mind that God expected me to be chaste and celibate until I was married. I never had sex with my boyfriends, and, in fact, I never participated willingly in a sexual relationship until years later when I was engaged to the man I would later marry. When I had a choice, I remained true to my own vow of chastity.

And so I was innocent in thought, in motive, and in action when my odyssey of sexual slavery to the perverse fantasies of two ordained clergy, who were both old enough to be my father, began. I did love John (you'll soon meet him, and then you'll meet Linc, the second clergy to sexually abuse me), but I loved him in the same way any girl loves the good father she has longed for, and he used my platonic idealization of him to prey on my innocent naiveté.

I never saw it coming. I was first blindsided and then stood dumb like the proverbial "deer in the headlights." I dissociated; I cried; on my knees, I begged God to make him stop. Ultimately, without exception, I did what he told me to do like the "good little girl" my mother had taught me to be.

And now, *Unholy Union*: a memoir; a documentary.

UNHOLY UNION:
A Memoir of Clergy Sexual Abuse Within the Salvation Army

CHAPTER 1

Silent No More

"I found it difficult to fathom why nobody, including myself, had done anything to stop this man. It began to dawn on me that the most mysterious dimension of this kind of betrayal might *not* be the fact that a certain number of men would always try to sexually exploit women in relationships of trust; this phenomenon, although unpleasant to acknowledge, is rather understandable. It was far more difficult to understand why so many of us, bystanders and victims alike, had remained silent in the face of these violations."

Sex in the Forbidden Zone **by Peter Rutter, M.D.**

DOES THE MOMENT ALWAYS, INEVITABLY COME WHEN ONE MUST TELL THE truth? When personal privacy no longer matters ... When protecting someone else's reality does not make sense any longer ... When the need to disclose, uncover, un-muzzle, unmask overcomes all of the commands to keep the secret ... remain silent ... tell no one?

I cannot say if that moment comes for everyone who has

suffered. I can say that moment has come for me. I must tell. The need to tell has become palpable. It is an ache. It consumes. It wakes me. It whispers in my ear when I would sleep. I must tell.

Unholy Union is my story. It is the story of a young girl who loved. Who trusted. Who wanted to be good. Who heard a call to serve others. Who entered seminary to fulfill that calling. A young girl who was unmarried, called by God, and pregnant with her minister's child.

How does such a thing happen? Was I bad? Did I set out to ruin him? Before the story ended, we were both ruined. The church determined that I was unfit to serve God in any capacity. He lost his vocation. His family suffered. Terribly.

I lived. Barely. Betrayed by the organization that might have helped. Exiled. Labeled.

I was defiled. I could be thrown away. I was disposable. I had no value. I was told that the church was for "good" people. I was shunned. Alone.

I am telling my story now because my conscience will no longer allow me to do otherwise. In order to find some meaning in the suffering I endured then—the suffering that continues—I will tell. My life was forever changed because of what happened to me at the hands of the man I trusted above all others. He was my intermediary, my way to God. He was everything I wanted to be. He was my mentor. He was my ideal.

He raped me. And then told me God wanted him to do it.

The girl I was then believed him. I must tell her story. She must be heard. When she has been heard, maybe the woman I am now can finally grieve her loss of innocence, celebrate her heroism, and embrace her miraculous spirit of survival.

PART I

A CHILDHOOD

CHAPTER 2

In the Beginning, There Was Daddy

"Dear God,
There are no words for the depth of my love for this child.
I pray for her care and her protection.
I surrender her into Your hands.
Please, dear God, send Your angels to bless and surround her always.
May she be protected from the darkness of our times."

Illuminata by Marianne Williamson

THE AIR WAS WARM AND CLOSE AND MUSTY. THE SMELLS OF LIFE. MY daddy was the author of that life. As I walked through the long aisles of incubators full of eggs and warming trays squirming with fluffy baby chicks, I felt my daddy's calloused hand holding my pudgy, three-year-old fist securely. Daddy was in charge in the hatchery. Our family lived in the apartment upstairs, but I felt most at home downstairs in the hatchery with Daddy.

I was fascinated by the baby chicks. I do not remember being told that they were fragile, but I saw the careful, tender movements of Daddy's hands as he adjusted the lights, checked the feeders, and primed the water bottles.

"There, there," he would soothe, "don't crowd. There's plenty for everyone." The voice he used for them was soft. A caress. I remember that voice.

When I was born, Daddy insisted that my name be Bunny. My mother wanted a more sensible name. Bunny could always be a nickname. My father won that argument. Bunny is my given name. I am grateful to Daddy that my name is not Bonita or Bernice—my mother's choices. It is Bunny. It is a connection to that one person to whom I felt special, chosen, selected. That's the way I felt then … when I was little … when I was safe in my daddy's world. His arms. The touch of his hands. The feel of the overalls he always wore. The man-smell of him that was different from any other smell. It was intoxicating to me then. The sound of his voice. A voice that called to me like music. Delicious. Heady. Perfect. My daddy.

Daddy was as gentle with me as he was with the baby chicks. He talked to me as we walked through the hatchery. "Don't worry, Pumpkin, you will always be my little girl. Did you know that I always wanted a little girl of my own?"

Being with him, I was content, complete. We lived in San Leandro in the Greater San Francisco Bay Area, but my world was my daddy. My world was peaceful, perfect. It was 1944, and the rest of the world was at war. But in my world, with my daddy, I was safe and loved.

My mother ruled the apartment upstairs. When I was with my mother, I remember feeling trapped. Trapped in her anger that I could not understand, could never appease. I remember anxiously listening for Mother, staying aware of her, trying to anticipate her moods in order to stay out of the way of her anger. I listened so I could be good. So I could be safe. So I wouldn't be hit. So I wouldn't be hated. I don't remember wanting her to love me. I had my daddy. I just didn't want to be hurt.

My older brother was a part of that world too. David was one year older than I was—I have always called him Buzz. I don't remember a lot about him when I was three. Maybe that is because my father was so much the center of my universe. He had always wanted a daughter and had freely admitted this when my brother was born. I think his open, unabashed love for me at that time bound me to him in a relationship that was so all-consuming that I had very little time or attention for anyone else. I was alive only when I was with him. I lived for that time.

My father read comic books … Captain Marvel. At night he would read to me. I do not remember Buzz ever being included in this special time with Daddy. I don't remember ever feeling that I had to compete for his attention. In my memory, the picture is of just the two of us.

Because the story I am telling you is true, I must tell the truth, even about Daddy. Especially about Daddy. I wish the truth were that he was always good and kind … that he was the father that every little girl needs and deserves … that he was someone I could depend on to be there for me throughout my growing up. But that is not the truth.

There was a last time with Daddy.

He was reading to me in bed, his bed. I felt warm and secure sitting on his lap, his arms around me. I knew I was special to him. I knew that I pleased him, without trying, without effort. As I lay my head against his chest, I felt his soft, worn pajamas against my cheek, and the air up close was like a part of him that I could breathe in and hold inside myself. He was mine. In a way that nothing and no one would ever be again. He was mine. Only mine. And I was his. Only his. Nothing else existed for me.

I remember my mother entering the room. The room is dark. I am in bed with Daddy. My nightgown is gone. My panties are gone. Daddy's pajamas are gone too. Daddy is holding me against him. I feel his skin against my skin. I like the feel of him against me. I do not remember him hurting me. I remember him holding me close and talking to me in that softest of voices, his breath against my face, against my neck, against my ear. Tenderly. I remember him touching me gently, caressing me, kissing me. I remember wanting him to do it. If I should have known, somehow, that what was happening was wrong, I did not. I loved him. I wanted to be his little girl. Whatever that meant. Whatever that required.

My mother's voice is angry. This is not unusual. She was angry about a lot of things every day. But her reaction to me that night, the hard set of her face, the way she touched me—not so much with anger as with distaste, disgust—instilled in me the cold bewildering knowledge that I had done something wrong, very wrong. Something so wrong that Daddy was gone and would never come back.

I remember being in the bathroom that night. All the lights are on. It is very bright. The walls are white. The glare of the light makes the walls even whiter. I am sitting on the toilet. The toilet is white. But in the water, in the white toilet, in the bright white bathroom, there is red. There is red and it is spreading. I am sitting on the toilet. Is the red, then, coming out of me? I do not remember hurting. I do not remember pain. I remember being afraid. So very afraid. And being unable to ask any questions that might have answered my fear.

Daddy is gone. And my mother is closed off from me in a more complete and frightening way than ever before. I am totally alone. At three years of age, I am without an ally. Alone and helpless, I begin trying to win the love of the only meaningful adult left in my life—my mother. My angry, punishing, vindictive, incomprehensible mother.

CHAPTER 3

And Then There Was Aunt Dolores

"A worthy woman, who can find? For her price is far above rubies."

Proverbs 31:10 *American Standard Version* (ASV)

WITH MY FATHER GONE, MY MOTHER MOVED US TO MODESTO, IN the central valley of California, where her sister Dolores lived. My Aunt Dolores was a widow with eight children ranging in age from eight to eighteen. We moved in with them in a big, old, ramshackle two-story house on F Street, near the train yard.

I don't remember missing my father. It is as though when I knew he wouldn't be back, a door closed in my mind and he no longer existed for me. I don't remember ever listening for his voice or his step. He was gone—everything about him was gone. His voice. His smell. His clothes were no longer in the closet. His work jacket disappeared from the hook on which it had hung inside the kitchen door. Most apparent of all was the absence of his work shoes. They no longer occupied their place on the newspapers near the backdoor. His shoes that had born his personal imprint even when they were empty of his body. His worn brown work shoes, at a glance, spoke of his presence or absence. They were gone.

I think it would have been too painful for me to imagine Daddy could come back if he wanted to. So instead of thinking of him as existing somewhere else, I thought of him as forever gone. I don't think I could have accepted the fact that he existed somewhere, but not for me. I don't remember anguishing about it. I don't remember asking my mother about it. I don't remember her saying anything about it. I never cried. About Daddy.

Aunt Dolores was a short, squat, homely woman. She would have been in her mid-thirties when we lived with her this first time. Her mouth caved in on gums already empty. Her faded red hair was cut bluntly at the chin line, her fleshy face was freckled and weathered, and her small eyes were sunk deep into the wrinkles that already wreathed her face. She wore loose-fitting, print dresses that exposed her oversized upper arms, on which large flaps of loose skin hung.

Inside this coarse body was an enormous heart so generous and genuine that the rough packaging was instantly unimportant. I could not pronounce her name, so she became "Lorse" to my brothers and me—a love name that would last her lifetime. She smiled most of the time. She laughed loud, smoked Wings cigarettes, and drank strong black coffee.

Because there was nothing hidden about her, because she had no secrets I had to guess, because she had no unwritten rules I had to anticipate, I loved her. To me she was beautiful.

Lorse was without material possessions of any significant nature. I remember transients coming to the backdoor and asking for handouts. Lorse would open a can of Campbell's soup for each of them. I never heard her criticize these men who were living off the charity of others little better off than they were. Something in her was kind and compassionate in the most offhand, natural way. I am sure she never thought she had done anything that deserved gratitude. She just did it and then went back to what she was doing without so much as a backward glance.

The house on F Street was an old derelict. A few scabs of paint still clung in haphazard fashion to the otherwise bare exterior boards, screens were missing or torn, and where windows were broken, cardboard filled bare frames. The yard was hard-packed dirt with an occasional scraggly weed too stubborn to die. The house was, in many ways, like Lorse herself—old before its time and hard used, but honest, open, and welcoming. Nothing was hidden. I was at home there.

My mother worked outside the home. Lorse took in washing and ironing and stayed at home with the kids. From my perspective, as the next to youngest in a mix of eleven children, I was immersed in a tornado of confused activity that seemed to whirl outward in all directions. My mother had exercised absolute control over the environment in our previous home. Lorse seemed to espouse an attitude of nonintervention, as long as no one was bleeding. Of my eight cousins, six were boys. Many were old enough to be building cars; some played on local baseball teams; we all went to church together. This was a family in a much different sense than what I had been used to. I felt at ease. I did not feel responsible for anything during this time.

Since my brothers and I were several years younger than the cousins, we were indulged and petted by everyone. We were allowed to tag along wherever they went. If we needed a boost over a fence or a hand up, it was always available. They accepted us as a part of the clan, and no questions were ever asked. I was never afraid that someone would be angry with me. I don't remember ever getting yelled at or being hit. The cousins seemed to welcome us much as their mother had. Several years later, we would live together again ... and there would be problems, ... but during this first experience of being a "family," I remember being happy.

All of the kids slept in a couple of bedrooms upstairs. The first floor of the house was the kitchen, dining room, and living room. Lorse never seemed burdened or grudging. She stood in the middle of all this and life flowed through her and into everyone and everything she touched.

I remember Sunday mornings, when all of us went to church. We walked the few blocks to the church building. I remember summer. Hot summer. Even in midmorning it would already be hot enough to make us sweat in our stiffly-starched church clothes. In the mid-1940s, there was a sense of community in small towns like Modesto. We would pass other families doing the same things we were doing—walking to church, playing in sprinklers, choosing sides for a baseball game in the school yard. We would smell bacon frying and hear screen doors slamming as mothers called to children. In the park we would see families settling in for a day out-of-doors. I felt a part of it all. I was not afraid.

We attended the Salvation Army's church in Modesto. The Salvation Army had been a part of our family history for several generations. Grandparents and aunts had given their lives as missionaries and ministers through the Salvation Army. Founded by William Booth in 1840 in London to minister to the poor and disadvantaged in God's name, the Salvation Army is set up on a military model. Ministers are officers and have ranks much like military personnel would.

My Aunt Frances—another of my mother's sisters—was an officer who died of leukemia while serving as the director of a Salvation Army orphanage in Hawaii during the Second World War. She was given the choice of returning to the mainland to die near family, but she would not. She never retired or quit. The Army has an expression for those who die in service. Aunt Frances was "Promoted to Glory."

The Salvation Army Corps in Modesto was housed in a small, white frame building just a few blocks from the business district. We loved Sunday mornings. Church was fun. Some of the cousins played in the band. I just liked the noise and the stories and all the people who knew and loved Lorse. She was like a star in the middle of some grand production. That's the way it seemed to me. I was always proud to be with her.

As soon as church was over, we took our Sunday shoes off for the walk home. The dirt was warm between our toes. We were free. Carefree.

Lorse fixed French toast after church on Sunday. She would coax a banquet for 13 out of a couple of loaves of Rainbow bread, a few eggs, a quart of milk, and an old coffee can full of bacon grease. I loved to watch her do it. Maybe because Daddy's leaving had left such a big hole in my life, the love I felt for Lorse was so intense that it was painful. I sometimes felt it would suffocate me. I do not remember my mother at all. She was there. I know she was. But I don't remember her. I remember Lorse. I soaked up the warm feeling of fullness that surrounded her. She wasn't mine in the same way that Daddy had been mine. But she was there.

Joe was 18 and the oldest of the cousins. Jerome was 17, Charlie was 16, Gilbert was 15, Alvin was 12, Cherrill was 10, Billy was 9, and Lei Lani was 8. Most of them had blond hair and blue eyes, and I thought all of them were beautiful.

Much of the time I spent with my cousins was dominated by Cherrill. Throughout my childhood she would remain a significant influence on me. Because she was several years older than I was and had the same outgoing personality that her mother had, I idolized her. I remember her taking time with me, in spite of friends who always wanted her attention. There were bunk beds in the room where we slept, and Cherrill and I shared one of the narrow bunks. She never seemed to think I was stupid or too young. She explained a lot of things I didn't care anything about—like where babies came from—and she taught me the first prayers I ever knew. She helped me name the baby doll I received for Christmas that year—Phyllis Ann. The most beautiful name I had ever heard.

Alvin engineered most of the group projects that we were involved in. He was the self-proclaimed leader of the seven younger kids. I can still see him in the overalls that hung loosely on his stringy body, his blond hair sticking out in irritated tufts, his face dwarfed by the huge bandage covering the nose broken by a bat that sailed loose from someone's hands during a sandlot baseball game. He was everything a good leader should be.

One of the most elaborate schemes we ever carried out was a tunnel that we dug from our backyard, under the back fence, under the alley, and into the junkyard that faced the opposite street. I remember how Alvin swore all of us to secrecy about the tunnel. When we were finished for the day, he would cover the entrance with a complicated camouflage of cardboard boxes, old feed sacks, and broken fruit crates. I don't know how the tunnel was discovered, but I do remember the day the police came to the door and talked to Lorse. The tunnel was destroyed. For years I fantasized about the tunnel. A part of me still does. While we were digging it, it seemed like we could do anything. We were powerful. There was nothing we could not do. We could escape from the limitations of our world. The tunnel was ours. It was a way out. And a way back in.

CHAPTER 4

Of Brothers, Big and Small

"... Am I my brother's keeper?"

Genesis 4:9 ASV

My mother adopted my little brother while we lived on F Street. Almost by accident. Pete's birth mother dropped Pete off, asking Mother to babysit for a few days. She never came back. I remember Cherrill explaining to me that Pete wasn't my real brother because he didn't come out of my mother's stomach. I was three years old at the time and had no idea what she was talking about. I never questioned the nature of my relationship with Pete. I knew he was adopted, but since I was too young to have any idea what difference that should make, he was just my little brother. Pete and I became the "kids" in the family. Buzz was only 13 months older than I was, but he seemed to enjoy an elevated status. He always seemed much older than his years. My mother treated him as though he were.

As young children, Pete and I developed an affinity for each other that would last throughout our growing up and into adulthood. As I understand it now, my mother looked on me as though I were flawed because of my femaleness. I had the ability to "ruin" people simply because of that one characteristic. A characteristic I could do nothing about. On the other hand, Pete was flawed because he came from "bad stock." His birth mother slept around. And, of course, that was something Pete had no way of remedying. Throughout our growing up, Pete and I had in common the fact that our mother looked upon us as something to be fixed. At any cost.

The very fact that our mother saw us as flawed was, in and of itself, the reality that would color everything else that happened to us. Our perceptions of ourselves, our fear of the rest of the world as being a dangerous place, our lack of trust, our feelings of trying to be what she wanted us to be, and the foreseeable rage we felt because we could never do that. She was asking something we could not do. We could not change who or what we were. The feeling of being wrong was maddening. We felt like trash that she would throw away if she could. Since she could not—or would not—throw us away, she made the reformation of us her life's mission. This could never work. I think Pete and I would have done what she wanted if we could have figured out in our child minds what that was. We only knew we were wrong in a deep and inherent way. My mother saw our lack of response to her rages as stubbornness. Pete and I were merely stunned—never knowing what to do, we cowered before her mutely and were paralyzed. This only made her more livid. And more determined.

Buzz, on the other hand, seemed to be separated from Pete and me as "her little man." She called him the "man of the house" from the day my father left. He would have been four years old at the time. And so Buzz had his own particular burden to bear. In a different way, expected to act and be something that was an impossibility.

I remember feeling separated from Buzz, and I remember fleeting moments of deep, dark resentment toward him—the favored one. Twice while we lived with Lorse on F Street, I threw things at Buzz. Not childish acts. Acts intended to harm. The first time, a group of us was playing in the backyard. I picked up an old cast iron stove lid with the tool intended for that purpose and looking at Buzz, I flung the lid at him, hitting him in the forehead. I don't remember the feeling that went with the act. Buzz ended up with a gash on his forehead, and I was severely reprimanded. I don't remember any physical punishment; ... I don't remember being beaten while we lived with Lorse. Maybe my mother felt enough support from Lorse that beatings weren't her immediate response when something went wrong.

The other time I lashed out at Buzz, some of us were playing upstairs in the house. I remember bouncing on one of the beds. I remember feeling murderous rage at Buzz. I have no idea why. I picked up a pair of scissors and threw them with everything that was in my three-year-old body—all my physical strength and all the energy of the rage I was feeling. The scissors hit Buzz in the eyebrow and blood gushed out. This time he was taken to the hospital for stitches. I remember feeling remorse this time. I remember feeling how wrong the act was, and I remember crying uncontrollably because I did not know how badly Buzz was hurt.

While my mother was gone with Buzz, Lorse talked to me and told me that I must never do anything like that again. I remember her telling me that I might have blinded or killed him. I don't know how much of this I understood, but I remember the conversation, and I remember feeling very, very sad. Buzz was my brother. I remember not wanting to lose him. When he came back, I remember feeling enormously relieved. He was not gone forever. I had not done that evil to another important part of my family. I never did anything like that again. What I apparently learned was that I didn't want to lose him. I didn't want to lose again.

On many occasions while we were growing up, Buzz used his influence with Mother to spare me a punishment or to at least ameliorate one. He literally stepped between the two of us at times so my mother would have to hit him if she wanted to get to me. He was larger than life to me on those occasions. He was my big brother. He was willing to sacrifice his own safety to protect mine. He never cried, and I don't remember him having much to say in these situations. He had the ability to stare her down. If that old rule about "whoever blinks first loses," applied, Buzz did not blink. Mother blinked. She would turn away, hesitate briefly, and then walk away. I think Buzz stepping into the picture may have provided her with a sanity check. She saw herself, at least briefly, as out of control. He was, after all, the other "adult" in the house. What he reflected back to her on those occasions mattered because of the role she herself had assigned him.

I don't ever remember Buzz comforting me. I don't think he could have touched me in kindness or explained my mother's actions to me. He was a "man" after all. The role assigned to him meant that he could display no weakness or tenderness. He could intercede, but only in a stoic, manly way.

I remember a particular time when I was being interrogated by Mother. She was demanding answers, and as was common in these cases, I was speechless. The crises centered on a pair of shoes. The soles on my shoes had worn out, but I had not told Mother about it because we never knew how she would react when something was damaged. Usually, even if it were a case of routine wear and tear, we were blamed as though we had done something intentional to make her life more difficult. So I concealed the shoes from my mother.

I remember Buzz noticing the sole of my shoe flapping loosely as we walked home from our school bus stop. I told him I didn't want Mother to know because I didn't want her to worry about buying me new shoes. We were constantly berated for costing her too much—another frightening quandary. We could do our best, but some things were beyond our young abilities to fathom and remedy. I don't remember him saying anything to me—I don't remember any advice being asked for or offered. He just listened.

As I write this, I am remembering that Buzz was only that mere 13 months older than I was. How did he handle the pressure that was placed on him—by Mother, who expected adult behavior, and by me, for whom he felt responsible without my ever asking? I do not remember ever asking him to help me with Mother. Perhaps that was part of the miracle of the deliverance he sometimes provided—it came unbidden.

But back to the worn out shoes: Having come across the shoes, Mother had called me into the kitchen and asked me repeatedly to tell her why I had not told her that my shoes were worn out. She went on to tell me that she knew I had done it—worn them when the soles were virtually gone—to shame her publicly. To openly humiliate her as a mother who did not provide the basics for her children. I knew I had no such motive. But I could not speak up on my own behalf. I could see her working herself into a rage, and I was too terrified to speak. I still believe that if I had opened my mouth to explain, she would have slapped me against the wall for making excuses.

There was no path open to me except to wait for the inevitable—the interrogation that would escalate into a rage, followed by a beating. The terror on this particular occasion was exacerbated by the fact that this prelude went on for so long. She had repeatedly called me into the kitchen and then sent me back into my room to "think about it" and admit that I had intentionally tried to humiliate her. As far as I can remember, I never said a word. It's difficult to say whether this made matters worse. Sometimes when we did not respond, she took our speechlessness as defiance.

This time she seemed to just be biding her time, and I know that she felt justified in what she was doing. She believed what she was accusing me of. No matter what the issue, she attributed to me the most devious motives ... never seeing that I was absolutely dumbfounded by the accusations and unable to respond because I did not even understand the convoluted thinking she was ascribing to me. I was, in fact, a child. A child who loved the mother she feared. A child who wanted nothing so much as to please her mother. A child who felt hopelessly alone. Frightened. Terrorized by the look in her mother's eyes. Eyes that glinted with loathing, disgust, rage. I was nothing in her eyes. I was a mistake. I was something to be broken so that I could be put back together properly. She felt her responsibility was to correct my nature, my very being. She honestly felt that what she was doing was for my own good. I cannot say she was evil. Because her motives were always to make me fit to live in the world without harming others. She could not see the desperate child. She saw only the mistake of nature that I epitomized for her. Somehow, I encompassed all of her worst fears.

When she called me into the kitchen one last time, I was ready for her to at last shift from her tightlipped anger into her white-hot rage. I was standing in the kitchen doorway, twisting my fingers in front of me, waiting, my eyes downcast. In the kitchen, because that was where I was told to be, but as far away as I could be while still complying—across the room from her. She was standing against the kitchen counter looking at me. I was stunned by the words that came out of her mouth. She dismissed me. After telling me to never do that again, she let me go. I was astonished. And then baffled. This was the one thing I had not expected. I was incredulous. Transfixed. Unable to move.

I looked up and saw Buzz standing there ... across the room ... not beside her ... but near her ... I knew he had interceded in my behalf. He did not indicate anything by word, gesture, or even a glance. But I knew he had performed the magic of which only he was capable. He had turned her wrath away from me. I knew he had done it. Why did he do it? He could have done just the opposite in order to further ingratiate himself to Mother.

He could have used his position of favor to destroy me. He could have reinforced her image of me as insidious, disgusting, cunning. But he didn't. He saw me as defenseless. He saw me as worthy of his defense. He empathized. Without any idea of what empathy was, he felt my pain. And he saw and felt the injustice. He was good and kind. He wanted to prevent hurt. He was old beyond his years. He never touched me gently. He never spoke to me kindly. He only saved my life.

Speaking of his experiences in Nazi concentration camps during World War II, Victor E. Frankl writes in *Man's Search for Meaning*:

> ... There was a sort of self-selecting process going on the whole time among all of the prisoners. On the average, only those prisoners could keep alive who, after years of trekking from camp to camp, had lost all scruples in their fight for existence; they were prepared to use every

means, honest or otherwise, even brutal force, theft, and betrayal of their friends, in order to save themselves. We who have come back, by the aid of many lucky chances or miracles—whatever one may choose to call them—we know: the best of us did not return.

Buzz did not lose his scruples. He never betrayed me. He saw me. He created some of the lucky chances that saved me. But, ultimately, Buzz "did not return." He was strong for me. But who was strong for him? When we were grown, I always thought of Buzz as the one who "made it." My mantra became, "Buzz made it, so I can make it." I saw him, my big brother, as master of his own fate; he made his own choices, lived his own life.

He was successful in business, had a wonderful family, had a daughter who graduated from Fresno State University, and had a reputation for perfection that earned him the admiration of many in his sphere of influence. He had hobbies—running marathons and biking double centuries. He was a wonderful uncle to my two boys as they were growing up—attending soccer games when they were small, building their first custom engines when they began to drive.

But who was strong for him?

Ultimately, Buzz did not return. My big brother. The one who spoke for me when I was speechless. The man who walked me down the aisle on my wedding day. The one who was always larger than life to me.

In 1991, at 50 years of age, Buzz committed suicide.

CHAPTER 5

On Our Own in a Pretty House

"And every one that heareth these words of mine and doeth them not, shall be likened unto a foolish man, who built his house upon the sand: and the rain descended, and the floods came, and the winds blew, and smote upon that house; and it fell: and great was the fall thereof."

Matthew 7:26-27 ASV

My brothers and I flourished during the time we lived with Lorse's family on F Street. We would never have chosen for it to end.

But the day came when Mother moved us out on our own. This would be the beginning of her restless searching for a "better place." We moved continually—from one small rental house to another. It never occurred to her that children need familiarity, consistency, continuity. Without exception, she based her next move on what was convenient or expedient for herself alone. We did not count. We did not have needs.

Usually, there was no reason given for a move. She was just not satisfied with what was at hand. She was continually searching for something else. Something that would soothe her. Something that would calm her. Something that would finally be right. Something that would appease the demons that drove her. This pattern continued throughout my mother's life. She never lived anywhere more than two years, under any circumstances, without becoming discontented, garrulous, fuming, impatient. Wherever she was wasn't good enough, big enough, small enough, clean enough, cheap enough, new enough. When we were grown with families of our own, my brothers and I moved her continually, never questioning the rationale. We just did it. It was always a painful process … because when she got to the "better place," she blamed us for the inevitable inadequacy and deficiencies she found there.

When we moved away from Lorse's house on F Street, we moved into a pretty house on Pine Street in Modesto. It was an older home and in excellent condition. There were three bedrooms. It seemed airy and spacious and full of light. My father's sister—my Aunt Toni—was living in Modesto with her family—my Uncle Harry and their son Michael. Michael was two years younger than Pete. Uncle Harry, who had been in the military during the war, had recently been discharged. They had not found housing in Modesto, so for a while they shared our house on Pine Street.

I never felt particularly close to Aunt Toni and Uncle Harry. They were always nice enough to us, but there was not the genuineness, the deep down acceptance of who we were that we experienced with Lorse. Nevertheless, we lived near them, occasionally with them, as we were growing up. Michael and his two sisters, who were born later, were the other cousins in our lives. They had a close and complete family.

We envied them the "Ozzie and Harriet" lives they lived. Two parents who coddled and pampered them. New clothes. Shiny shoes. A mother who walked them to school in the morning and greeted them happily when they came home. A father who had a respected profession … who came home at night and sat down to dinner with them … who read to them and held them. I envied them. I fantasized about Uncle Harry continually. I wanted him to be my daddy. I ached for someone to fill that role in my life. I ached for and I was afraid. I was extremely shy with Uncle Harry. Afraid that he would read my mind and be rejecting of what he saw there. He had his own children. I did not belong. And I knew it. I did not have a daddy. And I knew it. I was careful. I contained my neediness. I watched. I longed. I was careful.

Uncle Harry was a teacher, and he soon found a position at a school in Modesto. Aunt Toni became manager of a small, downtown restaurant. Not long after that, they moved into a house of their own. I was relieved when they left. It was hard to watch them love each other. To see up-close that relationship that was lost for me. I wanted what they had so badly. It was easier when they were gone.

On the surface, there was much to make a life happy on Pine Street—a pretty house, a nice yard, a good neighborhood. But it was not happy.

I remember Daddy living with us briefly there in that pretty house. He was there, but he was not there for me. He never looked at me. He stayed at our house, he came and went as though that were absolutely normal, he talked to everyone else in the house, but Daddy never looked at me. It was as though I were invisible. I did not recognize this person. I knew he was Daddy. But I did not recognize him. He was no longer familiar. He was a stranger. He did not look at me. He did not see his little girl. His little Pumpkin. The one he would always love. The little girl he had always wanted. She was gone. I was there.

And he was angry. He was angry like my mother was angry. He threw things. He punched holes in walls. He hated. He drank. He yelled. He was not safe. I was terrified of him. Who was this person? I had wanted my daddy to come back. Who was this person?

The final day with Daddy began with them shouting at each other. Mother was in the kitchen. Daddy was in the bedroom right off the kitchen. She was yelling at him for spending money. He told her to shut up. She did not. He came to the kitchen door. He was wearing only his baggy underwear. His arms hung at his side; his hands were in fists. He was swearing at Mother. She would not shut up. She was telling him he was no good, he never did anything right, he was worthless. She may have been right, but I did not want to hear her say that to Daddy. I did not want to hear him telling her to shut up. I hurt for both of them. I feared these violent strangers. I loved them both. I did not want them to hurt each other. The horrible fighting words they hurled at each other enveloped me. I stood in the doorway that led from the living room into the kitchen and listened and watched this drama unfold.

The words were loud. Filled with hate. There was not enough hate in the words to satisfy Daddy. He moved toward Mother. His fists flew at my mother. My daddy punched my mommy in the face, in the chest, in the stomach. She fell backward, hitting her head on the kitchen counter. She fell on her back on the floor.

I knew she was dead. I knew my mommy was dead. And I knew my daddy had killed her. I ran to Mother, threw myself across her, begging her to not be dead. I screamed, sobbing hysterically. I could not open my mouth wide enough … could not make my voice loud enough … could not tense my muscles tight enough to express the horror I felt. In my four-year-old child's mind, the unthinkable had happened. Mommy was dead. Daddy had killed her. In their war with each other, I was the collateral damage. I was alone. My mommy was dead. My daddy had done it. There was nobody left for me.

I don't remember Daddy going to Mother. I don't remember him helping me. When Mother regained consciousness, she was dazed. She roughly pushed me away. I retreated to the living room. I was in a stupor. I sat on an upholstered stool in the corner. The stool was red and blue. A familiar piece of furniture that was worn and shabby. I sat on that worn and shabby piece of familiar furniture rocking myself back and forth. I had seen my mother dead. Was she dead? I had seen her come back to life. Was she alive? I rocked myself back and forth and tried to sooth myself with words, with gibberish. And then I dissociated. I left what I did not understand and could not fix.

When I was again aware, I was still sitting on the red and blue stool. I had to help myself. No one came to me. No one helped me. No one held me and told me it would be all right. No one explained. I had to hold myself together. They were both too busy with their own misery to see what they had done to me.

Buzz and Pete were there that day too. I don't know what they saw, what they heard, how they felt. There were five people in that pretty house on Pine Street. Five people together. Each of us alone. We never spoke of what happened that morning. Never spoke. Never.

Daddy left. The man I knew but no longer recognized. He left. My father—the man I recognized—had left a year or two earlier. Now this man who hated and hit left. Which one was my daddy? Did it matter? They both left. I let go of them. I retreated into the world I was busy creating within myself. The only safe place I knew. I dissociated. I stood on the porch, looking out as far as I could see, knowing that Daddy was out there somewhere, and I let go. I just ... let go.

CHAPTER 6

The Watcher

"O be careful little eyes what you see.
For the Father up above
Is looking down with love,
So, be careful, very careful, what you see."

Traditional Children's Song

My cousin Jerome enlisted in the Navy when he was 18. Within a year, he was married and had a baby boy—Clayton. Because Jerome was aboard ship most of the time, when his wife Lois became pregnant again, she moved into a bungalow behind our house on Pine Street so that Mother could help with the new baby. Clayton was a beautiful, healthy, happy baby. Jerry, the son born shortly after Lois moved into the bungalow, was small, sickly, and difficult. Mother was more than happy to help.

Mother put a crib in the room Pete and I shared, and Jerry took up residence with us. He cried a lot. Mother would not pick him up when he cried. She was of the opinion that if she picked up a crying baby, the baby would be spoiled and demanding. Jerry was sick. He was small. He was born with an enlarged heart. He needed love. He needed to be fed. Mother ignored him. He would not be ignored. He cried so hard he choked and lost his breath and turned blue. Mother still would not pick him up. She came to the crib and shrieked at him. He cried louder. She picked him up and put his head under cold running water. He sputtered, recoiled from the shock, and then cried hysterically. Finally, my mother threw him toward his crib from across the room. He hit the wall behind the crib and fell in. He stopped crying. He whimpered. But he stopped crying. I watched.

Mother took Jerry's unhappiness personally. As though he were purposely doing something against her when he cried. He was just being a baby. A sick baby. He did not know how to be anything else. She took it personally. He was supposed to behave. He was supposed to know what she expected. He was a newborn baby, but he was supposed to take care of her feelings. Be good. He could not. So she beat him. In the night, I saw her do it. He was tiny, defenseless, totally at her mercy. She beat him. Her face a mask of rage, she beat him. I watched.

Mother potty trained Pete while we lived on Pine Street. Buzz and I had been quick learners. Pete was not. He had his own agenda. This infuriated her and made her more determined than ever to win this battle. Eventually, Pete got the message. Once he understood what the rules were, he seemed more than willing to do his part. It just took him a little longer. But he could not stay dry all night. He wet the bed. Mother was convinced that he could stay dry if he wanted to. So she would not put a diaper on him at night. He was expected to control himself. He continued to wet the bed. To punish him, she made him stay in bed, in the wet bedding with his face in the mess and the covers pulled up over him. He could not move. He had to smell it, feel it in his face. He cried. He sobbed. He felt humiliated. And he, of course, was sorry. He said over and over, "I'm sorry, Mommy. I'm sorry. I won't do it again." I watched.

I watched and I knew something was wrong. I knew Pete could not help wetting the bed. I knew he did not do it on purpose. As young as I was, I understood what my mother would not understand. She treated him as though he had wet the bed on purpose, specifically to spite her. He could not explain. He could not defend himself. So he suffered. I felt extremely sorry for him. On some level, I thought I should be able to protect him. He was my little brother. I saw him as innocent. Watching him suffer was in some ways more difficult than suffering myself. I *knew* how it felt when I was the one being punished. I could only imagine how Pete felt, and because he was younger, smaller, more fragile than I was, I was afraid he could not take it like I could. I wanted to help him. But I knew I could not interfere. I stayed near him as though my presence would be some help. I had no idea if it comforted him or not. It was all I knew to do.

Watching Mother with Pete, I became terrified that I would have an accident. That I would soil myself. That I would pull this particular form of her wrath down on myself. She was more vengeful, more full of righteous indignation, more sure of the correctness of her stand on this issue than on any other, it seemed. She would not flinch or back off. She was in this fight for the duration. She would cure him of wetting the bed. Or one of them would die in the process. I sympathized with Pete. I ached for him. And I was afraid for myself.

I became afraid to sleep. Afraid I would wet the bed. Afraid Mother would come in the room to punish Jerry. Afraid of all the unpredictable things that happened at night. Afraid that I would be punished. Or that I would be a witness. Nights became the enemy in that pretty house with the nice yard in the good neighborhood.

Mother could not accept the parts of Pete that were different from Buzz and me. He was genetically different. He had blond hair and blue eyes to our brown hair and eyes. He did not have the same parents that we had. There were bound to be differences. Buzz and I may have been better attuned to Mother *because* we were biologically related to her. We read her better. We were watchful. We understood the dangers. Pete did not. He was on another wavelength entirely. He was careless more often He was caught in some minor transgression more often. He was punished much more often.

Pete was small and delicately boned. Buzz and I were more sturdily built. Buzz and I ate what was put before us. We knew the rule. Pete was a picky eater. So sometimes he just did not want to eat. This would never work in Mother's system. Buzz and I knew this. Pete seemed oblivious. He did not internalize the rules the way we did. Or he just did not know he should. He listened to his own self better, perhaps. Mother took Pete's lack of interest in food as a criticism of her efforts to feed us. It became a personal vendetta.

Pete did not like oatmeal. He loathed oatmeal. He could not stand the taste or the way it felt in his mouth. The bowl would sit in front of him until the oatmeal was a cold, congealed mess. He was not allowed to move until he ate it. When he would finally put the spoon in his mouth, he would gag. He would choke down a few bites. And then he would vomit. This would enrage Mother. She would put the vomit back in his bowl. He had to eat it. By the time they reached this part of the drama, Pete would be pathetically sobbing. She would beat him for crying and then make him get back up to the table. The oatmeal had to be eaten. She could not, would not back down. That would be letting him win. That was unconscionable.

Watching this, I hated Mother. She was torturing Pete. She was ascribing motives to this tiny, vulnerable, desperate child that did not make sense. I knew she was wrong. There was no shred of doubt in my mind. She was wrong. I loved Pete. I knew there was nothing I could do. My heart hurt for him. I watched impotently. I learned some important lessons from watching Mother with Pete. At a very early age, I was mentally taking notes on mothering from my mother. I watched her and silently vowed, "When I am big, I will never hurt someone who is small." My mission in life became to *never* be like her.

One winter day, Buzz, Pete, and I were playing outside. It had been raining and there were great big, beautiful puddles everywhere. We were playing near the puddles, but we knew we were not supposed to get our shoes wet. We knew the rule. We had been told not to get our feet wet. It did not work out that way. In spite of the fact that we had been warned, in spite of the fact that we knew retribution would be quick and certain, in spite of all that, we were splashing in the puddles with abandon. All three of us were soon soaked. We were just kids who got lost in the moment.

Mother was watching us from the living room window. She called us in through the back door into the kitchen. She was holding a board. There was no doubt about her intentions.

I was made to watch as she beat Buzz and then Pete. There was no preamble this time. Merely the statement, "I'll teach you to disobey me." With that, she methodically beat them. It was not a spanking; it was a beating. Her face was contorted with rage. Whatever it was that possessed her on these occasions, she gave in to it. She withheld nothing. She used all the strength she had. She did not paddle. She beat. An adult with a weapon in her hand using all her strength against two little boys who could do nothing but submit. When she was through, she sent them to bed for the rest of the day. They were both spent, badly bruised, hurting, exhausted. Relieved that the worst part was over. But heartbroken. Bewildered.

Now Mother turned her attention to me. I was being set up, but had no idea what was going on. Why hadn't I been beaten when they were? She told me that she had not beaten me because she did not think I would do such a thing. In a wheedling voice, she asked me if I had gotten my shoes wet, apparently giving me a way out by saying that she did not think I had. I was uncomfortable with what was going on. I had seen what she had done to my brothers, and the ferocity of the beatings made me terrified for myself. I was trembling. I was confused. I took the out she offered. I said I had not gotten my feet wet. This was exactly what she had been waiting for. She coldly told me that she had seen me with my feet in the water, that she had been testing me to see if I would tell the truth. She told me that I had compounded my wrong by lying and that I was worse than the boys.

I had thought I might be spared. I tried to read between the lines. I tried to figure out what was safe. There was no safety. She grabbed me and unleashed a fresh, new fury on me. I remember lying in bed that afternoon, every inch of me burning, my legs covered with stripes. But the real hurt was in my heart. I knew my body would heal. It had happened before. I did not know how to make the hurt in my heart go away.

Was I really as bad as she said? I must be. But there was rage too. Rage that she did not see me. That she did not know. That she refused to see me. Rage because I could not satisfy. Impotent, blind, senseless rage. Rage on behalf of the little brother I loved. Rage because there was nothing that we could ever do. It was not that we *did* something that was wrong. I could understand that concept and perhaps do something about it. In her eyes, we *were* wrong. We could do nothing about that. We did not make mistakes. We *were* mistakes. That was the hard part. The maddening part. We could not change who we were … even for her.

The last time I was with Pete, we were in our fifties. He and his wife, Maureen, had come from Sacramento to visit me in Salinas. During that visit, Pete and I talked a little about our childhood. This is something we *rarely* did. Neither of us ever voluntarily revisited that pain. It had been several years since Buzz's suicide and both of us were still raw and hurting. Suicide does that. On this particular occasion, I asked Pete if I could share with him something I had written about Buzz. "Of course," he said. We were sitting on the upper deck off the second-story great room in the beautiful house my two sons and I built. We were overlooking lush, green lawns and exotic rose gardens. The warm September morning was clear and cool, with just a hint of a breeze. And it was one of those perfect moments when Pete and I felt totally comfortable in each other's company.

I went into the house and came back with the manuscript to this book. I read Pete the chapter about Buzz. The chapter where he saved me from Mother in the kitchen. When I finished reading, my fifty-five-year-old brother, my little brother Pete, whom I had loved without reservation, looked at me and—choking with sobs—said, "You always took care of me, Bunny." It was the most beautiful gift he ever gave me. I knew that protecting him was my overriding concern during our childhood. But I never knew if he realized how hard I tried. He suffered so much at the hands of our mother. There were so many times I failed. But he remembered the times I did not fail. Four months later, in January of 2000, Pete died.

CHAPTER 7

Too Young and Not Ready

"Once anxiety over safety becomes a child's orientation, s/he will use his/her long-range senses (sight and sound) as buffers between self and experience. S/he will try to predetermine the probable value and outcome of the experience in an effort to keep distance between him/herself and possible harm."

Magical Child by Joseph Chilton Pearce

I ENTERED KINDERGARTEN AT FOUR YEARS OF AGE WHEN WE LIVED ON Pine Street. I was under the age required for admission, but my mother prevailed on the school to allow her to enroll me, because it would simplify her life—less babysitting required. I was too young in every way—especially emotionally. It was the beginning of the nightmare of uncertainty that marked my tenure in elementary school. Coming from a home where chaos and brutality were the rule, I expected the worst at school also. I knew no one. I felt isolated and alone. Fearing reprisals for asking questions—which was the way things worked at home—I suffered in silence. I was, without exception, afraid of my teachers. At the end of each day, I was exhausted from the effort to understand what was, for me, largely incomprehensible. My mother enrolled me in school and then expected me to be able to navigate all the intricacies of schoolwork and socialization on my own. I held on to my sanity by switching. I let "others" in my personality system go to school. Some of them where quite good at it.

By the time I entered school, my dissociation had become a habit. It was the way I coped with the total lack of control I felt. I could have some control by not being there. When I later began an extensive therapy to deal with my dissociation, I could easily identify eight different alters who helped me navigate the dangerous pitfalls at home, at school and then in the relationships with John and Linc. This book is not primarily about Dissociative Identity Disorder, but that is a part of who I am, and during times of uncertainty and trauma, it was essential to my survival.

Kevin is the seven year old alter who attended elementary school for me. He was polite, careful, and thorough. Within my personality system, he had an older brother named Curtis who watched out for him at school and made sure he was not picked on by bullies. Curtis was also the repository for anger and rage that could not be openly felt or expressed. This was the way I coped in a world that I was not equipped to face.

One of the problems my brothers and I faced was my mother's obsession with packing up and moving. There was no pattern. It would happen haphazardly. When she became restless or discontent, the boxes would come out, and we would be moving again. We never knew where. We certainly never knew when. It might begin in the middle of the night and we would be gone by morning. Or we might have a little warning. It happened when she was ready.

She would take us to a new school, register us, and then turn and walk away. We had to make our way alone. A constant fear of my childhood was that I would be unable to remember the way home. One time she registered me for the wrong grade. I was in a classroom where everyone was smaller than I was, and I was sitting in a desk that was many times too small. The teacher was exasperated and had no idea what to make of me. I felt awkward and afraid because the teacher was looking at my large frame with disgust. Someone finally figured out that my mother had registered me for second grade while I belonged in fourth. Again, I merely did what I was told as best I could. I had not been prepared to speak on my own behalf, to ask questions, to reach out to others. I approached school every day as though it were a place of torture—because for me, it was.

The one bright spot I remember was reading. It came easily. I don't remember ever being confused about what was expected. Words made sense. And reading was something I took with me, no matter where we went to school. Math and social studies were awful. I remember sitting in a desk at yet another new school with a book open in front of me and not being able to participate in anything that was going on. I had never seen this social studies book before. The teacher was impatient because she thought I should know the subject matter.

This was normal. I was expected to know something that was totally foreign. During my elementary years, instead of school being a respite from home, in many ways, it held its own set of horrors. Math is a subject that requires systematic, step-by-step processes. I dreaded arithmetic. Again, it was Kevin who learned arithmetic. Little by little, we acquired the rudiments of numbers and were able to put the pieces together. We struggled. It seemed that everything was a struggle. Working together as a team, though, we survived. By the time I was in fourth grade, my personality system consisted of six alters who pitched in and helped at school when things were just too much for any one of us. It worked. And there were moments when we thrived. We found within ourselves the support and friendship that existed nowhere else.

CHAPTER 8

A Bigger Move This Time

"Subsequently, however, a cessation of parental love through death, abandonment or chronic rejection, has the effect of making the child's unrequited commitment an experience of intolerable pain."

The Road Less Traveled by M. Scott Peck, M.D.

BY THE TIME I WAS IN THIRD GRADE, I HAD ATTENDED A HALF-DOZEN schools in Modesto. Like a mother cat with a litter of kittens, my mother picked us up and moved us at her whim, but never very far—always within the same town. That year, however, we learned we were moving to Salinas—about a hundred miles away.

Once moved, life was pretty much as it had always been—except Lorse and the cousins were no longer immediately available. We had come to depend on the time we spent with them for relief from my mother's moods. While we lived in the same town, even if we did not live in the same house, there were opportunities to be together. We went to church together, we ate at each other's houses, and we always spent every holiday together. That was no longer the case.

In Salinas, the odyssey of constant moving continued. Dumpy little house after dumpy little house. Intimidating new school after intimidating new school. I was dazed and lost most of the time. I paid close attention so I could find my way home, but beyond that, life was a nightmarish haze. My mother began working nights when I was in fifth grade. This terrified me. When we were much too young to be alone, that's what she began doing—leaving us alone from 10:30 at night until 7:30 in the morning. She had obtained her nursing license and was now working at Monterey County Hospital on the graveyard shift. I was always awake when she left for work. I would watch her go down the front walk and the night terrors would begin. My brothers slept. I was petrified of the dark; I knew I could not complain; and so, again, I switched. My system now included Delia, the caregiver for everyone who was afraid of the dark.

And my mother's rages continued. In her anger and desire for absolute control over everything my brothers and I did, there was the implicit message—if we did not obey immediately and without question, she would leave us as our father had left us. Now that Lorse was nowhere near, we felt particularly vulnerable to her dark moods. She used us as the objects on whom she took out every real and imagined wrong ever done to her. We received the brunt of her frustration. She reminded us constantly that we were the reason for her every disappointment and hardship.

After my mother began leaving us alone at night, my father reentered my life as the voice on the other end of a phone that rang in the pitch darkness—always in the middle of the night, always from a bar, and he was always drunk. The phone calls continued for years—sometimes two or three times a week, sometimes after months of silence. His speech was slurred, his tone of voice accusatory, and the conversations always centered around the same few issues.

"This is your old dad. I just called to tell you that I'm writing a song for Hank Williams, and I'm going to be rich." He was always going to be a famous songwriter. He was always going to make a million dollars. He would challenge me to disagree with him. "You don't believe me, do you? Well, I'll show you. I'll show everybody.

"You think you're my real daughter, but you're not. My real daughter has blond hair and blue eyes and she is beautiful. I buy her beautiful clothes to wear." I had brown hair and brown eyes—like my father. I looked a lot like him. How could he expect me—or any daughter—to have blond hair and blue eyes? Hearing him say this, I wondered just how many ways I could possibly be wrong. I had no control over my hair or eye color. I wanted to please him, but I had no way of becoming what pleased him. I wanted to be his. I wanted to be loved. His words cut deeply into what little memory I had of being special to someone.

"I want to take your name back. I want to name my real daughter Bunny. I had to name her Bonnie for now, but I want to give her her rightful name. She is my little Bunny, not you." In saying this, my father was taking back the specialness I had always felt because he had named me. He had given me his "love name." Now, if he could figure out a way to do it, he would take that away too.

I stood in the dark, cold house and listened to my father. He never gave me a chance to say anything. He just babbled on in his drunken gibberish. My father. My father the millionaire songwriter. My father who had another daughter he loved. My father who wanted to take my name back. Somehow, I knew even then—as a young child—that the million dollars and the "real" daughter were figments of his drunken imagination. The true part of those calls, however, was the fact that he—like my mother—had no place in his heart, his mind, his life for anything but his own miserable ruminations. He, too, was wrapped up in self-pity and loathing. And I was nothing to him. Nothing.

I was a lost little girl with brown hair and brown eyes who was afraid of the dark.

CHAPTER 9

Thanks to Mr. Froehlicher and Miss Buehler

"This is to mother you,
To comfort you and get you through ..."

This is to Mother You lyrics by Sinead O'Connor*

WHEN I BEGAN JUNIOR HIGH SCHOOL, WE LIVED IN THE ALISAL DIStrict of Salinas. This was an unincorporated area that was populated by lower-middle-class families and the working poor. There were a lot of us. I attended El Sausal Junior High along with all the other kids in the area. Things improved in junior high for a number of reasons. Mr. Froehlicher was one.

I was nervous about junior high. It was a huge school, as far as my experience at the time was concerned, and there was no preparation for the transition from elementary school. From the very first day, though, I felt at home.

---

* O'Connor, Sinead, *This is to Mother You*. 1997 by Chrysalis Records Ltd. Audio CD.

My first period on the first day was seventh grade math. The teacher, Mr. Froehlicher, put a problem on the blackboard, turned around, faced the class, and asked, "Who knows how to solve this problem?" I immediately raised my hand because the answer seemed obvious to me. To my surprise, not one other hand was raised. He asked me how I would solve it and I answered. He looked at me and said, "You're very bright."

I will never forget that moment. No one, *no one*, had ever said that to me before. In that one moment, the amazing Mr. Froehlicher had seen something in me no one else had ever seen. Junior high, thus begun, was wonderful for me. I *was* bright. In everything. I made excellent grades, had many friends, and was universally liked by my teachers.

Even before seventh grade was complete, of course, my mother was packing the boxes again. I was heartbroken when she told me to go to the office and check out of school. We were moving across town, and I would have to attend the one other junior high school in Salinas. I went to the office and talked to my school counselor and told her I needed to check out. She asked why, and I told her we were moving into the other school district. She extended a lifeline to me. She said, "We would hate to lose you, Bunny. If you can find a way to get here, we won't make you transfer." This was Miss Buehler, my school counselor, who extended herself to keep me.

I learned to ride the city bus. We moved again and again—that did not change—but I rode the city bus, and I—for the first time in my life—had the continuity, structure, and consistency to flourish at school. The violence at home did not abate. As the three of us became teenagers, my mother became ever more demanding and grudging. She could not countenance our having any life outside her sphere of tyrannical authority. It was natural for us to need connections outside the family by this time. The fact that home had never been a happy place made getting out even more compelling to us. She seethed.

CHAPTER 10

Captain and Mrs. Irby of the Salvation Army

"There is a way of being in the world that transcends the world, a way of being regular people and miracle workers at the same time. We become the lamps that shed the light that emanates from the electricity of God."

The Gift of Change **by Marianne Williamson**

As I was happily navigating my way through seventh grade, Captain and Mrs. Carl Irby became the new corps officers of the Salvation Army in Salinas. They sought out my mother and came to visit us in our home. They wanted to invite all of us to become involved in the new programs they were starting at the corps. My mother was gruff and off-putting with them. Neither of my brothers was interested. I certainly was. To me it represented a valid reason to be away from home. School was good now, but I still had a lot of time and was more than willing to spend it anywhere but at home.

From that first invitation, I became involved in everything that went on at church. The Irbys took on the responsibility of picking me up, because my mother made it abundantly clear she would not provide transportation—to her, it would just be a waste of gas. I went to Sunday school and Holiness meetings on Sunday morning. On Sunday evening I attended Salvation meetings. Wednesday night I attended Girl Guards—a program similar to Girl Scouts but with more of a religious spin. There were prayer meetings each Thursday evening—I don't remember actually being interested in prayer, but I loved spending time with the Irbys and was happy just being away from home. Friday night I attended Corps Cadet classes—a program designed to prepare young people for possible full-time service as Salvation Army officers—and later on Friday evening, there was youth group. Again, I was good at all of it.

My mother rarely let me out of her control, but I found the one exception to be church. She interfered with friendships and forbade me to join groups at school—she thought I should be home every minute I was not in class. By the time I was in junior high, I was spending all day Saturday cleaning and ironing, and many evenings were spent doing other chores she delegated to me. She looked on all of us as her possessions. We owed her everything. She told us this regularly. She begrudged any activity that did not directly benefit her. But she made an exception for God. When I wanted to attend church, she let me go. I had to be careful not to be too enthusiastic about my growing attachment to Captain and Mrs. Irby, though. She had a proprietary jealousy about any relationship that she imagined supplanted her position as the absolute authority in my life. She was jealous of every relationship—my friends, teachers, everyone. And so I was careful. Very careful.

Under that carefulness, though, I quickly responded to the Irbys' caring tutelage by transferring all my longing for loving parents to them. They were young—in their mid-thirties—attractive, outgoing, full of life. While they were in Salinas, their daughter Lynnea was born. I was even more bonded to them then. I babysat whenever I could, and they took me to conventions and conferences with them so I could help with the baby. For me, this was heaven.

Little by little, it became apparent that I was spending more waking hours with the Irbys than I was with my mother. And, of course, she noticed. She kept score. I had to be careful. I had to make it abundantly clear to her that I was doing it all for God. I wasn't, of course. God was a part of the picture, but I didn't want a Heavenly Father. I wanted parents I could see and touch and love confidently and without constraint.

At that time, the Irbys were those parents to me. To some extent, it seems certain they were aware of this. But I did my best to hide my neediness. I wasn't sure how transparent I could be. Could they take the full burden of my neediness? Probably not. They were kind and good. But they had their own family. I realized this, and so I was careful with them too.

The Irbys' house was on my way to the bus stop after school, so I would sometimes stop and say hello. On one such occasion, I stayed a little too long and missed my bus home. They told me to call my mother and tell her that I was going to stay and eat dinner with them and they would then bring me home later. To them it seemed like a small thing, but I wasn't sure about it. I knew my mother did not want me to spend "personal" time with the Irbys. The relationship was supposed to be confined to church events only. The Irbys insisted. I called my mother. She went into a raving tirade at me while I was standing in the Irbys' living room, holding their phone to my ear. They could hear her raging. They felt terrible and they were perplexed. What was the big deal, after all? During her tirade, Mother told me I could not accept a ride home from them. I could wait for the next bus or I could walk. It would have taken me hours to walk. So I waited for the bus. I left the Irbys' house because I was embarrassed by what had happened. They saw my discomfort and did not ask questions. I couldn't even look at them as I left.

When I arrived home, my mother was out on the front lawn watering. She stared at me with a look of the utmost, malevolent hatred on her face. "So, you'd rather spend time with them, would you? You don't have time for the old bag who took you out of the gutter and raised you, do you? You make me sick. Get out of my sight." So I came home because she told me to, and I wanted more badly than ever to be anywhere other than there.

I began to fantasize that my mother would die. I wished her dead. I wanted her to just get out of my life. I knew that would never happen unless she died. I wanted Captain and Mrs. Irby to be my parents. I was sure they would adopt me if only my mother would die. Captain and Mrs. Irby told me about such a situation in a nearby town. The boy's parents died and he was adopted by his Salvation Army officers. I envied that child. I hated him for having the chance I lusted for. I ached with the need to belong to someone who loved me, who would actually take care of me, who would hold me and cherish me.

Still, I was careful not to betray the depth of my neediness to the Irbys. I felt destroyed by the desire to not be part of my mother's life. But I was embarrassed by my own neediness. And so, even with the Irbys, I was careful.

CHAPTER 11

Pete Copes ... Or Doesn't

"He bonds to his mother, to her anxiety and her value. His natural instinct for taking his cues from her grows; whereas in natural development, it should fade as autonomy unfolds."

Magical Child by Joseph Chilton Pearce

While I was busy with school and church, Pete was more on his own. We no longer attended the same school. My junior high school was seventh, eighth, and ninth grades. He was three years behind me in school. So he would enter junior high just after I went on to high school.

I was happy to be more on my own. Pete and I had been constant playmates as young children, but we were also watchful and traumatized—never knowing when the next catastrophe would strike or where it might come from. My being gone so much meant I was not as much a part of what went on at home. This was good for me. But things did not get better for Pete.

Pete became secretive and withdrawn. He had friends and he

was very attractive to the opposite sex. Buzz and I did not have the same magnetism he had, and dating for us came much later. Pete sneaked away from home to be with his friends. He lied when he needed to—something he was never very good at. Mother continued to beat him.

Pete was as tall as Mother the last time I remember her beating him. I don't remember anything about what led up to the beating. I remember being in the kitchen of the tiny house in which we lived. This house had only one bedroom—which Mother and I shared. Buzz slept on the couch in the living room, and Pete slept on a cot in the kitchen. I remember seeing Mother with a board—this was not a stick, it was a club. Heavy. About 18 inches long. She went at Pete. He put up his hands to protect himself. She was swinging the board at his head, his arms, his torso. Because Pete was tall now, and strong for his age, he was able to ward off most of the blows. But he was crying. This great big handsome young man was crying. And he was trying to talk to her. "Don't, Mama. Don't do it. Please, Mama, don't." Between sobs he was trying to reason with her. But she was not reasonable. She never was. He could have hit her. He was strong enough now to take the board away from her and beat her the way she had routinely beaten him all his life. I remember being afraid he might. But he didn't. He cried and pleaded. He did not strike out at her.

In dodging her blows, Pete lost his footing and fell to the floor. She followed him down, still flailing the board. They were rolling around on the floor. Pete trying to avoid her. She determined to finish what she had started. She was so enraged by this time that she was choking and incoherent. For the first time, he was not her helpless, submissive target. He was not standing still, and I think she knew that she might be in over her head for the first time.

When I could take it no longer, I began to scream at her. And I began to sob hysterically. This did it. She looked at me and shrieked, "Do you want the neighbors to call the police? Shut up! Just shut your mouth." The thought of someone calling the police was enough to break her terrible trance. She came to. She got up off the floor. Pete sat there for a long time, just crying. Shaking his head, rubbing his arms where Mother had hit him and crying. I ached for him. We were both crying. Together. Alone. Brokenhearted.

No wonder I didn't want to be at home.

Pete was the vulnerable one. He was the least equipped to deal with Mother, so in some perverse sense, it is logical that he was often the one on whom she took out the worst of her rage. I have heard that chickens will form a mob and attack any member of their own flock on whom they see blood. Their answer to perceived weakness is brutality. This seemed to be the way Mother operated.

But no one—not even the "man of the house" was entirely safe.

While we lived in this same house, I came home from church one Sunday night to find Mother, Pete, and Buzz sitting in the living room. As soon as I walked in, I knew something was very wrong. No one was saying anything. On the contrary, they were sitting there in absolute silence. I looked around. Pete's face was streaked with tears, Mother was staring before her dazed and unresponsive, and Buzz had a huge gash on the top of his head.

Mother, in a fit of fury, had picked up a lamp—ostensibly to throw it on the floor—and "somehow" Buzz's head got in her way. She split his head wide open. She, being a nurse, shaved his head around the cut and stitched it up. No Novocain. She just stitched it up. Buzz was stoic before, during, and after. He never said a word. Never made a sound. He was still the man of the house. Men don't cry.

Pete was the one who told me what had happened. I stood there in the aftermath of this savagery, and Pete took it upon himself to tell me what happened. Mother and Buzz remained silent—each in his or her own tragedy—and sweet Pete told me what had happened. And then, with tears rolling down his cheeks, he sobbed, "We all promised to do better." Sure. That'll work …

CHAPTER 12

The Dog Bite

"The dread of abandonment comes from premature autonomy being forced on the child, that is, when the parents make the child aware of, and feel responsible, for his/her own survival."

Magical Child by Joseph Chilton Pearce

Buzz was in high school, I was in junior high, and Pete was finishing sixth grade when all of the events in the previous chapter took place. We lived in that tiny house on Garner Avenue in the Alisal district, and Mother was working nights at the hospital. She became ever more vengeful and unpredictable. It seems like things should have been better for her. Her work was steady. There certainly wasn't a lot of money, but finances were better than they had been when she was waitressing. Buzz was doing well in high school, I was loving junior high, and Pete was a popular kid in the neighborhood. We were all three doing our share at home. She had a lot to be thankful for. She never saw it that way.

Things should have been easier for her. But she was possessed with some demon that gave her no peace. She brooded, she seethed, and she erupted. Without warning or provocation, she erupted.

It is difficult to describe how alone a child feels when living with someone like Mother. The very person who should be available, who should provide support, who should be on your side, is the most dangerous person of all. And this is the very person you *must* go home to every night. This is the enemy you must sleep with.

No matter what happened, we were blamed. It did not matter what the chain of events was. It did not matter how innocent of motive or cunning we were. We were seen as guilty on every occasion.

One warm early summer afternoon, I found myself running home from school on my lunch hour to get my gym clothes. I had gym class right after lunch, and it was Monday, and I had forgotten to take my gym clothes with me that morning. Not having the correct clothes meant disappointing the teacher, losing points, and not being able to participate that day. I wanted none of that. I just had time to get home and get back without being late for class. I got home, grabbed the clothes I needed, and then began the rather long run back to school. As I passed a house about a block from mine, a large dog broke loose from his tether, ran up behind me, and bit me hard on my buttocks. I was astonished, terrified, and hurt. My clothes were not ripped, but the bite was extremely painful.

The dog wandered off, and I quickly went back home to look at the damage he had done. What I saw was a huge chunk of torn flesh and long abrasions where his teeth had gnashed on my flesh. It was horrible-looking and my underwear was torn and bloody.

And this is the point I want to make: My mother was at home sleeping because she had worked the night before. Worse than the damage the dog had done and as upset as I was about the large wound, I was more afraid of waking her than I could ever be of the dog. I knew I would be blamed. As unreasonable as that sounds, I knew it. There was no way I could tell her what happened. Even when I had been badly hurt, I was afraid to tell her. I knew she would fly into a rage and I would be blamed

The prospect of facing her was worse than anything else I could imagine. I wrapped my underwear in an old paper bag to throw away elsewhere, washed off the bite, which was angry-looking and beginning to swell, and hurried back to school. My butt felt like it was on fire, my heart was heavy with shame, but I sucked it in and went on back to school. I hid the wound from everyone. I could hardly sit down, and I was scared to death, but I hid the wound from everyone.

During the ensuing weeks, I assumed I would die. I had heard just enough about rabies to know that it came from dog bites and it was always fatal. I did not know that not every dog bite leads to rabies. Not knowing this, I expected to die. I took care of the bite myself, was careful to conceal it from notice, and silently waited to die. I accepted the inevitability of death rather than take the chance of talking to my mother. For me, the expression, "I would rather die than talk to her," was literally true. I did not want to die, but death was preferable to facing my mother's unpredictable irrational fury. Eventually, I realized I probably wasn't going to die. But I never told my mother about the bite. Never. I remained afraid of repercussions long after the scabs were healed.

But the fact that I had no idea of a mother who would help me, who could correct my misconception and tell me I wasn't going to die—who might actually champion me by contacting the owner of the dog and taking action against a danger in my environment—*this idea did not exist for me.* I knew whose side my mother was on. *The other side.* No matter the issue, I remember not one example, throughout my entire life, of my mother going to bat for me. Even when I was savaged by a Salvation Army officer, she blamed me for "ruining a good man." She never knew about the second Salvation Army officer. Why would I tell her? I don't remember ever, even once, intentionally doing something wrong. I was a good person. But I knew my vindictive mother saw me as otherwise.

CHAPTER 13

High School Years

"Jesus called disciples—students of life—to learn from him how to live in God's world God's way. Constantly learning and growing and evolving and absorbing. Tomorrow is never simply a repeat of today."

Love Wins by Rob Bell

I GRADUATED FROM THE NINTH GRADE IN JUNE OF 1956. I HAD DONE brilliantly in my three years at El Sausal. I aced my classes, made many friends, experienced the joy of learning from teachers who were smart, encouraging, and even funny at times. Staying in one place because of the generosity of Miss Buehler and my own determination to make the city bus system work for me, I became the excellent student I always had the potential to be. I left El Sausal with more than a little nostalgia.

But I got off to a rocky, tremulous start in high school.

During August of 1956, we spent the three weeks of my mother's vacation visiting with Lorse and her family in Modesto. While we were there, Cherrill had the Asiatic Flu—the first wave of these virulent new flu viruses. She was just getting over the really acute phase of her illness when we arrived. Of course, I spent most of my time with her, and by the time we were back home in Salinas, I began to feel sick.

I developed a high fever and had severe pains in my chest. Breathing hurt. I could not remember ever feeling so miserable. My mother was not particularly concerned. She was skeptical when we were sick and expected us to get over it on our own. She always planted the idea that we were just pretending in order to malinger and exact sympathy. I had been a victim of childhood migraines. I would get so sick I could not stand any light and would be so nauseated I could not eat, and I vomited even water. She remained oblivious—never offering so much as an aspirin. Thousands of people became very sick in the summer of 1956; many died. My mother remained oblivious.

When the first day of school came, I wanted to go to school. All my friends would be there, and I did not want to miss the first day. But getting up was an impossibility. I was just too ill. I missed the first few days and then decided I was well enough to go. When I arrived at the huge high school building, I was overwhelmed. There had been no orientation for incoming students, I did not have any idea where the classrooms were, and I did not feel well at all.

My friends were already busy with their own schedules and were over the worst newness of the situation. I felt totally lost. I made it to where I needed to be, but as the day wore on, I became weaker and weaker. I was still very sick. I still had a temperature. I began to doubt that I could make it through the day and then walk home.

Again, I knew I could not call my mother and ask her to come and give me a ride home. She just did not do that kind of thing. That would be encouraging us to be weak. Once, in my senior year of high school, I was bleeding so hard from my period and having such severe cramps that I almost fainted during my last class. I called her that day, and she came to get me, but I paid for it. She was derisive and dismissive, stating that I "didn't know what pain was."

On my way home from that first day of high school, I remember carrying the large stack of books that had been assigned to me, putting one foot in front of the other, and getting within a couple of blocks of home. I had exhausted every ounce of reserve by that time, and I really did not think I could make it those last few blocks. My body was too involved with the illness by that time to listen to my head, which said that we had to keep going. There was no choice. I knew I was on my own. I made myself keep going.

I made it home. I collapsed on my bed, curled up, and, literally, passed out. I did not remove my clothes until sometime in the middle of the night. And then I collapsed again and was in and out of consciousness for days.

I was in bed for two weeks. I do not remember my mother being concerned or offering help of any kind. We never went to the doctor. It was not so much that we could not afford it—we had health insurance through her work—but she never saw us. She never saw how seriously ill I was because she never thought about it.

This flu was a new phenomenon. People were dying from it. But I knew if I complained at all, she would minimize it. She would belittle me. She would honestly think I was faking to get attention. I knew that. So I said nothing, and I slept. Every part of me hurt. Getting up to use the bathroom took a supreme effort. But I masked all this as much as possible when Mother was around. I masked my hurt—the physical and the emotional. I knew people were dying. I was afraid I might die. But I was more afraid of Mother.

Eventually, I did get better. When I returned to school, I was still weak, but I was so relieved to be alive that the residual weakness did not seem important. By this time—roughly three weeks into the semester—my friends were established in their own routines and were busy with other people. I had to begin the process of finding my classrooms again when everyone else looked like they had been doing this forever. I was behind in all my classes, of course. That whole first semester was ragged. But, gradually, things got better.

I remember my typing teacher most of all. Mr. Muncy empathized immediately with my plight. All the other students were well on their way to memorizing the keyboard. I knew nothing. He encouraged. He took the time to work with me individually. He never seemed too busy. He believed I could catch up. He believed in me. I caught up. I went on to become one of his most proficient students ever. Because of his kindness, I opened up to the possibilities in this new situation.

Mr. Muncy will never know what his kindness meant to me. What he modeled for me solidified my determination to be *that* kind of person. I scanned my environment constantly for caustic, exacting people—like my mother. And there were a few of those—my American History teacher, for instance. But there were many more like Mr. Muncy. People who were kind all the way through. It was not something they put on like a suit of clothes. It was who they were. The kindness was real. And I was able to see that. Thank God I could see these people. I had not been blinded to the possibility of kindness.

In spite of my high grades, my obvious intelligence, and my enthusiasm for all my studies, I was not in a college preparatory track at school. My mother made it abundantly clear that we were expected to get jobs as soon as we finished high school and begin to pay her back. We would pay room and board or we would leave. And she did not expect us to leave. She expected us to pay. I enrolled in business classes.

In the 1950s most high school classes were challenging. There was a pretest before I could enroll in shorthand. Shorthand was a fast-paced, difficult course. It was like learning a new language and forgetting everything you ever knew about written English. I loved it. I was good at it. I learned fast. I set records. Received certificates. I felt very good about my ability to decipher this new code. My teacher during that first year of shorthand was Mr. Haggblade. He was young and new to teaching, and he doted on me. And, of course, I loved him. I savored his attention. And I was careful not to let him know that I idolized him. I was interested and attentive during class, but I never made more of his interest in me than it was. By this time, I knew that my attraction to people like him came from deprivation. His interest in me was purely as a teacher gratified by the student who really gets it. I knew that. I am glad I knew that. The feelings that surfaced when I was with someone like Mr. Haggblade could take my breath away, give me dry mouth, make me lightheaded. I was careful to keep the feelings to myself. I knew they were inappropriate. Most of his students liked him. I was careful with my friends to conceal my excess of emotion. I knew what was appropriate. And I was an expert at concealing. Concealing. One of the important skills I learned at home.

There were no advanced placement classes back then, but there was a group of us who were kept together. The classes we ended up in were more challenging. I remember requesting Business English in my schedule because it seemed a logical choice for me. My counselor called me in and asked me why I had chosen that over the English class the rest of my group would be taking. I told him I thought I needed it to go with the rest of my business classes. He just shook his head and told me there would be nothing in that class for me. He assigned me with the rest of the group. What a mind-boggling, dazzling, spectacular stroke of genius that was. I can remember that conversation with my counselor; I remember exactly what he looked like, but I don't remember his name. In that one casual indication that he saw me as gifted, he made a huge difference in the rest of my high school career.

That special English class during my junior and senior years of high school was taught by Mr. McLennan. He was a retired Presbyterian minister. He loved sharp, inquisitive, eclectic minds. He expected all of that from us. He taught nothing predigested. He wanted us to think for ourselves. He enjoyed goading us into challenging our assumptions. And his. He actually expected to learn from us. Don't get me wrong. He was pretty sure he knew a whole lot more than we did. But he was open to whatever came his way—without prejudice or preconceptions.

Mr. McLennan was one of those rare individuals who demanded the best from whomever he cared about—and he cared deeply about his students. What he received in return was a hodgepodge of brilliance and inanity, and he took the best we had to offer to enrich his own experience. He relished it. Nothing was ever thrown away. He took the stuff we gave him from our minds, our hearts ... the stuff he dug out of us under extreme duress ... and he really thought about that stuff. It did not bounce off him and fall unused to the floor. He examined. He thought. He valued. He valued our stuff. We were rank amateurs. He was the sage, the prophet. Maybe that is the mark of a great prophet. The ability to see the profitable in others.

Mr. McLennan was the first person who ever told me that I had the ability to make people feel what I wrote. I took his writing assignments seriously—and there were plenty of them. I wrote for him. I wanted to impress him. He read my ideas, my sophomoric abstractions, my naïve propositions. He read it all. And he admired my ability. He was a giant. He mattered to so many. And he let me know that I mattered. I mattered to him.

The time I spent with Mr. McLennan is available in my memory for review at any time. He gave me a sense of potential. Other teachers saw me for who I was, and that was important—very important. Every teacher who did that for me filled a part of the huge hole I felt inside because my mother never saw me. She never knew me. But Mr. McLennan went beyond that. He saw the potential, the imaginable, the treasure worth mining. He gave me no gifts. He referred me back to myself. "The gifts are there, Bunny. They are yours already. Go after your gifts. They are implicit. You are one of the most gifted students I've ever taught." I did not fully understand what he meant at the time. I did not argue with him. But I had no idea what he meant. I could not yet imagine for myself. I was so far short of seeing what he saw. He saw greatness. He saw spirit.

I saw broken. He saw whole. I saw ugly. He saw beauty.

Mr. McLennan brought a bag of seemingly unrelated, disjointed issues and threw them at us in random fashion. Or so it seemed to us. Before our eyes, the disjointed formed a pattern. The discord became a melody. The pieces—odd, broken, queer in and of themselves—formed an intricate quilt, where every fragment had a purpose and lent its bit to the beauty of the whole. How did he do that? I was a good reader. Reading words was easy for me. I had never read ideas before. I graduated from *Black Beauty* to Dostoevsky. I never looked back. He inspired. Breathed into us. I know only part of what I learned from Mr. McLennan. The knowing has been a lifelong journey. We could not have known it all at once. I continue to know in small part what I learned from him. I will be learning what he taught us for the rest of my life.

Coming from a religious background, he challenged our easy acceptance of routine and regurgitated religiosity. There were students of all persuasions in the group. Mr. McLennan did not need the trappings of a formal institution. He was spiritual. He was not necessarily religious. I found this very threatening. I needed the rules and regulations. I needed the institution. Most of us did, I think. He knew this. We were just kids—16 or 17 years old. He was telling us the question we would all ask someday. He did not presume to tell us what our answer would be. I am just now—53 years later—asking the questions. I have no idea yet what my answer will be; such was his impact on my life. There were no trivial moments with Mr. McLennan.

When I married, he read the notice in the newspaper. He took the time to write me a personal note. I had not seen him for the five years since I graduated from high school. He told me that Buzz (yes, Buzz had been in his class a year ahead of me) and I were two of the shining accomplishments of his teaching career. I had been through so much in those five years. His note took me back to a feeling that I associated intensely with him. The feeling of being known, seen, and valued.

Mr. McLennan's class was easily the high point of my high school career, but I loved every bit of it. I had a group of friends. We had fun. But I was first and foremost a student. I was too shy with boys, too serious about my studies, too bookish to date. I averted my eyes from the boys. I felt awkward and unattractive around them. I did not want to try something that seemed so outside my experience. I did not know the rules of dating. I had no information. No one had ever explained that world to me. I was confident with my books, my girlfriends, the teachers who liked me. That was enough for me.

I graduated number twelve in a class of over 700 students. I was proud. I graduated with honors. I won the Outstanding Student Award for my graduating class; I received a scholarship to the local community college; a special seal on my diploma documented my three-year tenure in the National Honor Society. I was excited to be in the front row during the honors assembly. My mother did not attend the assembly, but Captain and Mrs. Irby did. I felt so proud for them to witness me as one of the best of my class. And they were proud of me. They said so.

Mother never once acknowledged my accomplishments in any way. She may not have been aware that what I did was exceptional. She seemed not to notice or care.

CHAPTER 14

Preparing for Ministry

"Spiritually evolved people, by virtue of their discipline, mastery and love, are people of extraordinary competence, and in their competence they are called on to serve the world, and in their love they answer the call."

The Road Less Traveled by M. Scott Peck, M.D.

Throughout my high school career, I remained active in church. The Salvation Army had become a second home—the good home—in every sense of the word. Captain and Mrs. Irby had nurtured the corps, and there had been growth in overall numbers, and there was a significant number of young people my age and a little younger. Captain and Mrs. Irby took us to rallies and camps, they taught us the Bible, and they made us laugh. They were loving, hardworking, and passionate. I became, more and more, the leader of the younger youth because Captain and Mrs. Irby enabled me. They never pushed, but they were ready to stand beside me when my natural leadership skills became evident under their guidance.

The Irbys were perfect exemplars of who and what God is in this world. They not only kept us safe, but they also pushed us to find our own spiritual wings. We flourished in their care.

For me, high school was a time of relative ease. School was good, church was a place where I was thriving, and I was routinely babysitting for the Irbys and others. Perhaps the best benefit of all this for me was the fact that I was not at home very much. It was during this relatively stress-free time that I began to discern with a new conviction that God was calling me to full-time service as a Salvation Army officer. I spoke with Captain and Mrs. Irby about this often. They were, without exception, encouraging. They were unabashedly proud of me also. With their recommendation, I was invited to enter Bible competitions, lead prayers, and participate in other small ways at territory-wide conferences usually restricted to those already ordained. I began to be noticed and encouraged by higher-ups within the Salvation Army—especially the Divisional Youth Secretaries, Captain and Mrs. Lincoln Upton.

The summer after my graduation from high school, Captain Upton invited me to work at the Army's youth camp in the mountains outside Santa Cruz, California. I was thrilled with the opportunity. This meant five weeks away from home doing something I loved in a most spectacular setting. It took some talking to win my mother's permission, but the fact that I would be paid finally convinced her that there was benefit in it for her. The money could be used to buy my own clothes and other necessities. This made sense to her.

The five weeks I worked at Redwood Glen Camp were idyllic in every way. I became acquainted with a wide variety of people from throughout the Western Territory of the Salvation Army. I was living with other girls like myself—girls who felt the call to follow a spiritual path that included working with underprivileged children. I was awed by the beauty of the setting, the generosity of the officers under whom we worked, and the close connection with the God I knew I would serve for the rest of my life.

Captain and Mrs. Upton were the camp directors. They were supremely suited to the position. He was funny and whimsical and was a compelling Bible teacher. She was organized, efficient, and a planner. Under Captain Upton, programs were always fresh and engaging, and I soon became his willing disciple. I was completely in my element. I loved being with the children, and I was gaining ever more experience in an area I foresaw as my vocation. Again, I saw in the Uptons a couple in the most complete sense—their two children were just a little younger than I was, they obviously enjoyed each other, and they found time for others, myself included.

After I had completed my five-week commitment, there was an unexpected opening in the subsequent five-week series of camps. The opening was for Dining Room Hostess. At age 17, I would be very young for this job. The hostess oversaw all of the youth who worked in the dining hall, worked closely with the cooks planning meal service, and attended all staff meetings to speak to all issues regarding the feeding of the 200 campers during each weekly session. In short, it was a job for a self-starting, mature adult. I did not imagine myself in this position, but Captain and Mrs. Upton did.

It was on the last day of my duties at camp that they called me into the office, explained that the hostess had to leave unexpectedly because her child was ill, and asked me if I would consider staying at camp to fill that position for them. They both expressed their absolute confidence in my ability, and Mrs. Upton told me that she would work closely with me until I was completely trained and at ease in the position. I jumped at the chance. I was thrilled just to stay at camp, let alone be given such a position of responsibility.

Best of all, I would be working with the Uptons—they were the "cool" leaders who combined spirituality with zany fun. Everyone wanted to work for them. And the pay was good too. I immediately said yes but told them I would have to talk to my mother. At the mere thought of talking to her, my stomach clenched in a familiar knot.

What would my mother make of this? It was a compliment, for sure, to be considered for this position. But my mother had a way of turning anything positive that I wanted into a slap in her face. I knew this, and I dreaded making the call. This question required immediate resolution, so I would not have time to do my usual routine of placating my mother and winning her approval by inches. Mrs.

Upton imagined the call home to be a mere formality. She encouraged me to do it immediately so they could put the plan in place.

I called my mother. I tried to keep my voice steady, relay the information without conveying too much enthusiasm, and emphasize the fact that I would be making good money for the rest of the summer. This would be my first real full-time, adult job.

My mother listened until I was finished. She was ominously silent for a heartbeat. Then she said, "So, you want to stay up there, do you? You're choosing to spend your entire summer with strangers? I have one vacation a year—remember me, the one who raised you when no one else would—and you won't even be here. I've given my life for you, and this is the thanks I get? Who do you think you are? Well, if that's what you want, just don't ever show your face around here again. You can stay with them for all I care. I don't want you." And she hung up the phone. The reality. I had a dream for a few minutes. This was reality.

Of course, I called my mother back immediately and told her I wanted to come home. I begged her to forgive me. I honestly did not want to hurt her. This was the bind that we—my brothers and I—were always in. We really did not want to hurt her, but she found a way to turn our most innocent requests into some kind of a vendetta against her. I had to go home. I knew I couldn't figure out the rest of my life while standing there in the phone booth at camp. Never go home? On one hand, that's exactly what I wanted, but I was 17 years old and caught in a toxic bond with this woman who was anything but a "mother" and, yet, was just that. I had to go home.

When I told Mrs. Upton that I could not stay, she was incredulous. What mother wouldn't want her daughter to have a chance like this? The Uptons saw this opportunity the way I did: a very young woman with the opportunity to grow in a safe environment. It would look great on any resume. They saw it as a plum that they had offered to me and to my mother by extension.

Therefore, Mrs. Upton misunderstood what had gone on between my mother and me. She said, "Bunny, if you just don't want to stay, you can tell us that. We won't be angry with you. But please don't lie about it." She could not imagine my mother standing in my way, so she thought I was lying about her withholding consent. She thought I was just using my mother as a way out. I tried to explain, but she expressed her disappointment, not in my mother, but in me. I walked away and packed my few belongings. During her tirade on the phone, my mother had told me to find my own way home—she would not come and get me. Home was 40 miles away.

I found someone at camp who would give me a ride to the Greyhound bus station in Santa Cruz. The bus left the depot at 2:00 that afternoon. I was packed and ready well ahead of time, but I was so upset by the conversation with my mother that I hardly said my goodbyes to the people I had engaged with so joyfully all summer. I kept to myself.

As the early afternoon wore on, I became nervous about making the trip to Santa Cruz in time to buy a ticket and get on the bus. By the time we were finally underway, I was pretty sure it just wasn't going to work. Sure enough, we got to the depot, my ride left me, I went inside, and I found that the bus had left 15 minutes earlier. There would not be another until the same time the next day.

I had to call my mother. She was livid.

I sat on the train tracks behind the bus depot. I sat and I cried. I was as heartbroken as I had ever been in my life. For a few moments, while the Uptons were talking with me, the world was my oyster. I was a young person who was valued. I was someone with a future. That's what it seemed like. I loved the Salvation Army, I loved working with children, I had bonded with Captain and Mrs. Upton, and I was making a step toward following a path of lifetime service. This was what they offered me. My mother smashed the dream and my heart.

She did come to get me. She was absolutely disdainful of me, of the Army, of the Uptons—of anything or anybody she felt usurped her absolute power over me. Who was I to want anything or anybody but her?

CHAPTER 15

Community College and Boys

"'I want to have only good things in my life. So I work on having positive thoughts because I know my thoughts are going to be creating whatever happens in my world.'"

Wally "Famous" Amos as quoted in *One Person Can Make a Difference* by Gerald G. Jampolsky, M.D.

I WAS NOT THE LEAST BIT NERVOUS OR INTIMIDATED WHEN I BEGAN classes at Hartnell College in the fall of 1959. I had my scholarship, I had preregistered and I knew many of my friends from high school would be there too. Hartnell was Salinas' version of a community college. Although my friends who went directly on to four-year colleges and universities called it "Hartnell High," it was exotic enough for me. After all, until I won the scholarship, I had absolutely no hope of attending any college. I was full of joy and enthusiasm as I walked onto the pleasant campus knowing that school had been one of the brightest spots in my life so far. I expected nothing less at Hartnell, and I wasn't disappointed.

Because I tested very high on the entrance exams and had

an excellent GPA coming out of high school, I went directly into English 1A, German, American Government, and Comparative Religions. It was all intriguing, but the very best was in the area where I always excelled—English Literature and Composition. Miss Perry was the instructor, and she was brilliant. I am still not a Shakespeare fan or aficionado, but she opened up to me the mysteries of this long-ago, still dynamic library. My term paper was a character study on Gertrude from Hamlet.

When Miss Perry returned our papers to us, she told the entire class that mine was the best paper she had ever read on the subject. Mine was not long, but it was terse and to the point, stayed on subject, cited valid sources, and was grammatically perfect in an age before spell and grammar check. I was a little embarrassed by her praise, but I was also exhilarated. Somewhere, I still have that paper. I loved the class and I loved this peculiar older lady who wore a wig because she had lost her hair to some dreadful childhood illness and who had an unapologetic love for Shakespeare.

With Miss Perry there was a mutual admiration that I recognized as that same old longing for the good parent. Miss Perry exemplified that for me. She was plump and witty, with a dry sense of humor. She loved my writing, and she freely acknowledged what she saw as exceptional talent. What's not to love? She was, of course, not my mother, but I somehow believed that she wouldn't have minded that role at all. That had to be enough.

I discovered boys at Hartnell. It didn't take long. I was now in a mix of students from all over Monterey and San Benito Counties. Hartnell was the only college within 50 miles at that time. I was no longer constrained by the image I had in high school—the "brain" who studied so hard she never had a social life.

By this time, I was working enough to buy my own clothes, and so I was finally able to buy clothes that looked good on me. I was small—barely five feet tall—and had the perfect hour glass figure. I had always been self-conscious of my ample bust line—in seventh grade, when my friends were stuffing toilet paper into their training bras, I was already wearing a C cup. I had such a poor self-image that I always covered myself completely and wore layers to conceal all the curves. Now, for the first time, I realized I could be attractive.

All of a sudden, I was being shown a lot of interest by the opposite sex. I could have my pick and go out as often as I wanted. And so I went out a lot. But I remained aloof to the idea of sexual intercourse. Kissing, even petting above the waist, but nothing going on below. The sexual revolution had not happened yet, birth control was brand new and not always obtainable, and I just didn't want to have sex anyway. It did not seem peculiar at all that I wanted to "save myself for marriage." I never waffled on it. Boys I dated either accepted it or went elsewhere. For me, it just wasn't negotiable. I liked being desired, but I found it easy to set boundaries with these boys and remain in control of my own values. I never sold out.

During my first semester at Hartnell, Captain and Mrs. Irby were transferred to another assignment, and new corps officers were posted to Salinas. I was sorry to see the Irbys go, but I was in a whole different space once I started college. I was looking at all kinds of new ideas, making new friends, and exploring the physical side that had previously not mattered to me. And so, when the Irbys left, I left the corps. The new officers, Captain and Mrs. Peacock, called me a number of times, but I wasn't in the least bit tempted to get to know them. They were strangers to me, and I was more than willing to put my calling on the back burner while I opened up to a new kind of freedom.

I was now working for Reed's Janitorial Service—doing bookkeeping, answering phones, and processing payroll—during the swing shift. Since the business operated at night—cleaning offices when they were closed—the hours were perfect for me. I finished my classes, did all my homework for the next day, showed up for work at 3:00, and worked until 9:00. At 9:00 I would meet up with friends. As soon as I began working, my mother required that I pay half of what I earned to her for my room and board. This would always be the case. There was no free ride with Mother. Everything had a price.

I had a succession of boyfriends—mostly casual, sometimes a little more serious. But I was not shopping for a husband. At that time in American culture, it was unusual for a woman to stay single much beyond 20. Many of my friends were already married and had begun having babies. I did not feel any pressure to follow suit.

In spite of the fun I was having in my classes, at work, and dating, there remained in the back of my mind the possibility of reengaging with the Salvation Army and going to The Salvation Army School for Officer Training in San Francisco to realize what had been a firm commitment to serve others. For me, I had to be single to do this. The Salvation Army requires both members of a married couple to attend seminary, be ordained, and serve together. I had rarely dated anyone within the Salvation Army and had never met anyone who seemed an appropriate partner. I wanted to enter training as a single woman, because it seemed more would be open to me that way. Single women were not discriminated against in the Army. They competed for opportunities alongside men, and appointments and promotions seemed to be based on ability, not gender. I believe I had an idea that I would meet that certain someone while at Training School. In that way, our future together would be assured.

My two years at Hartnell were a mix of social and intellectual growth. I had led a cloistered life of home and church up to that point. Extracurricular activities had been virtually nonexistent. I found out that I could let go, relax, enjoy. I began to believe that a normal life was possible. Now that I was grown and doing life on my own, with very little supervision from Mother, I began to think that I could separate from her without the overwhelming emotional consequences. What I had overlooked was the fact that I had changed, but she had not. She still saw me as her possession. I was still an extension of her. I might go my own way during the day, but I belonged to her. My home was with her. She still owned me.

I graduated from Hartnell College in 1961 with my Associate of Arts Degree.

CHAPTER 16

A Further Word About Dissociative Identity Disorder

"The traumatized child repeatedly enters into contextually determined dissociative states of consciousness that acquire a history of experiences and affects and a state-dependent repertoire of behaviors. Over time, these states are elaborated into alter personalities."

Diagnosis and Treatment of Multiple Personality Disorder by Frank W. Putnam, M.D.

During the settling relationship with Captain and Mrs. Irby, I did not need to dissociate as much, but there were times of stress even in that relationship—just the ordinary give-and-take of any relationship—and during those times, my child parts were hypersensitive to any perceived signs of rejection on their part. There were times when my, by this time, fully developed child alters felt in jeopardy of losing again. This inevitably led to switching.

Captain Irby was always much more important to us—my

alters and myself—than Mrs. Irby was. The hunger for a father was much more compelling than the need for a good mother. We ached for a father—my conscious self as well as the eternally watching inner parts. We spotted potential candidates everywhere. Besides Captain Irby, there were multiple opportunities, at school in particular, to engage closely with positive father figures—Mr. McLennan being a major one. I knew when the child alters were involved in this transference phenomenon—their neediness was palpable. These stand-in "dads" were wonderful, but the kid parts craved the real thing. There is a difference between a caring teacher and a totally available parent. My child alters were stuck in a dynamic that needed an all-caring parent who was unlimitedly available. And they craved touch.

It is now widely known that touch plays a huge role in healthy growth in young children. My kid parts wanted to be held, to sit on daddy's lap, to be hugged. The need for the physical display of affection from a man in authority over them was another of the elements that set us up for predation. It's interesting to note that physical displays by boys of my own age did nothing for the child alters. The groping, hugging, and petting with these boys was not what they wanted at all. They weren't even interested. It bored them. They were absent during these situations—they had no desire to be present at all.

When we were in the presence of a father figure, on the other hand, I felt the kid parts at full attention, aware of every nuance. I felt their neediness and their desire for physical contact. I was *very* careful. I knew what they wanted was inappropriate and would be seen as an aberration. I knew their innocence, but I also had a firm grip on what was socially acceptable. I contained their neediness when I could, and when it became too much, I removed us from the situation. There was never any inappropriate touching by Captain Irby or by any of the teachers we were fortunate enough to be nurtured by. This was the way it should have been. There also was *never*—and I mean *never*—any inappropriate acting out on my part or on the part of any child alters. I made sure of that.

By this time, my internal world contained eight distinct alters.

I never interacted with them. I heard their voices and I felt their needs. I also stepped aside and let them out when it seemed necessary or expedient. I was aware of two little girl alters who were three and four years old—Phyllis Ann and Claudia. Their need was for the daddy who left them. There was Kevin the seven-year-old boy who went to school and learned arithmetic and who also ached for a father. There was Curtis, the 13-year-old boy who was patterned directly after my older brother. Curtis was totally self-contained, needing no one—much like my brother. Curtis watched out for the younger parts, and he also contained the rage for everyone. His was a big responsibility. I became accustomed to internal "hurricanes." These were episodes when the rage just could not be secreted away quickly enough or contained tightly enough. These episodes were triggered, without exception, by interactions with my mother. These hurricanes were a nightmare for me. I knew I had to stay in control.

There were also several adult alters. Delia, as mentioned earlier, was the caregiver for all the little ones. She was patterned after my Aunt Dolores—my wonderful Lorse. Josie was an African American woman who stood as a filter to ward off danger. She was foulmouthed, outspoken, and combative. There were times—with boys who wouldn't take no for an answer, for instance—when Josie was the needed enforcer. There was Bunny Too, who was the party girl who loved to date, do a little drinking, dance, and make out with the boys. And there was Charlotte in full Salvation Army uniform—the moral police person who kept us in line and helped us avoid the worst confrontations with Mother by staying vigilant and reminding us of the rules.

And so there was much going on below the surface, even during the relatively placid times. On the outside I was seen as a bright, outgoing, high-achieving teenager who was dedicated to her studies and to God. On the inside a significant part of me was struggling with arrested developmental issues that were not easily contained. The need for a father was a part of every action I took, every word I uttered, every achievement I aspired to. If I was good enough, smart enough, pretty enough, I would finally achieve that ultimate experience—I would be some daddy's little girl.

PART II

BETRAYAL

CHAPTER 17

John

"*Trust* ... refers to the assumption by the person with less power in forbidden-zone relationships that the person with the greater power will act in her best interest. This assumption has its inner source in the model of the parent-child relationship. The tendency to trust is reinforced, even invited, by the professions themselves, which have codes of ethics asserting that the interest of the patient, client, student, congregant or protégée must be held upper-most, and that sexual contact is not permissible."

Sex in the Forbidden Zone by Peter Rutter, M.D.

INTO THIS MAELSTROM OF NEEDINESS CAME CAPTAIN JOHN HART—THE answer to my prayers and the destroyer of my dreams. He took what no man has any right to take. He gave what no man has a right to give.

In 1962, when Captain John Hart came to Salinas as the new corps officer for the Salvation Army, he entered what was still a small town along the central coast of California. These were relatively simple times in this agricultural "home town" of working class people. He brought his wife, Peggy, and their four children with him. His was a picture-postcard family—wholesome, outgoing, musically talented. Everything a small congregation of eager followers could want in a pastor. When he came into my office at the Community Chest that first time to introduce himself, I did not know there was another side to John. A side I would come to know as he revealed himself to be much more than I wanted or expected and much less than I hoped.

He was 45 years old when he came to Salinas. I was 20.

I was secretary to the executive director of the Community Chest. The Salvation Army was a member agency. When John came into the Community Chest office for the first time, it was not to meet my boss. It was to introduce himself to me. Some of the members of the corps had told him about me, and he wanted to meet me for himself. I was flattered that he thought me important enough to warrant his personal attention. I was immediately captured by the intensity with which he connected with people. With a few words, a ready smile, a warm handclasp, and eyes that said, "No one is more important to me than you are," he imprinted himself on mind and heart.

From that first meeting, I wanted to be near him. I craved what I saw in him. I knew he had something I wanted. I pointed my face toward that almost forgotten dream of being what he was—a Salvation Army officer. The very next Sunday, I attended worship at the corps and recommitted my life to Christ in the Salvation Army. I felt God had sent John specifically for this purpose—to reengage me on the path that had always been right for me. I would finally answer my calling.

There was nothing physically attractive about John. He was short, overweight, balding. That was soon forgotten as one felt his personal energy, his vitality, the fervor he brought to each moment. I don't remember ever hearing the word charisma before I met John, but that is exactly what he had. Whether he was speaking to one person or to an entire congregation, he projected an intimate interest in his listeners. Being in his presence was being drawn into his experience, savoring his reality, wishing to be nowhere else.

I was not the only one who felt this. On the contrary, our congregation flourished under his leadership. The numbers grew to be sure, but there was more to it than that. Each person felt more important. We each felt that we were involved in something of great consequence, a cause of inestimable value. And we had a leader who knew the destination and desired that each of us make the journey with him. He wove a spell of hope and optimism. To a person, we loved him. We willingly put our lives in his hands.

From the very beginning, John made it clear that I was important to him. He invited me to his home at every opportunity. I quickly learned to love Peggy. She was warm and welcoming in a quieter way. Where John was flashy, Peggy was settling, soothing, calming. Where the relationship with the Irbys had grown and matured over time, my engagement with the Harts was breathtakingly immediate. There was no period of discovery. My dissociated child parts had contained their yearning until the moment that the perfect consummation was at hand. When I pledged my life to Christ anew, these small, watchful, needy parts inside saw only John and Peggy. Their allegiance was immediate and complete. They weren't interested in God. They wanted John and Peggy. These were the ones. We had found our family. At last. I fully bought into this myself. I was totally unguarded in this new relationship that seemed to promise everything we needed.

Between the two of them—John and Peggy—there seemed to be the perfect balance for a life freshly consecrated to God. The fact that they also encapsulated the parents I had hoped for was a deeply felt bonus—but my commitment to God this time was the mature decision of a ready heart with an exceptional talent for ministry to children. I wanted to fulfill my destiny.

With my recommitment to the spiritual life came vulnerability to any and all instructions from my commanding officers. I wanted to please; I wanted to get this whole dimension of my life right this time. And so my discipleship began.

Peggy seemed content to provide the serene space in which

John and I generated our grand plans for whatever project was at hand. Because he had singled me out to be his prodigy, I was with him constantly. He took me seriously. He recognized and encouraged my abilities. He told me with his words and with his attention that I was an integral part of his every plan for our corps. I felt alive with him. Alive in the world. Alive in my devotion to a just and good cause. I was touched by his zeal for God and for man. I wanted to be like him.

And he made it clear that he wanted to teach me. To mold me. To help me become the minister that he was. I idolized him. I was his adoring subject. Everything else in my life became uninteresting, trite, boring. I wanted what he had to teach. I lived for the time I was with him—watching him, helping him, assisting him in this great cause.

While I was oblivious to all else but my calling, had he always had ulterior motives? Was his purpose from the moment we met to win my devotion so that he could use me? I will never know for sure. Because of the nature of our relationship—based on a commitment to serve God and mankind—I trusted him without qualification. I never once thought I was unsafe with him. I was young and idealistic. And I was starved for the kind of attention he gave me.

CHAPTER 18

John's Family

"All of us have desires to be babied, to be nurtured without effort on our parts, to be cared for by persons stronger than us who have our interests truly at heart. ... Each one of us ... looks for and would like to have in his or her life a satisfying mother figure and father figure."

The Road Less Traveled by M. Scott Peck, M.D.

JOHN AND PEGGY'S FOUR CHILDREN ACCEPTED ME INTO THEIR LIVES AS readily as their parents had. Because John saw me as someone instrumental to the growth of the church and worthy of his time and effort, his children—each in his or her own way—received me without reservation. There was no hesitation. I was immediately one of them.

Pauline was the oldest of the four. She was approximately my age. She was beautiful. Curly dark brown hair, skin like porcelain, small, even features, and a diminutive figure. Her physical presence was arresting. But, more than that, Pauline was one of the sweetest spirits I have ever known. She was quiet like her mother, but she had a depth and purity, a maturity of spirit that was far beyond her years. I never heard her speak hastily or harshly. Every word out of her mouth and every action seemed an extension of the pure and sweet nature that set her apart from the rest of us. I was in awe of Pauline. I loved to look at her. Her beauty was absolutely natural and she seemed totally unaware of the effect she had on others. She seemed far ahead of me spiritually. I mentioned this to John. He made light of it. Pauline and John did not have a particularly close relationship, although the unique father-daughter intensity that I found so compelling was definitely present. Pauline seemed ill at ease with her father's directness and his unabashed enjoyment of life. Hers was a more measured approach.

Pauline's religion was a very personal one, even then. John and I needed the group experience. We needed a religion that encompassed, consumed, and drove us. Pauline meditated on what was holy and was quietly nourished by it.

I believe that Pauline wondered about her father's motives with me from the beginning. I felt that. If she had any reservation about who or what I was in connection with the church, her family or her father, she would never have voiced it in a way that would hurt. But long before there were any sexual overtones in John's relationship with me, Pauline questioned the time we spent together. She was very close to her mother, and perhaps she was voicing what Peggy could never bring herself to think or question. Pauline looked at me with concern. I do not believe that she begrudged me the time with her father. I think she was worried.

Jackie—younger than Pauline and me by a year or two—was a female version of her father. She was outgoing, boisterous, demanding of herself and others, vigorous, enthusiastic. She was an elf—short of stature, curvaceous, with a cherub's round face and a pug nose. I loved her instantly. We became close friends, coworkers in the church, and competitors for her father's attention.

I identified closely with the relationship that Jackie had with John. That was the relationship I wanted. She teased her father mercilessly, challenged his concepts, poked and prodded him physically and intellectually. She took nothing for granted. She took everything for granted. She had a security and self-assurance that were like magnets to me.

Jackie whined at restrictions that her mother tried to impose on her impulsiveness, looked at her father with a twinkle in her eye, won him over, and captured the heart of anyone who tried to dampen the vitality that defined her. She never seemed to consider that she should not have her way in whatever she wanted. And, mostly, she wanted what was good. Her motives were always the best. It was her methods that were sometimes outlandish and ill thought out.

Because of Jackie's natural effervescence and her refusal to take others' opinions seriously, she found success within herself. She seemed well satisfied with who she was. Others found it easy to forgive the brashness that sometimes could have gotten her into trouble. Because she was comfortable with who she was and because she seemed always to be looking outward and forward, I found her irresistible. I think she found in me some of the seriousness, introspection, and caution that she needed for balance.

When I was a visitor in their home, I remember being always aware of the relationship of mutual adoration that John and Jackie shared. They were openly affectionate in an obvious, in-your-face way that seemed independent of anyone else in the environment. They really saw and appreciated each other. They listened to each other. They laughed often and took great joy in each other. They argued constantly with great enthusiasm and even greater affection. They pushed each other. And when Jackie pushed John too far, they could end up on the floor wrestling. This seemed totally innocent and healthy. They would wrestle until they were both physically spent and senseless from laughter, intoxicated with the abandon they both brought to every experience.

I envied Jackie. I envied her that exclusive relationship with her father. I loved Jackie. I idolized John. And I think one of the things that drew me to both of them was the bond they shared as a father and daughter who openly valued and loved each other. I wanted what Jackie had with her father. I do not remember wishing her away. I wanted to be included in that experience—not to supplant it. My friendship with Jackie brought me as close to that experience as I could ever imagine being. But I watched her with her father and I was hungry. As stated earlier, my dissociated kid parts craved the touch of a father. We all envied her the attention she received, the petting, the intense eye contact, the acknowledgement that she was immediately important—a part of his world that was joyful and sought after.

My child parts wanted what Jackie had. I felt their hard knot of desire when we watched them together. We wanted to be somebody's little girl. I wanted to be somebody's big girl. We all wanted somebody to be proud of us. We wanted somebody to love us as completely and as innocently as John and Jackie loved each other.

It would be that need—to be loved, cuddled, held, protected—that would later set us up for a different kind of attention entirely. I can clearly say that I never wanted to take Peggy's place in John's life. I never looked at them as a couple and wanted to be in that role. I never aspired to the position Peggy held. I loved Peggy and longed for her as a mother just as I longed for John as a father. I never thought of her as competition for John's affection. Their relationship with each other, their "couple-ness," made it safe for me to enter. I wanted to be one of the kids. One of their kids. I wanted them both. I wanted a family. Not an affair.

Donny was three years younger than Jackie. He was pensive and petulant. He was open and honest. He was cute and funny. He was outspoken, headstrong, and not easily discouraged. He had a crush on me. He was outspoken about the fact that he loved me. He was sure that we were meant to be together. At 15 years of age, Donny protested an undying affection that became almost an obsession. I was always gentle with Donny. I was flattered that he saw me as someone worthy of his first real love. And Donny was always respectful of me as a person. He never assumed anything. He waited patiently for me to discover what he already knew for a fact—that we would someday be together. When he had money, he bought me gifts. I accepted them. I knew that part of the reason for Donny's interest in me was the position that I now held as youth director in the church. He was talented, a born leader, and saw in me some of the abilities he himself had and wanted to develop. My relationship with Donny was the reverse of my relationship with John. Donny looked up to me and craved my attention. It was a classic case of puppy love. I always knew this. And I knew that Donny could easily be hurt. I cared about Donny. I did love him, but in a platonic way. Because I loved him, I took Donny seriously, never belittled his affection or questioned his certainty that our future was meant to be shared. He came to me with his heart in his hand, and I handled that heart with tenderness. I was very clear with Donny about the nature of my affection for him, and he seemed to accept that—for the moment. He told me he would never leave, never let go, that someday the truth would be apparent to me. Until then, he was willing to wait.

Later, when everyone else turned on me ... when I had no friends left ... when I had been despised and reviled by the church I loved, expelled from the congregation of people who had been my extended family, and coldly and deliberately hated by everyone else in John's family ... when my own mother would not listen ... Donny was the exception.

Donny was the one who said, "I know you, Bunny. You would never do the things they say you did. I will never believe anything bad about you. I believe in you. Remember me? I'm the one who loves you. I always will."

And so, finally, Donny was right. He did love better, more completely, with more maturity than anyone else. His was a love that never entertained doubt, that believed the best, that sought the highest.

When Donny was 21 years old, he died in a surfing accident almost within sight of the home I then shared with my husband. I never saw him after that last protestation of belief in me. But he loved me. In the highest and best way, he loved me.

Robin was the youngest of John and Peggy's children. He was probably ten years old when I met him. As the youngest, he clung to his mother, and Peggy seemed to dote on him. He was small for his age but articulate and able to hold his own. I knew Robin less than I knew the others—perhaps because he was too young to belong to the teenage youth groups and was seldom involved with us. He was as musically talented as the rest of his family; he was sweet looking—almost pretty—but reticent and not as eager to participate in what was going on around him. He seemed satisfied to be with himself, and when he needed more than that, he usually turned to his mother.

Peggy was loving with all her children. I never saw her unhappy with any of them. But I saw the tender side of her as a mother most in her relationship with Robin. She accepted him as he was, touched him gently, let him be happy or unhappy with life without seeming to take any of it personally. She was always aware and available. And that seemed enough for Robin.

Watching Peggy with Robin, I remember thinking, "That's the way a mother is supposed to be. She loves him enough to take care of him, even when he's not perfect. That's the way I will be when I am a mother." And ten-year-old Robin soaked up Peggy's availability, leaned on her during sermons that, to him, were boring, and whined at her when we were on our way to yet another youth rally and he would rather have stayed home. He was ten. She allowed him to be just that. To me that seemed a miracle.

I will always be grateful for the time I spent with John and Peggy and their family—before things changed between John and me. I was a part of a loving family. I grew. I thrived. I watched how they related to one another. We worked at the church together. We prayed together. We sought each other out for relaxation, inspiration, consolation. We discussed important issues. We planned God's work and we talked about the eternal. It was important. It was essential. For me, it was heaven. I felt rich. I felt close and full. I wasn't restless. I felt satisfied, content. We were on fire for the Lord, but we had the cool refreshment of each other's presence. I thought I had finally found home—with them, with the church, with my calling to enter ministry.

Even after my relationship with John became sexual, I treasured moments of normalcy when we were all together at church or at their home and I could "forget" about what John and I did when we were alone. I needed his family. I clung to the naïve illusion that things could go on as they had before. I dissociated when we had sex. I pretended that the sex did not happen. I pretended that it would never happen again. I pretended that we could be pure and good and holy. I pretended that he would see me. That he would realize. That he would know what I could not tell him. I wanted a daddy. Is that the way a daddy acts?

CHAPTER 19

Sex in the Forbidden Zone

"There is a category of sex that is very dark. I mean rape, incest, molestation, abuse of any number of varieties, centered around sex, then lodged like a knife in people's souls."

Illuminata by Marianne Williamson

I HAD KNOWN JOHN FOR ABOUT FOUR MONTHS WHEN THE FIRST SEXUAL contact took place. I refused to believe what had happened. I dismissed it from my mind. I convinced myself that I had misunderstood. Or imagined. Surely what I thought had happened had not happened. That one incident—the incident that changed everything—remains isolated, disconnected, separate, encapsulated.

If I had allowed myself to look closely at that incident, I would have had to admit to myself that the hopes I had built around this man for the future I wanted were false. By the time John made his first sexual demands of me, I had already made a huge investment in who and what I thought he was. He was important to me. His opinion of me was important. I needed the recommendation of my corps officer in order to enter training school. Looked at in this way, he had me just where he wanted me.

That one incident was the signpost at a fork in the road. Perhaps if I had reacted differently ... if I had stood up for myself ... if I had recognized the incident for what it was ... if I had protected myself from unwanted invasion at that first hint of his uncalled-for expectations of what my role in his life was to be.

But I did not react that way. I was blindsided. I did not see it coming. And then I was like a deer caught in the headlights.

I told him I did not want it. I watched him take his clothes off. His fat body was repugnant to me. His face was not the face of the mentor I idolized. This face was a blank mask—no emotion whatsoever. He calmly took off his clothes and then he instructed me to take mine off. I cried. I held myself and told him I would not. I told him I did not want him to see me naked. But I did not scream or run. I never even thought about doing either of those things. This, after all, was John, the man who loved God and alongside whom I worked to minister to the marginalized. The unimaginable was happening, and I still could not imagine that he would actually do this. Was this some kind of a test?

I told him again that I would not take my clothes off. He said that was okay. What he wanted did not require that my clothes be removed. With his blank face, his big belly, and his erection, he approached me. I kept my arms crossed in front of me. He pushed me down on the sofa and pulled my skirt up, exposing my underwear. He laid himself on top of me. He then grabbed my panties and pushed them aside. Within seconds, he was inside me.

I begged him to stop. I pleaded with him to let me go. He was probably 225 pounds to my 110. I could not move once he was on top of me. I did not scream. I did not hit, bite, or scratch. I did not fight. I begged. And then I dissociated. I checked out as I had done 17 years before with my father. The dynamics of the two relationships were remarkably similar. I loved them both. I trusted them both. I wanted to be special to them both. I did not know how to defend against either of them. I did not know that was an option.

I offer the following quote from *Diagnosis and Treatment of*

Multiple Personality Disorder, in which Dr. Putnam discusses reactivation of dissociative symptoms after rape:

> In most of these cases, the patient appeared to have been functioning well prior to the rape ... and had a significant deterioration in function following the trauma. Often the trauma reactivated nightmares and flashbacks of previous incest or sexual abuse, which were followed by increasingly frequent dissociative experiences such as time loss or minifugue episodes.
>
> "In some of these cases, the history given by the personalities suggests that the patient had achieved some level of integration or at least stability in the personality system, which was shattered by the sexual assault and the subsequent reactivation of dissociated memories and affects from prior sexual abuse.

As mentioned in the foreword, the manuscript for *Unholy Union* was complete before I read Dr. Putnam's book. When I read this portion in his section on "Patients with Posttraumatic and Pathological Grief Reaction," it perfectly mirrored what happened within me during John's first attack and during subsequent months when he took great pleasure in perpetuating his abuse.

While he was writhing on top of me, John told me that I was not pretty, that there was nothing special about me. I heard the words. What was his purpose in saying this to the young person who was now lying dazed and hurt beneath him? I think he wanted me to think this was not about the obvious—lusting after a woman's body—because that is prohibited in the scriptures. I think he wanted me to believe that what he was doing was ordinary, nothing to be upset about. It was just a different part of the relationship we had been building over the past several months.

To further document the inappropriateness of John's behavior—no matter what my mental state may have been—I offer the following quote from Dr. Peter Rutter's thoughtfully written, very powerful book, *Sex in the Forbidden Zone*:

The forbidden zone is a condition of relationship in which sexual behavior is prohibited because a man holds in trust the intimate, wounded, vulnerable, or undeveloped parts of a woman. The trust derives from the professional role of the man as doctor, therapist, lawyer, clergy, teacher or mentor, and it creates an expectation that whatever parts of herself the woman entrusts to him (her property, body, mind, or spirit) must be used solely to advance her interests and will not be used to his advantage, sexual or otherwise.

"Under these conditions, sexual behavior is always wrong, no matter who initiates it, no matter how willing the participants say they are. In the forbidden zone, the factors of power, trust, and dependency remove the possibility of a woman freely giving consent to sexual contact. Put another way, the dynamics of the forbidden zone can render a woman unable to *withhold* consent. And because the man has the greater power, the responsibility is his to guard the forbidden boundary against sexual contact … (Italics from original author.)

I never wanted sex with John. I never touched him inappropriately. I never dressed in a provocative manner. I never said one word that could be construed as an invitation for sexual intimacy. I followed all the same rules with John that I had followed with teachers, with Captain and Mrs. Irby. My child alters were hungry for the father relationship, but their neediness was contained within my internal system. I had become expert at this. I was circumspect.

I had willingly placed my life, my spirit, my soul in John's hands, believing they were safe with him. I never wanted sex. He did not ask for my consent when his interest in me became sexual. His actions were taken in a most ordinary way. As though we were equals. As though there were no special relationship of trust for which he was responsible. As though he were not married. As though I did not already love his wife. As though there were nothing unusual or particularly important about his sexual interest in me.

He told me God wanted him to do it.

He had prayed about it.

He had prayed about this?

I offer the following from *Sex in the Forbidden Zone*:

> The power of the pastor over the congregant is tremendously enhanced by his authority, if he wishes to exercise it, to describe to a woman her status with God. A sexually abusive clergyman can easily exploit this authority by telling a woman that her sexual involvement is part of a *divinely ordained plan*. Even sophisticated women can have difficulty resisting this argument *if they are devoted to the religious vision that the clergyman represents*.

When John was finished, he got off me, calmly put his clothes back on, and told me that he was ready to take me home. He said that if I thought about telling anyone about what had happened, he would say I was lying. He told me that since he was my corps officer, it was my responsibility to obey him in all things. He also said that since he was an officer and I was nobody, he would be believed and I would not. And then he added a threat to harm me and/or my family if I ever told anyone.

He also told me that he knew I wanted it as much as he did.

I listened to what he was saying and had no response whatsoever. I was stunned, hurt, and ashamed. I was in a fugue state—watching, listening, but unable to assimilate what had happened or what he was saying. This is another side effect of dissociation—having more than one personality processing the situation, thus putting the whole system on overload. John's sexual acting out with me to satisfy himself with no thought of the effect on my life was tantamount to the incest visited on me by my father.

This first encounter happened at the corps after a youth group meeting. All the other kids had gone home, and John had asked me to stay and help him get ready for the Sunday worship service.

This was not unusual—it had become a routine. What happened when the others were gone this time was anything but routine.

In the back of the building was a room the kids used to hang out in. There was a sofa and a couple of big chairs in the room. I was arranging song books and Bibles in the pews when John called to me and asked me to come back there where he was. I walked into the room, and he asked me to sit down on the sofa because there was something we needed to talk about. We did not talk.

When he took me home that night, I was bereft. Thankfully, my mother was at work and neither of my brothers was at home. I took a bath, curled up in bed, held myself together as best I could, and rocked myself to sleep.

Thus began a year of obedience to the demands of my corps officer that included things that are still very difficult for me to write about. Throughout it all, I tried to maintain some semblance of normalcy. I was so ashamed of what was happening that I feared someone finding out as much as John did. I believed what he said about no one believing me. I knew I could not tell my mother—my fear of her was greater than any despair I felt for myself. I did not want my brothers to know. The shame and guilt were overwhelming.

Dissociating became a way of life. Whereas dissociation had served its purpose when I was a young child, it had become less important during my teen years when I was more in control of my life at school and at church. From that first experience with John, I began to use dissociation to get me through when I saw no way out. I was desperate to retain some sense of normalcy. I needed to carry on as if nothing were amiss. I did this by dissociating when the sexual activity took place. And I put on a brave face for the whole world. Sometimes it's very difficult to be brave. I paid a heavy price. There was no peace for me.

For the victim of sexual abuse, there can be no peace.

Late one night, I came to from a period of dissociation and found myself in my mother's car driving around Salinas. I knew one of my alters had been drinking. I allowed the drinking to take place. Drinking was one way of distancing ourselves from the pain for a while. I drank after I had been with John. I could not drink at home. My brothers would have wondered what was going on—I had them to deal with even if I drank late at night when Mother was at work. Ostensibly, I was going into the ministry. Drinking was not compatible with to that objective.

So, after I had been with John, I would get in my car and just drive, and I would drink. More than once, I entertained the idea of having a terrible accident to end everything. I thought about being arrested for drunk driving. I wanted someone, something to stop me. I did not feel like I could stop what was going on. I wanted someone to take over—to take control and make it stop. I drank. I drove. And then, drunk out of my mind, I went home. And slept. If I was drunk enough, I could sleep.

Years later, drinking again became a problem. Drinking had never been something I routinely did—I had no taste for it—but it became a problem when I was finally processing all of this with my psychiatrist. Alcohol as a coping mechanism had lain dormant for 30 years, but it became an issue when we (my alters and I) were finally in a deep and comprehensive therapy to free ourselves from the burden of guilt, shame, and despair the relationship with John—and then Linc—had left us with.

During that therapy, my teen alter, Curtis (who carried the anger for us all), drank to escape the trauma of recalling and retelling. We often went to our therapy sessions after drinking eight ounces of straight vodka. Eventually, I was able to tell my psychiatrist what was going on, and we entered into a contract with him that we would not drink before, during, or directly after our sessions. Therapy offers resolution, but there is a cost. I experienced many overpowering compulsions—drinking, suicidal ideation—and had to deal with it all without acting it out in my current life. It was worth it. But it was hell. Thirty years after I last saw John or Linc, I was dealing with the legacy of their predation.

While ensnared in the relationship with John, death became a welcome idea. It beckoned to me. I would drive to the alley behind the corps building and just sit there and cry and cry. I sobbed my heart out. I was so alone. I needed help but knew no one to whom I could turn. I fantasized about suicide. I did not want to die. I had been taught that people who suicide go to hell. I did not want to go to hell. But I did not want to live either.

Because there was no resolution of my victimization when it came to light within the Salvation Army, because I was told to go away and "tell no one," I carried all the pain of my victimization with me throughout my adult life. Flashbacks plagued me. When some small thing—sometimes totally unrelated—would bring the relationship with John to my mind, I would be back there again. I would feel the gut-wrenching shame and guilt, the sense of hopelessness and helplessness. Despair.

My husband's gun became a way out. I found myself in our back yard pressing his gun against my temple. On other occasions, I came to with suicide kits in my car: a length of hose, duct tape, a towel. There was a part of me that thought that was the way out. I could pay for what my minister had done to me with my life.

The effects of sexual abuse run deeper, somehow, than other types of abuse. I had endured verbal, emotional, psychological, and physical abuse from my mother, so I would be in a position to know this. It is as though sexual abuse is so inside the victim that it can never be erased. There is a feeling of filthiness that is inherent to the experience. This is the gift that John gave me.

CHAPTER 20

Did it Really Happen?

"Many forbidden-zone relationships fatally reenact such scenarios: a woman, closed down to herself but adapted to meet the expectations of others, puts hope and trust in a male therapist, teacher, pastor or lawyer. When he attempts to sexualize their relationship, the woman, by deep inner training, is preadapted to numbly turn over her body and sexuality to his needs."

Sex in the Forbidden Zone by Peter Rutter, M.D.

WHEN I SAW JOHN ON THE SUNDAY AFTER THAT FIRST EXPERIENCE, he was the John I had known and loved. He was absolutely without guile. I avoided personal contact with him during worship and did my best to behave normally also. I began to doubt my own perception of what had happened. Had I imagined it? Surely it had been some bad dream—a nightmare from which I had awakened and which I would never need to visit again.

Dr. Putnam says in *Diagnosis and Treatment of Multiple Personality Disorder*, "Even if the patient is not completely amnesic for all of his or her dissociative episodes, the dissociative process still produces a distortion of recall so that memories of a dissociative episode may have a distant, detached, and dreamlike quality that makes the patient question whether or not the experience actually occurred." This aptly describes my effort to erase the episode entirely by choosing to not be present when it happened and then to squirrel away the memories to lessen the pain of knowing what had been done to me. This technique allowed me to hope.

This respite lasted for two weeks. All of the usual activities transpired, but there was no effort on John's part to single me out for any kind of out-of-the-ordinary personal attention. I remember being relieved. I went into a mode I had always used with my mother—a Pollyanna belief that if I was good enough, the bad stuff would never happen again. I believed that because I had to pretend I had some control over my life. I believed because I had to go on putting one foot in front of the other

I began to relax with John. I wanted to think that whatever had happened was over and would never happen again. I was again enjoying being with his family. These family times were rich times for me, and I began to believe I could still have them. I wanted to hold on to the illusion of family. And so I hoped.

And then, one evening when John and I were in the office at the corps, he led the conversation around to our relationship. There were others present in other parts of the building, so I did not feel threatened. He offered me a lot of the predictable justifications for his behavior—such as the fact that he and Peggy had not had a sexual relationship for a long time. He said that's why God had brought me into his life. God knew he needed sexual release. I was there specifically for John's use. He was not bullying or threatening. He was talking in a conversational tone. He said he knew that I would understand and that the experience could be good for both of us. He again stated that he knew I wanted it as much as he did, and he told me he could teach me things that would be good for me. Absent from the conversation was any interest on his part in how I felt about all of this.

I know I felt trapped. Here I was, where I belonged—in church in front of God—and what was being proposed by my minister was against everything I had ever been taught about goodness and holiness. He asked me what my mother would think if she knew what I had "encouraged him to do." He was playing mind games—manipulating me in my weakest area. By this time, he knew what my relationship with my mother was like. As counterintuitive as it sounds, to this day, I was more afraid of my mother than I was of John. And I think he knew that.

During this conversation, John kept his tone warm and personable. I listened to him and began to believe that I could bear anything until I was able to leave Salinas and go to training school. I asked John if he thought I would still be able to go to training. He answered, "Of course. This has nothing to do with that. I would never stand in your way. I just want us to enjoy each other during the time we have left together."

John also "apologized" for the first episode in the back room. He said he would be kinder and gentler with me from now on. He said the first time is always hard and he just wanted to get that out of the way. He told me that our relationship would go on in every way as it had before, except that this new dimension would become a part of it—a special part that would be kept absolutely secret between the two of us. He did not directly threaten me this time, beyond the comments about my mother's possible reaction. For me, the mere mention of my mother was enough.

And our lives went on pretty much as John said they would. I was able to separate our sexual relationship from the sacred relationship that was already established. I had to separate the two. I had to perpetuate the charade because I did not want anyone to know. And so dissociation was my survival strategy again, as it had been when I was a small, trapped child. With John, I felt as trapped as that small child had been all those years ago.

CHAPTER 21

Please, God, Make Him Stop

"Flee from sexual immorality. All other sins a man commits are outside his body, but he who sins sexually sins against his own body."

I Corinthians 6:18 *New International Version* (NIV)

My perceived relationship with God suffered terribly as John coerced my cooperation in his sexual fantasy life. When John took me home after he had sex with me, I would do everything I could do to cleanse myself of the filthiness I felt. I took a bath. I scrubbed myself. I washed every part of me. I used soap, mouth wash, shampoo, the hottest water I could stand. I put on clean pajamas. I huddled in my bed and tried to forget. I dissociated. I clung to myself because I felt I had no one else to cling to.

And I prayed. I asked God to forgive me. There is a scripture that I had been taught from the time I was a small child. It states, "There has no temptation befallen you than that which is common to man, and God will—with the temptation—also provide a way of escape." We were taught that this meant we never had to sin.

There would be an escape provided. If we did not take the escape God provided, then we were willfully sinning.

I kept trying to understand what this meant for me. Since I felt powerless to stop what was going on with John, I felt that I was damned and would go directly to hell if I died. To avoid this possibility, I asked God to forgive me for the sin I had committed. I asked for forgiveness over and over. I was so torn because I knew what was happening was wrong; I knew God blamed me because the scripture said I was choosing to sin, and yet John held all the power and was perpetuating the wrong. I had no hope he would ever stop on his own. I had been able to handle boys my own age. I felt totally powerless with this man who was old enough to be my father.

And so began whole nights spent on my knees in prayer. I knelt beside my bed with my hands folded and my eyes closed. I begged God to make him stop. I pleaded with God. I told Him I did not know what to do. I wanted to be good. I wanted to serve Him. I did not want to have sex with John. I begged God to help me. I confessed my confusion, my pain, my horrible guilt and shame. I asked God to make a way of escape. When none came, I began to feel that I must be guilty. If I was not the guilty party, God would surely help me.

God did not help. I was so broken. I was caught in a situation I did not choose, and I did not know how to get myself out of it. During those nights of prayer, I never felt God near me. How could that be true? How could He leave me alone to figure this out on my own? It was very difficult to conceive of a loving "father" God who could let one of his children suffer like I was suffering. I thought if I prayed long enough, hard enough, with enough fervor, I could get God's attention.

It did not happen.

I heard other people talk about God answering their prayers. I read stories about miraculous interventions. I read about angels who kept watch. I never had an answer, an intervention, or an angel keeping watch.

God turned his back. God was not available to me. Eventually, I gave up. I just endured what John did.

And what John did was more than sexual abuse. It *was* sexual abuse, to be sure, but it was also physical abuse, mental abuse, emotional abuse, psychological abuse, verbal abuse, *and spiritual abuse*. He was my minister. He was ordained. He was my pastor. He was my shepherd. He was the agent of God appointed over me by my church. What he did when he misused the trust that all of those roles elicit was spiritual abuse of the most heinous kind. Because of the lies he told me about God "wanting" him to use me sexually, because of his blatant disregard for the state of my mind, my soul, my spirit, because of my inability to find recourse directly from God, I have struggled throughout my life with who and what God is. John took what was my island of calm and respite—the church. He took the one thing I was sure of—my relationship with God. He took what had been my light and turned it into the most desolate darkness of all. I was alone. Forsaken.

CHAPTER 22

What About Peggy?

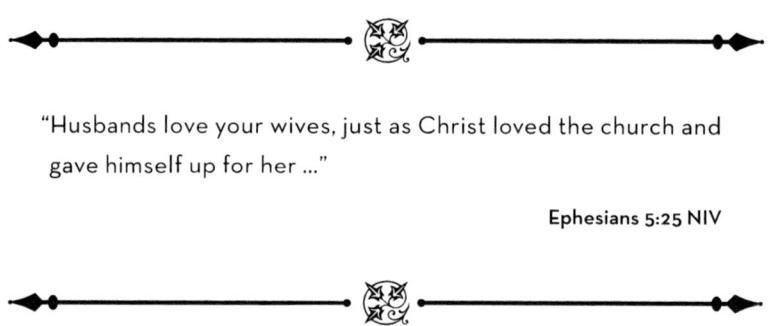

"Husbands love your wives, just as Christ loved the church and gave himself up for her ..."

Ephesians 5:25 NIV

IN THE BEGINNING OF OUR RELATIONSHIP—BEFORE ANY SEXUAL ELEMENT was present—John had confided in me many things that he was not particularly proud of in his past. He had recovered from a drinking problem that had almost cost him his family. Salinas was his first appointment since he had been clean and sober. He said he had left his past behind and he was ready to be used by God. It was a new beginning for his family too. None of them ever told me anything about any hardships they might have suffered during John's drinking days. They were too close a family and too honorable in their commitment to each other to do that. But John intimated to me on a number of occasions that they had been through a lot with him.

Salinas was the opportunity to put all this behind them. They came full of hope. At last, they were involved in something that mattered to all of them. At last, John was using his obvious gifts for the One who had created those gifts in him. His family sometimes seemed a bit concerned. As John freely stated, they had been through many beginnings with him. Surely this time they could believe. Surely this time they could believe in him. But there was often concern in the way they looked at him. Without exception, John laughed off their uneasiness as though he had not a care in the world.

John never told me anything about extramarital affairs in his past—or even the slightest allusion to anything of that nature. He told me about other things he had done. He seemed candid and open and willing to talk about his past. It did not seem like he was withholding anything. I never asked him about his past, but it seemed it was something he needed to talk about. I was interested because, at that time, I was interested in everything he said. And I felt privileged to be his confidant. He talked to me about his past when we were alone working on some project, and there was an air of intimacy, of connection, that I treasured during those conversations.

I had never had a parent who talked to me about life in a nonjudgmental, open, and honest way. I loved these conversations with John and the relationship they affirmed. I felt important. I finally felt special to someone who treasured me the way a parent might. I drank it in. Thirstily.

I do not remember any mention of sex in any way … in the beginning. I am sure I would have been uncomfortable if there had been. I wanted to be his child. I wanted to fit into his family. I *felt* like his child. Any mention of sex—in relation to anyone in his life—would have been a blatant misstep on his part. It did not happen. I felt close and safe … in the beginning.

I cannot help but wonder, from the perspective of what our relationship eventually became, if these intimate conversations were planned to build toward a different type of intimacy entirely.

From the first sexual encounter, John knew that I was deeply troubled spiritually by what we were doing. I cried a lot. I cried while he had sex with me. I cried after he had sex with me. I cried in the car when he took me home. I cried a lot. He would be alternately reassuring and then impatient with me. He told me there was nothing wrong with what "we" were doing. When he brought up his relationship with Peggy with me, I only felt worse. I loved Peggy. She was beautiful. She was sweet. She was the perfect mother I never had. I didn't want him to discuss the intimate details of their lives with me.

Peggy was innocent. She was a victim of what he was doing. John could not convince me that he was not sinning against her. I did not want to have sex with John. But it was happening anyway. It was hurting Peggy. I knew that. I had no illusions about that. What John was doing was wrong for many reasons—especially as respected Peggy's role in his life. And because the sex was happening with me, I felt guilty: I knew I, too, was betraying Peggy.

In spite of the fact that John was having sex with me, I wanted to believe that he loved Peggy. I wanted him to love her. I had never wanted that kind of love from him. I wanted him to find it with Peggy. I saw Peggy regularly. I admired her. I ate at her table. I freely partook of her hospitality. I savored her quiet, gentle presence. I loved her.

As ironic as it may sound, I wanted Peggy to hold me and let me cry it all out to her. I'm sure my kid parts thought she could kiss us all better exactly like she did Robin.

My preoccupation with Peggy, of course, made what was going on with John even more difficult. I had never wanted to supplant Peggy. He minimized all of it. According to John, she held no place in his affections.

His trivializing of Peggy as a person, as his wife, as the mother of his children, explained a lot about the way John could rationalize any behavior on his own part. It was all part of the complex set of "rules" he had concocted to validate any action he took. He deserved whatever he wanted—no matter the price others paid. God told him so. Believing this, he did not have to take responsibility for the hurt he was causing everyone in his environment. There were so many victims. He saw none of us.

CHAPTER 23

Rich Love

"Then Jesus said to his disciples, 'If anyone would come after me, he must deny himself and take up his cross and follow me.'"

Matthew 16:24 NIV

I HAD BEEN GOING STEADY WITH RICH LOVE FOR SEVERAL MONTHS WHEN John was appointed to the Salinas Corps. Rich and I met through mutual friends. He lived about 50 miles away in San Jose. After our first date, we found we were interested in many of the same things—water skiing, movies, music, dressing up and dining out, or just dragging main with our friends. He came to Salinas often, and between his visits, we talked on the phone for hours.

Rich became serious about his interest in me very quickly. I was not so sure. I loved being with him, he was fun, and he was good to me. He was a thoughtful boyfriend—often sending me flowers and bringing me other small gifts. He was never pushy about sex. He seemed okay with waiting for that. When Rich asked me to marry him, I hesitated. He wasn't pushy about that either, but he was persistent. Eventually, I agreed, and we picked out an engagement ring. We began to make plans for our life together.

It's interesting to note that when we became engaged, I bought Rich a Bible. It was a beautiful leather-bound edition, and I had his name engraved on the cover. The woman at the religious book store where I bought it commented, "That's a very appropriate name for the cover of a Bible." I glanced down with new eyes and realized she was right. "Rich Love" was an appropriate name on a Bible.

I think when Rich and I became serious about our commitment to each other, I needed him to know something about the spiritual part of life. We had never discussed religion, and I wasn't sure what he would make of my gift. He liked it. We had never discussed religion, but we knew we had similar values. Values that were not necessarily embraced by many of the people we ran around with. My concern with keeping sex within marriage was one example. I knew he was a nice guy who listened and valued other people. He found a lot of the same traits in me. In that way, we were well matched, and he happily accepted the Bible.

And then came my re-involvement with the church after that first meeting with John in my office. Because I immediately felt that I must obey the calling that I had put aside three years earlier, I assumed I must break off the engagement with Rich. It seemed that the two were incompatible. Since we had never actually talked about the spiritual, I now saw Rich as a part of the world that I must forsake in order to do what was right.

Breaking up with Rich was one of the first things I talked to John and Peggy about—asking for their guidance. Peggy told me to listen to my heart—there might be room for both God and Rich there. John was more outspoken. He saw real value in terminating the relationship because it was "of the world." I found it easy to agree with John. In this first new conversion zeal, I felt I must be free of worldly encumbrances. Rich seemed like an encumbrance—a part of the world I had chosen instead of God for the past several years.

I called Rich and told him about my newfound faith in God and the reaffirmation of my calling to full-time service. He would not take the ring back. He refused. But he did accept the fact that we were no longer engaged to be married.

And then Rich promptly immersed himself in the church. I felt he was doing it just to be near me. I thought it would be a momentary thing—he would stay only until he saw that it would not change my mind about marrying him. Rich became active in the San Jose Corps of the Salvation Army, and he proclaimed his intention to enter training school and become an officer. I did not take him seriously—I was just too close, I think. I saw this as yet another effort to win my affections. But I was happy for Rich, and I felt a deep responsibility to encourage his new faith. And—putting marriage aside—we were very good friends. That had always been true. I loved to see Rich when he came to meetings at our corps, and when John and I took the young people from the Salinas Corps to youth events at the San Jose corps.

Rich remained determined that I would eventually take his calling seriously and we would ultimately marry. We were great friends. He was good to me, and he was good for me.

When I re-involved myself in the church, John—without hesitation—asked me to become the corps youth leader. It was something I had done in my teens, and it seemed perfect for me. It was in this effort to work with the youth that I found my deep connection with John. I had natural abilities. People were attracted to me. I was a born organizer, mentor, and overseer. I could innovate a program and then turn it over to someone else to run—staying involved as a guide and facilitator.

We had activities at the building almost every night of the week. There were youth groups for all ages, Bible study groups for deep study, sports activities for the more physically inclined, and band practice for the musically gifted. It was a constant flurry of activity, and I embraced it all.

When not working, I spent virtually all my time at the corps. And John was always there too. He encouraged me, challenged me, and smiled at the successes. He also helped me dust off my ego when things didn't work. During this first flush of involvement with the corps and with John, I never saw any indication that he had the ability to influence and encourage and then use that influence and encouragement against me.

Rich worked with the youth at the San Jose Corps. Not with the same intensity that I did, but he was looking at ways of serving. He seemed much more interested in being involved with us in Salinas, though, and we gladly accepted him. He helped with youth camping trips, rallies, Christmas food drives. He did whatever was asked of him. He had an aptitude and willingness that I had not given him credit for. I was happy for him. I wanted to see him succeed.

Rich found his spiritual mentor in the corps officer of the San Jose Corps. His officer there had no preconceived notions about who or what Rich was. He saw Rich as a pure and unspoiled babe in Christ. He never doubted Rich's calling to enter the ministry. He encouraged him. As much as I continued to value Rich's friendship, I now saw him as the ex-boyfriend who was following me around. I think we were both right. God uses many different means to attain the desired end.

Rich did enter training when I did, and he continued to be a great friend to me. He also still harbored the hope that we would eventually marry. We did not. But the friendship never flagged. He was as good a friend as I have ever had. I took him for granted. He was the boy who would always love me. And, with good friends, that is true. Sometimes, the love of a true and honest friend is the truest love of all.

Rich would show just how true and pure his love was when I confided in him that I was pregnant with John Hart's child just three months into our first semester at training school. And he would show that same truth and purity of spirit yet again 47 years later. Rich and I had no communication for those 47 years—when I was told to go away and tell no one, Rich was one of the people I lost. But, eventually, because the truth must be told, I did contact Rich to corroborate my story. He was as true and as honest and as pure a friend those 47 years later as I remembered from 1963. Some people can be counted on. Rich was one of those people.

CHAPTER 24

Together More and More

"A man in this position of trust and authority becomes unavoidably a parent figure and is charged with the ethical responsibilities of the parenting role. Violations of these boundaries are, psychologically speaking, not only rapes but also acts of incest."

Sex in the Forbidden Zone by Peter Rutter, M.D.

After that meeting where John laid out the ground rules of our relationship, I convinced myself that I could do what he asked me to do. It would only be a small part of what we were doing. I would still be working with the youth in the corps. John had even offered to let me deliver the sermon during Sunday morning worship on some occasions. He also stated that he would put forth my application as a candidate for officer training for the fall of 1963, and he would walk me through the rather daunting application process.

He was dangling opportunities in front of me that he felt would make it more palatable for me to cooperate with his sexual expectations of me. It would be a tradeoff. If I helped him, he would help me. Since I could imagine no way out for all the reasons already enumerated, I began to rationalize that it wouldn't be so bad. I knew I wanted to be a Salvation Army officer. I would work toward that goal and enter training in the fall. That was only 12 months away. I could do whatever it took for that period of time. Then I would be gone from Salinas. I would be doing what God wanted me to do. And surely then John would have to leave me alone.

With the new twists that John had put on our relationship, he took a proprietary interest in my personal life. He questioned any time I spent away from him. He questioned my involvement with anyone he perceived as a threat to the position he now felt was his in my life. I had already broken the engagement with Rich, but John was very interested in any contact that Rich and I had. He questioned me constantly about what Rich and I did together, what we talked about. By this time, I was glad that Rich and I were no longer relating on a romantic level. I knew I could not be in an ongoing relationship with a boyfriend and yet be involved with John sexually. Things were difficult enough for me, and I knew I did not want to involve Rich. On the other hand, there were times when I wondered if I could call on our friendship and tell Rich what was going on. I quickly dispelled this idea, because I was too embarrassed and full of shame to talk to someone who I knew to be pure and blameless. And I was afraid of John.

John began coming to my home at 11:00 at night, when he knew my mother would be gone to work. He would park in front of the house and wait for me to come out. I was supposed to look for him every night. If he was there, I would get in the car with him, and we would go visiting—usually to his parents' house. It is inconceivable to me now that no one wondered what we were doing.

His parents had moved to Salinas to be supportive of John and his family. They were wonderful people who had also been Salvation Army officers—their service was in Scotland, which had also been John and Peggy's original home. The older Harts seemed to love everything about John and his family and the work they were doing at the Salinas Corps. But when John would show up on their doorstep late at night with me in tow, it seems like they should have questioned what was going on. They looked startled and perplexed at times, but it never went any further than that.

John would be laughing and jovial and say that we had just come by for a "cup of tea." His mother would make the tea, and we would sit around and talk. I was always awkward and uncomfortable with these late-night liaisons. Again, I wanted somebody to just "know." I wanted someone to be the "adult" who would stop us. I wanted out. I didn't know how to find my way out, so I continued to hope someone else would find it for me.

Sometimes during these late night meetings, there would be sex, but usually not. There would always be sexual touching while we were in the car. He now felt he was entitled to whatever liberties he wanted to take. By this time, I believe I had been brainwashed into compliance. I cried, but I no longer thought about physically resisting him. I just hoped that touching would be enough this time. Later on in the relationship, John would come up with a place where he felt there was the secrecy and privacy necessary for an ongoing sexual relationship. It would have been risky to do it in the car where someone could easily come by and see us.

John would also come up with reasons that we needed to spend Saturday together. I knew what this meant. Highway 101 runs through Salinas. It is a four lane freeway with many on- and off-ramps throughout town. When I got in the car, John required that I take off all my clothes below the waist. He was titillated by the fact that he was driving around in broad daylight with a seminude young woman in the car. He would pull onto the freeway, and we would drive for hours. He would avail himself of my body at will—pawing over me with his right hand while he drove with his left. I dissociated. I sat beside him mute. This did not seem to bother him. He wasn't looking for conversation.

I was terrified that we would be discovered. The station wagon we were in had the Salvation Army logo on it. John would usually be in uniform. Perhaps he thought he would not be noticed for that reason—people recognize and accept the Salvation Army logo as indicative of good works. And I think the chances he was taking were an additional source of arousal for him. Sometimes he would put my underwear in his pocket as a "reminder" of our time together. I would never see them again, of course. They were trophies to what he had gotten away with. I always felt lucky if we did not have actual sexual intercourse. Having him touch me was bad enough, but I felt that I had somehow won when it went no further than that.

There were many times, however, when we were in the building together at night—usually after some activity that ended at 9:00. Then he would take his family home as others were leaving, and he would instruct me to "finish up" and he would take me home later. This was a common occurrence. Again, I wonder why no one questioned. Peggy would put up some small protest, but he always overrode her. These were the times I dreaded. I knew it meant he was coming back for one reason only.

I would be crying when he came back. He would tell me to go into the youth room where the sofa was. I would try to dissuade him by talking about God and sin. I would beg him to let me just go home. He found this compelling, I think. If he had just wanted sex, there were other places for him to look. I think he enjoyed the conquest every time. When we were in the room, he would calmly begin to take his clothes off, and he would tell me that when he was finished he was going to undress me. He told me he knew I did not want to take my clothes off, so it would be easier and better for me if he took them off. He said he liked to do it. He said it was better than a strip tease because he was in control.

When John was naked, he would come over to where I was seated on the sofa. He would put my hands at my sides and tell me to leave them there. Then he would begin to fondle me through my clothes. He paid particular attention to my breasts. He would tell me that he was going to be careful, that I could relax, he was not going to hurt me.

I cried.

I knew that if I resisted, my clothes would be torn. He was determined that I would be fully unclothed—this was the rule now. He would remove my blouse or sweater. He would slip his fingers in and out of the cups of my bra. By this time, he would be in a state of high arousal. He would be making guttural noises, and he would be transfixed—totally absorbed in what he was doing and, seemingly, no longer aware of me as a person. At this stage in the drama, he no longer addressed me or looked at my face. I did not recognize anything about him in these moments. He became someone else altogether, and I was afraid of this John. When I cried, he seemed not to notice or care.

When John removed my bra, he would lean back and just stare, cupping a breast in each hand. And then he would nuzzle and suckle. I had not chosen this fat old man for a sexual partner. His naked body disgusted me. He had no right to my body. His grunting and panting hot breath were disgusting. He was so lost in his own experience, I don't think he even noticed my reactions at all.

John had me stand so that he could remove my skirt or jeans. I would usually be trembling by this time. I knew what was coming. He did not look at my face, my eyes, but he began what would become a litany—he said he wasn't going to hurt me. It had hurt that first time, but it would never hurt again. He was going to help me, teach me. When he pushed me back on the sofa and began to mount me, I dissociated. I checked out. I went to a safe place within myself.

The first part—above the waist—was not the same as sexual penetration. The penetration was the part that was inside me. I felt fouled and dirtied by it in a very profound way. I hated his discharge. I was not a willing participant in any of what he did. But it was the penetration and bodily fluids that were unconscionable for me.

I never touched John when he was having sex with me. I had never touched that part of a man's anatomy, and that was something he could not have forced me to do. I don't remember our ever talking about this. I never touched him. He seemed content with what he initiated and carried out without my active participation.

I remember him kissing me on the mouth only once. His mouth was large and flabby and soft and rubbery. It was disgusting. I did not hide my disgust—quickly wiping my mouth with the back of my hand. After that, there were other things he was more interested in anyway. I could not have faked the kissing part—I was too repulsed by it.

And it seems that kissing is something that people do when there is a genuine, mutual attraction and attachment present. I never kissed him. I never touched his penis. I never told him I wanted to have sex with him. I cried.

CHAPTER 25

In a Secret Place

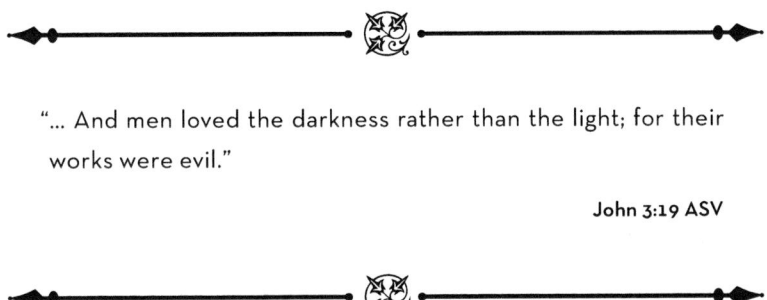

"... And men loved the darkness rather than the light; for their works were evil."

John 3:19 ASV

JOHN RENTED AN APARTMENT SO THAT THERE WOULD BE A SECRET, PRIvate place for him to have sex with me. He called it a flat. It was in a rundown old Victorian near the central business district of Salinas. John would park in a narrow alley behind the house. There was no yard to speak of—just a scrubby area between the house and the sidewalk. Everything about the house was dark and sad. There was an unlighted stairway that we used to get to his second-floor apartment. The building stank of old food, body odor, animal excrement. The hallway was rough, rutted, and time worn.

Once we were inside his flat, there was light, and it illuminated a hodgepodge of junk and garbage. He told me he obtained authorization to rent the space because he told the divisional office that he needed additional storage space. In an apparent effort to justify this, there were old broken chairs, leftover remnants of furniture he had removed from the corps building, boxes of files, and stacks of old papers and magazines. There was a small kitchenette complete with leftover food and dirty dishes. I never knew if they were his or if they had been left by the previous tenant. The whole setting was reminiscent of the use John was to make of it—dank, dark, dirty—just as his motives and actions with me were.

In the main room, there was a shabby, worn, old sofa. John brought an old quilt to put over it. In that grimy place, I was thankful for this one small courtesy.

Within this space, John would enact the scenarios I described as taking place in the back room of the corps building. He never did it at the corps once he had rented this space. We always entered the flat long after dark, and if there were tenants in the other parts of the large old building, I never saw or heard them. John never forbade me to cry when he was using me—it actually seemed to increase his pleasure—but in this space, he told me to be quiet about it.

There was one big difference about the sexual activity that John required of me once we were using the flat. He required that I be on top at the beginning of each episode. He would lie down on the sofa and command me to sit on his groin so that he could enter me and fondle my breasts at the same time. When he was satisfied with this, he would roll me over and finish on top of me.

Now that our assignations had become routine, his warnings to me became routine also. Each time we were together sexually, he warned me to keep my mouth shut about "our little secret." He continued to warn me that if I ever said anything, he would deny it and he would be believed because, after all, he was in the official position of authority.

He would cite my alleged complicity in what was going on:

"I know you want it as much as I do."

"I'm teaching you things you'll thank me for."

"You led me on. It was your idea."

"You keep coming back for more, so you must enjoy it."

"You use your body to make me do these things. It's not my fault."

"What would your mother say if she knew what you were doing when she's at work?"

He told me that if I did not do as he wanted, he would not put forth my application for training school.

There was always the mention of God. God was allowing him to appease his sexual appetite on me. I was put into his life by God for this purpose. God endorsed this way of release for him so he could be a better servant of God.

And, more and more, a part of this litany would be the threat of physical violence against me and my family.

"You can never leave me. I would find you."

"Don't ever think you can get away."

"I won't hurt you as long as you do as I tell you."

"You don't want your family to get hurt do you?"

As more information about this type of coercion has come into our social consciousness, it is easy to recognize John's behavior as typical of abusive spousal perpetrators associated with battered wife syndrome. The woman continues the bond with the perpetrator in spite of all the abuse, because she is threatened with ever worse consequences if she does not. Paradoxically, she feels dependent on him for her safety even though he is the source of the abuse.

I was suffering from all the symptoms of Post-traumatic Stress Disorder by this time. When I was not with John, I clenched my mind to prevent flashbacks from interfering with my daily life. And I never considered crossing him anymore. With his constant threats, I was just trying to hold on one day—sometimes, one moment—at a time.

I was dissociating regularly, even when I was not with John—it was becoming more and more necessary just to get by. And because the episodes continued, the trauma was compounded over and over again. I dreaded each recurrence, suffered during each reenactment, and then had to find a way to go on as if nothing had happened. And I dreamed of a time when it would be over. Would it ever end?

CHAPTER 26

During Worship

"... Whatever you do, do it all for the glory of God. Do not cause anyone to stumble ..."

I Corinthians 10:31-32 NIV

John seemed to need to add the element of danger to his sexual acting out. He was constantly daring someone to find out what he was doing. His was the kind of arrogance that believed he deserved a special dispensation because of his lofty position. And so he rarely used what would seem like rational discretion. On the contrary, he seemed to feel that he was above the rules for other common folk, and he enjoyed flaunting this feeling of entitlement. He found the danger titillating. I say this because he habitually brought this air of disdainful smugness into his behavior with me.

When he picked me up late at night to visit his parents.

When he had sex with me in the church building.

When he drove for hours with a seminude woman in the car with him.

When he came and went to his apartment at all hours in the company of a woman not his wife.

And John orchestrated another situation—perhaps the most blatant and disrespectful of all—for his sexual pleasure.

I had become John's worship assistant soon after I rejoined the church. I led the hymns, introduced the scripture, led the responsive readings, and then introduced John, who would preach the sermon. I loved doing this. I had a natural stage presence and was unusually articulate and welcoming. I embraced this role and felt that God was using me to institute a feeling of family within our community of believers. I was confident and enthusiastic—engaging everyone in our corporate worship.

A half hour before worship began, all those who participated actively in leading worship met for prayer in John's office. This included the band leader, soloists, prayer leaders, and all of John's family. This was an intimate time of dedicating ourselves to God and asking that everything we did would be used for His glory. For all of us, it was a richly holy time.

After John became sexual with me, he nuanced this prayer time to include 15 extra minutes for John and me to pray alone together. He always had a glib explanation that sounded so high-minded when he came up with an idea like this. He brooked no questioning of his authority. He said that he and I needed to be especially infused with the Spirit.

Having heard this, everyone else left his office, with the understanding that the band would begin the service at the appointed time. After our "prayer time," John and I would enter the sanctuary from his office—which opened onto the stage—and together, we would begin the service by welcoming everyone to worship.

Of course, our special time was not used for prayer. We did not spend that 15 minutes being infused by the Spirit. There was nothing holy about it.

While everyone else was assembling for worship just one thin wall away, John was leaning back in his big desk chair, his legs apart, unzipping his fly, exposing his erection. He required that I take off my panties as he fondled himself. He then raised me onto his lap, facing him. As I came down on his erection, his eyes glazed over. He would mumble, hold his breath, clench his teeth. His face would become red. The first time this happened, I thought he was having a heart attack. I came to understand that he was trying to prolong the moment by not climaxing too quickly. Apparently, this took effort on his part.

I think this situation was particularly erotic for John because of the close proximity to a large group of people who were, for him, vicarious witnesses to what he was doing.

While the situation was thrillingly erotic to John, it was ultimately shameful for me. I was in my Salvation Army uniform. John was in his. Ostensibly, we were the leaders of God's flock. We were there to model what was good and holy. I had to gulp down the shame and guilt. The show must go on, after all. I could not refuse. I could not tell.

John kept a damp towel in a drawer of his desk for me to clean myself with. That accomplished, we opened the door onto the stage and entered worship … hallelujah …

CHAPTER 27

Getting Away

"'Come, follow me,' Jesus said, 'and I will make you fishers of men.'"

Matthew 4:19 NIV

W<small>HAT I DESCRIBED TO YOU IN THE LAST SEVERAL CHAPTERS WAS MY</small> life for the twelve months after John initiated the sexual part of our relationship. During the day, I was working full-time as a legal secretary. I fulfilled my duties at home. I participated in everything at church.

I continued to act as a mentor to the children and youth at church. I felt privileged to be a part of their lives. I never flagged in my enthusiasm for activities to enrich their physical and spiritual wellbeing. We attended youth rallies, we learned Bible stories, we went camping, we took trips to amusement parks, we went swimming and bowling.

As testament to the work that I did with the kids, I would like to relate an incident that happened when I was 55 years old. At that time, I was the manager of the personal lines department in a large insurance agency. I loved my job and the team of young women who worked in my department with me. Georgia was a new hire in the commercial lines department, and her manager was very controlling—telling Georgia that she was not allowed to speak to me or anyone in my department for fear that she would waste time on idle chatter.

Georgia's desk was near the ladies room in the agency. One day, as I walked past her desk—being careful not to engage her in any way because I might cause repercussions with her manager—she spoke to me.

"Bunny, I know you don't remember me, but I remember you. You were my youth leader at the Salvation Army when I was a kid. You were wonderful to all of us. We all loved you. I'll never forget what you did for us." What a gift.

When Georgia said that to me, I was struggling with my therapy—beginning to face all the mess with John Hart and Lincoln Upton and the Salvation Army. What Georgia said to me that day allowed me to believe that I had done good; according to her and others like her, I had done *much* good. Her face lit up when she told me how much I had meant to her and the others. That, I hope, is my legacy. There was so much that was not good. But the things I did willingly, passionately, with all my heart and soul—the things I *chose to do*—when I was not acceding to John's demands—were good and honest and perhaps holy.

In all honesty, I did not specifically remember Georgia, but her comments reminded me of just how busy I had been with those kids. When I was with them, in that context, I had been able to put the sexual relationship with John out of my mind. That's one of the advantages of dissociating—amnesiac boundaries are constructed that partition off experiences to defend against complete mental, emotional, and psychological breakdown. Much of what I have described to you about the sexual activity with John is recovered information stored within my personality system that I had to face during the 15 years of psychiatric therapy I completed in 2008.

It's interesting to note that John took great pride in my work in the corps with children like Georgia. There was still that side to him—the mentor who thrived on my successes and encouraged me to do more. On the few occasions when I delivered the sermon in worship, he beamed like a very proud parent. That was true even after he had routinely staked a claim on the parts of my life and body that he had no right to.

And John kept his word about putting forward my application to enter training. There was a comprehensive application process that required much paperwork on my part, and it required the recommendation of my corps officer and at least one other adult in the corps. Each local corps has a Corps Sergeant Major—the highest ranking non-commissioned officer in the corps. Our Sergeant Major was Rita Muther. My two best friends in the corps during my teen years with Captain and Mrs. Irby were Rita Muther's twin nieces, Sharon and Karen. So she became "Auntie Rita" to me. She wrote me a stellar recommendation letter. One year later, she would reach out and wound me in a most cruel way. But before everything came tumbling down, Auntie Rita wrote a beautiful recommendation letter for me

I had saved as much money as I could, but I did not have the full tuition, so I had to apply for a scholarship. John helped a great deal with this part.

I was very nervous about the required physical exam. I looked at the form I was to take to my doctor, and it required a gynecological exam. I had never had one before—that was bad enough to contemplate—but I was afraid of what he might find. Would he know I was having sex? Would he ask questions? Would he put that on the form? I went to the doctor my mother had first introduced me to when I was an older teenager. He was a warm and caring person. I don't know what he knew when he examined me, but he asked no embarrassing questions, and when it was over, he wished me well.

My last worship service at the Salinas Corps of the Salvation Army before entering training school was memorable. I did not have any idea at the time that it would be the last of my lifetime. I would never be allowed to worship there again.

Peggy—who had a magnificent soprano voice—sang my favorite hymn for me. The band—including Donny and Robin—played beautifully. Everyone in the corps was very proud of me—it had been a long time since a cadet was sent to training out of the Salinas Corps. Gifts were given, and enthusiastic well-wishes and promises to keep in touch were exchanged.

There was a strict list of what I could bring to training with me. I would be sharing a dormitory room with two other young women; space was limited and—remembering the military model—everything had to be shipshape at all times. Inspections were routine. I packed my bags. I was on my way at last. The bad part was over. Now it was time for the good part to begin. Of course, I had no way of knowing that, though the bad part *was* over, the worst was yet to come.

CHAPTER 28

Finally, I'm a Cadet at Training School

"Do your best to present yourself to God as one approved, a workman who does not need to be ashamed and who correctly handles the word of truth."

II Timothy 2:15 NIV

SAN FRANCISCO IS A TWO-HOUR DRIVE FROM SALINAS. IN SEPTEMBER of 1963, I loaded my bags in the trunk of my mother's little Dodge, and we headed to the Salvation Army School for Officer Training on Van Ness Avenue in San Francisco. To say that I was nervous is an enormous understatement. This was a momentous step for me. Although I was thrilled to be on my way, I had never lived away from home before, and I had absolutely no idea what to expect from the officers in charge of training. I knew Rich would be there, and that helped, but other than him, I knew no one.

The instructions I received said that I should arrive at training in full dress uniform—including the traditional bonnet. When we arrived, my mother never got out of the car. I got out, retrieved my bags, and she was gone. A woman cadet one year ahead of me had been assigned to watch for me and make sure I made all the right connections on my first day. It was a big relief to meet someone who was there specifically for me.

She showed me to my dorm room, told me I could take my bonnet off and dress down, and then she gave me a tour of the campus. It was not a large facility—the training school is a two-year program—and there were probably 100 cadets in all. It was not without its charms—a solid old building, well-appointed and snug, with a beautiful chapel and a spacious dining hall full of light. The classrooms brought back cherished memories of Hartnell. It was not long before the warmth and security of this new, yet familiar setting began to ease my jitters. I felt welcome. I felt right.

Because I had been observed in leadership positions in my corps and at rallies and meetings throughout the territory, it was not long before I was called into the office of the Women's Chief Side Officer, Major Doris Fisher, for a special assignment. I was asked to deliver the welcoming address on behalf of the single women cadets at the Territory Welcome Banquet, which began each new session of training. All of the territory and divisional staff would be there. This was a very big deal, with a reporter from the Salvation Army's national periodical covering the festivities. It was an honor to be asked to speak.

I remember my address to this day. Major Fisher had told me that it should be no longer than seven minutes and that I should keep it light. I was nervous because of the setting, but this was my natural element. When I was introduced and welcomed to the podium amid polite applause, I looked at my notes and gave it everything I had.

I started with an aside about the Salvation Army's Trade Department—it is notoriously behind on orders at all times—and my good-natured chiding intentionally played on the frustrations everyone felt from time to time. There was a fraction of a second of stunned silence after these introductory remarks, and then the room erupted in laughter, applause, and stamping feet. I had them on my side from that moment on.

As I continued, I homed in on our session's name: "Proclaimers of the Faith." I used the scripture where Jesus—just before He ascends to heaven—asks Peter, "Peter, do you love me?" Jesus asks Peter this question three times, and Peter answers, "Lord, you know I love you." Finally, Jesus replies, "Then feed my sheep." I closed with this quote, challenging everyone in the room to truly be Proclaimers of the Faith and to do as Jesus asked—feed His sheep.

When I finished, there was an immediate standing ovation—these were the brass from the seven western states, Alaska, and Hawaii—and they were giving me a standing ovation. When I returned to my seat, the master of ceremonies, Colonel Parkins, lieutenant commissioner of the territory, called me back up to the podium to take my bows. It was a truly intoxicating moment for me. The applause went on and on.

That night a group of us jumped on a bus and went to downtown San Francisco to celebrate—I'm not sure now where we were, but there was a fountain and we just ran around, feeling alive and free and exhilarated. Rich was there, and he was proud of me—I was the hero of the moment, fielding congratulations from everyone, and he was my best friend and seemed glad of it. I knew this was the way it was supposed to be. I was in the right place, and I was a natural fit for the demands of this high calling.

And so as training began, I thought I had finally found home. At last, I was in the home of my soul. Here not only would I be safe, but I would have the joy of using my natural gifts openly and honestly among people who recognized and valued those gifts. At long last, I was out of my mother's oppressive darkness. I was away from John's immoral domination. I could accomplish great things for God and, by extension, for the Salvation Army. Goodness and mercy had won over evil and cruelty. Grace could now be my way of life. I was finally free to be good—which is the only thing I ever wanted to be.

CHAPTER 29

Mind, Body, and Soul in Action for Good

"I define love thus: The will to extend one's self for the purpose of nurturing one's own or another's spiritual growth."

The Road Less Traveled by M. Scott Peck, M.D.

THE SUCCESS I ENJOYED AT TRAINING SCHOOL WAS REMINISCENT OF ALL the successes I experienced from junior high through college. It was not only that I was an apt pupil, it was also that I loved learning. I ate it up. All of my classes were challenging—much that was new and some that I had studied before at the corps level, but here presented in a more challenging and engaging manner.

I had studied the Bible in a very nonchalant and casual way. This was different. It was in-depth and detailed, and required much critical thinking—finding the message beneath the language. And we moved at a dizzying pace. The class met daily, covered huge chunks of information, and there was an exam every Friday. There were six or eight of us who pulled all-nighters every Thursday. We read, quizzed each other, made flash cards, drank coffee, and took No-Doz. We were wired and we were determined. I aced every Bible exam.

After lunch on Fridays, we had housekeeping duties. We each had an assignment that had to be completed—the cadets did all of the routine janitorial duties on campus. After housekeeping, we were off for the rest of the day. This was our only "for sure" time off during the week. We could count on Friday afternoons. We went exploring around San Francisco, ate exotic food, and came home exhausted from no sleep the night before—hard work and harder play—and crashed. We slept the sleep of the innocent.

I was a natural at homiletics. I enjoyed public speaking, but this was my first formal education on the building of a good sermon. It was a bit intimidating because the purpose of the "speech" was the most important element. I was awed by the responsibility as presented by our instructor. We were taught all of the basics—using scripture, using stories and examples, using personal experience. I did well in homiletics.

History and doctrine of the Salvation Army was not as interesting as some of the other subjects, but being, as always, a perfectionist in my studies, I learned what I needed to know to excel on exams. There was a lot of memorization. I can't remember one of the Salvation Army's doctrines now, but I remember that it all made sense at the time. I mastered the material because I did not know any other way. I wanted to be perfect at everything.

There were about eight of us who were in a special English class. From our entrance exams, it was evident that we did not need basic grammar or composition, and so we were in a group segregated out and steeped in the Great Books. We read and discussed great ideas presented by the classical thinkers of western civilization. I remember we started with the Declaration of Independence. Being a student in a seminary setting gave a whole new meaning to some of the language regarding God's part in creating all men equal and endowing them with inalienable rights.

I remember being amazed when our instructor, Major Dexter, asked us if that was true: "Are all men created equal? Is there such a thing as an inalienable right?" I had never questioned any of this before. And looking at it dispassionately, there are many ways that men are not equal at birth. There is a range of potential even then—some more gifted than others in many different ways. Is this equality? And what about rights? Where do rights come from? When are they tempered with responsibility? Is everyone's definition of "rights" the same? If not, who gets to arbitrate? This was eye-opening for me, and the discussions in this class have remained memorable to me throughout my life.

In public speaking class, of course, I was in my element. I was chosen to present speeches at events within the training school and at meetings in other venues. Because I felt I was engaged in something of inestimable value, I was, without exception, an inspired and inspiring speaker.

Music was never my long suit, but I tried out for the school chorus and was surprised when I was chosen to participate. I enjoyed being part of this vibrant group—many of whom were very gifted.

Drama was another area in which I excelled. The cadets of the training school put on a public performance at the huge Veterans Memorial Building in San Francisco each spring. I took part in auditions and won a place in the cast.

Overriding the intellectual stimulation was the fact that this was all spiritually directed. We were engaged in something of eternal value. The day began with chapel. It was not just a rote exercise. We were deeply connected to the spiritual. There was a unique spirit of camaraderie that permeated everything.

Occasionally, John came to visit me. I never knew in advance about his visits. There were no cell phones, of course, and we did not have phones in our dorm rooms. There were payphones available, but I never called him. He would just show up and check in at the office. He usually came late in the afternoon, knowing that I was more likely to be available. The office would get a message to me that my corps officer was there to visit me. There never was any particular notice taken of this, but I was aware that very few of the other cadets had this type of repeated visit.

I never left campus with John. I refused to do that. We would find some spot on campus to have a private conversation. I was extremely uncomfortable with him. He was nothing to me now, except a reminder of the bad old days. I wanted nothing to do with him. His visits were short—he seemed ill at ease, uncomfortable. I don't remember wanting to share any of my victories, my enthusiasm for training, with him. I was virtually tongue-tied, having nothing to say to him. And I was afraid of him in my new world. Could he still ruin things for me? There would be veiled warnings about my remembering to keep my mouth shut. He didn't need to remind me. Why would I say anything to anybody? It was over and I was happy to put it all behind me—that's where it belonged. I was relieved when he turned to leave. I looked at his retreating back—this fat, little man waddling away seemed to have absolutely nothing to do with my new life. I was content to put in what little time it took and then just watch him leave, go back where he belonged. I *knew* where I belonged.

Part of our responsibility at training school was representing the Salvation Army in the greater San Francisco Bay Area. We distributed the Army's periodical, *The War Cry,* in businesses throughout downtown. We frequently paraded through areas of the city—fully uniformed, bands playing, colors flying, chorus singing—to recruit and proselytize. We were on fire for the Lord. We witnessed to the saving power of the Gospel of Christ. We visited jails and prisons and conducted worship services. We also became active in all of the Army's charitable outreach programs—homes for unwed mothers, alcoholic rehabilitation facilities, soup kitchens, Red Shield youth clubs.

It all mattered. We were called to minister to the marginalized and the down-and-out. This was now our bailiwick. We came back from these field trips energized, thrilled, excited. This was the real thing—no more theory; no more hypothetical questions. We were engaged in a war to win the souls of those who were routinely overlooked by the religious organizations of that day. We truly were the army of God. That's the way it felt. "Onward, Christian Soldiers" meant something back then, back there.

CHAPTER 30

A Growing Suspicion

"Unable to understand how fully she has been victimized, she turns the blame and subsequent self-hatred on herself."

Sex in the Forbidden Zone by Peter Rutter, M.D.

I DON'T REMEMBER WHEN EXACTLY IT WAS THAT I REALIZED I HAD NOT had my period since coming to training. It began to niggle me. When had I last menstruated? Was it in August or the first part of September? I couldn't dismiss this growing concern, because I had always been regular in my cycles—never late, never missing a period for any reason. I had brought tampons in my supplies when I came to training, and there they were in the drawer as Halloween approached—unused. By that time, there was no denying that I was overdue.

There was a big Halloween party, and everyone on campus—staff and cadets—were encouraged to dress in costume. My good friend Mary Lee and I thought it would be funny to go as imps or demons. It just seemed to be a good, ironic touch. We wore red body suits and tights and came up with horns and forked tails. The costumes were very formfitting, and we both looked good. I rationalized that if I was pregnant, I would have some physical indication, wouldn't I?

There was a flurry of activity as Thanksgiving approached. We would not be going off campus for Thanksgiving because that is a big weekend for the Army. It is the kickoff of the Red Kettle Campaign—the Salvation Army's most visible and time-honored fundraising effort.

The traditional red kettles on street corners and in shopping centers throughout the world are great fundraisers, but they are also a wonderful public relations opportunity. This campaign visualizes for many what Christmas is all about. We—the cadets of the Salvation Army training school in cosmopolitan San Francisco—would be stationed throughout the city, manning these kettles. Some would be bell ringers, some would be in strolling brass ensembles, and others would be carolers. There was a lot to smile about—it got us out and about, it was fun, and it engendered in us the spirit of this holy season. When this campaign began, I was at least three months overdue for my period.

CHAPTER 31

It All Comes Tumbling Down

"For the law was given through Moses; grace and truth came through Jesus Christ."

John 1:17 NIV

WITH THE GROWING KNOWLEDGE THAT I WAS PREGNANT, MY LIFE IN training school took on a two-sided effect, with which I was all too familiar—the torture of maintaining the façade of a highly functioning, mentally gifted cadet, while internally I was growing more and more desperate. I had no idea how to approach this crisis that was literally growing inside me. One week into December of 1963, I knew I would need to do something. It would be impossible to continue as though nothing were wrong. The anxiety I was suffering caused an extreme loss of appetite and I was sleeping little. I had not gained any weight, and I could not detect any obvious changes in my body, but I knew I was pregnant. What other explanation could there be?

All of the cadets and staff attended a Sunday morning worship service at the Oakland Citadel Corps—I no longer remember the occasion, but it was a large celebration of some sort. When the altar call was given, I went forward and knelt before God in the presence of all those people who had become so important to me. In that public arena, I mutely begged God to please, please, please provide a way of escape. I was overcome with all of the shame, guilt, and regret I thought I had escaped when I left John behind in Salinas. I knew, now, I had brought a token of our relationship with me. A token with a life of its own. A token that could no longer be ignored

That evening, in my room, I played with the idea of using a coat hanger to cause a miscarriage. I had heard of such things. I did not know exactly how it was accomplished, but I knew that there could be devastating consequences to such an action—infection, excess bleeding, even death. I went in the bathroom. I punched myself in the stomach over and over, hoping that this might cause a miscarriage.

I did not feel any empathy or concern for the life within me. I felt only desperation. I just wanted to be rid of it. It never occurred to me that this life was of any consequence in and of itself. I only knew that this life would ruin my life, my new life, totally. And this after I had thought I was safe, free of all the stumbling blocks I had faced and dealt with, alone, all my life. I had gotten through so much alone. Now I was in a situation I had never anticipated. John used withdrawal as a means of birth control. Knowing very little about it, I assumed this meant I could not get pregnant. Obviously, this was not the case.

Late that night I got a message to Rich asking him to meet me outside. I can't remember now exactly where our meeting took place, but it was in a small cramped space. It was after curfew, and we were both taking a big chance meeting alone. I had a reason to take that chance. Rich had no reason except he cared about me.

I told Rich that I was pregnant with John Hart's child. His reaction was not surprise or disbelief. It was a sort of resignation: "I wondered about him, Bunny. I always had a bad feeling about the way he seemed to dominate your time and attention. I'm sorry. I'm just so very sorry."

It All Comes Tumbling Down | 133

I did not cry. I think I was too overcome with the enormity of my situation to cry. I just needed someone to know. I needed a friend. I turned to Rich. We did not embrace. I do not remember any physical contact at all. I know I stood opposite him in the tiny space, too ashamed to even look him in the eye. And then Rich reached over and took my hand in his hands. Without the least bit of hesitation, he said, "We can get married, Bunny. We'll say it's my baby. If we do that, maybe they'll let us get married and move into the married cadets dorm. That way we can both stay in training. This isn't charity, Bunny. You know I've always loved you. I want to marry you, Bunny."

Then I cried. Never had such a thought occurred to me. Never had I dreamed that a friend could be this caring, this selfless. I had no experience whatsoever with this type of love. As Rich took me in his arms, I felt a rush of love and gratitude for this young man who extended to me a lifeline in such a matter-of-fact manner. No negotiating, no hesitation, no bargaining—asking absolutely nothing in return. He was freely offering himself. I was drowning. I had no hope. I saw no way out. And then there was Rich Love.

With hope in my heart for the first time since I began to suspect I was pregnant, I gratefully accepted Rich's offer. This could work. We were both in excellent standing in school. We were both adults. Together, we could do this. We agreed that we would see the Women's Chief Side Officer the following morning after breakfast.

That night, I slept. I never wondered if Rich would regret his offer. I knew him well enough to take him at his word. I had never known him to be anything but a good friend, a person of honor. It is written that Jesus said, "Greater love hath no man than this, that a man lay down his life for his friend." That night I felt that Rich had offered to give up his life—at least insofar as he had thus far known it—to save my life. It seemed miraculous. That night, I slept.

The next morning, Rich and I went to see Major Fisher. As we walked into her office together, she asked us to take the two chairs facing her desk. She folded her hands on the desk in front of her and asked, "How can I help the two of you?"

It was Rich who spoke first. He reached over and took my left hand in both of his. Without any hesitation, he told Major Fisher that he and I had been engaged before we entered training, that we loved each other, and that we were asking permission to be married immediately because I was pregnant with his child. I remember Major Fisher glancing down at her hands. She had never been married. I wondered how she would react. Would she see us as evil fornicators? Would she report us to higher authority and have us both expelled? Rich and I both knew this was a possibility, but we had gambled that she would see the possibility for the good that could come of this.

She looked at me and asked if I was sure I was pregnant. I told her that I had not had a period since I came to training. I was sure. She asked me if I was in agreement with what Rich was proposing. With my heart in my throat, I said I was. Afraid to breathe or hope, I looked at Rich. He squeezed my hand and gave me the semblance of a smile.

Major Fisher did not lecture or belabor. She said that there were others she would need to talk to, but she appreciated our honesty and our desire to do the right thing. She further stated that she could see no reason that it would not work out to the benefit of everyone involved. She rose and extended her hand first to me and then to Rich. She said that she would get back to us quickly so that we could take the needed steps so that a marriage could occur during the semester break, which was coming up in two weeks.

Rich and I left her office and melded back into the normal activities of a busy December day in training. I was assigned to a kettle in downtown. It was cold that day and windy. I remember tentative, fluttery relief. It was going to be okay after all. Our lives would be different than I had thought—I would be a married woman with a baby—but we would be a normal married couple. I would not be a pariah, a sinner. Thanks to Rich, I would be an honest woman.

Perhaps the hardest part to explain in all of this is what happened that night after I went to bed. There had been something nagging at the back of my mind since Rich first offered to take responsibility for the life growing inside me. I kept pushing this nagging something back—I didn't want to jinx the solution that Major Fisher was now busy brokering for us.

But now, after dark, in the quiet of my room, in the stillness of my own heart, I could no longer ignore that still, small voice gently whispering that I was doing something very wrong. This baby was not Rich's baby. To say it was and to enter into a marriage based on that lie, I would be committing a terrible sin against Rich. It would be hypocrisy of enormous proportions. Every time someone commented on the baby, every time I looked at the child, every time we visited Rich's family and presented "his" child to them, we would both be lying to the child and to everyone in the child's life. How could that be okay? In order to save myself, I had been willing to sacrifice Rich. That night in a cold moment of stark terror, I knew I could not do it. No matter the consequences to myself, I could not embrace a lie that would potentially bring great harm to someone I loved. I could not let Rich lie for me. When I realized this, there was a moment of peace. I did not know what would lie ahead, but I knew from that moment on, I would tell the truth.

The next morning I got Rich's attention and we found a spot to have a private conversation. I told him I could not go through with it. I told him about the night I had spent. I told him I realized that two wrongs could never make a right. I told Rich then that I cared too deeply about him to take unfair advantage of the sincere, loving friendship he had always displayed toward me, even in this most dire situation. I told him that I had to repay his loving friendship in kind. I had to tell the truth. I could not let him lie for me. I told him that I was going to see Major Fisher.

Rich's response? He told me that he would not let me do it. He told me he was going to watch me, and if he saw me heading toward Major Fisher's office, he was going to stop me. He told me that he would affirm that the baby was his no matter what I said. He was convinced that the plan we had made was good and honest—the best way for all parties concerned. He said that if I went through with my decision to tell the truth, I would be self-destructing. He said he would not let me do that.

Later that morning, between classes, as quietly and unobtrusively as possible, I made my way to Major Fisher's office. I had just sat down in front of her when her office door flew open and Rich charged in. He said, "Don't believe a word she says. She doesn't know what she's saying. No matter what she tells you, the baby is mine."

Major Fisher calmly asked Rich to sit.

I looked at Rich and said, "I can't do it, Rich. I have to tell the truth. I love you too much to do anything else."

Rich looked down at his hands in his lap. All the fight had gone out of him. He stood up, looked at me one last time, and slowly walked out of the office, closing the door behind him.

CHAPTER 32

Punishment Sure and Swift

"Women who report any of these violations are often subjected to further humiliation and brutalization as they try to enlist the aid of authorities in bringing their victimizers to justice. Thus the cycle continues."

Sex in the Forbidden Zone by Peter Rutter, M.D.

MAJOR FISHER SAT FOR SOME MOMENTS NOT SAYING A WORD. THERE was no sound. Her office was on the second floor of this solid, old building. It was still. For some moments she was content to allow that stillness.

I had been sitting with my hands in my lap. I never doubted what I needed to do. I finally had to tell the truth about John. The whole truth. Rich only knew about the baby. He knew nothing more. He did not know any of the details about the life I had lived for more than a year. He did not know the subterfuge, the betrayal, the guilt, and the shame. He did not know about the lies, manipulation, and threats. I had not wanted anyone to know. But now I would tell. Because someone had to know the truth. About John.

Eventually, very gently, Major Fisher asked, "So, Bunny, what is the truth you need to tell me?"

I looked toward her, not in her eyes exactly, but toward her. She was sitting up straight in her chair, her gray hair illumined by the early-morning sun coming in the window behind her, and she was expectantly looking directly at me.

"The baby is my corps officer's child, Major Fisher," I said. "My corps officer forced me to have sex with him for over a year. The baby is his."

Everything changed. There was a long pause. And then, in a very businesslike tone, free of any hint of emotion, she asked me my corps officer's name and I told her. She asked me if anyone else knew about this affair. I told her no one knew except Rich. I then told her about the meeting with Rich two nights before and his idea that we would be married and he would claim the child as his own. I told her that I had confided in Rich because he was a close friend and I was desperate. I further told her that being married was Rich's idea—I had never asked for nor expected such a gesture. I had initially accepted this solution but then realized I could not live that kind of lie. I needed to tell the truth.

Major Fisher told me she did not need or want to hear any more for now and that I was to tell no one else about this. She reiterated this, "Bunny, you are to tell this to no one. When we need to know more, we will ask. Other than that, you are to remain silent. You would be doing your fellow cadets and the Salvation Army a great disservice if you spoke this abroad." She asked me to leave her office and go back to my classes. When she needed to see me again, she would let me know.

When she called me to her office later that day, she told me that the pregnancy needed to be medically verified. She gave me the name and address of a doctor who would examine me. And then, the elaborate, convoluted planning to protect the organization began. She told me that the next morning when all of the other cadets were boarding the bus that would take them to their kettle assignments, I was "to dress in civilian clothes and *hide somewhere in the building.*" I would most likely be missed, and someone would be sent to search for me. *I was to remain in hiding until they gave up and left without me.* Then I was to go outside the campus, catch a bus, and make my way—alone—to the doctor's office and submit to the examination. She was totally deadpan and dispassionate while telling me all this. She said the doctor would report his findings to her.

From the moment I opened my mouth to tell my truth to Major Fisher, the atmosphere around me changed. I was no longer treated as a person. I was treated as a problem to be dispatched as quickly and quietly as possible. I did not immediately realize this. When Major Fisher began giving orders, I shifted into an automaton state. I asked no questions. I did as I was told. It did not occur to me that what they were doing was wrong. I did not ask why I had to hide, why I had to keep a doctor appointment alone, why she no longer even looked at me when she spoke to me. I felt like garbage. The thought occurred to me that I deserved this treatment. Because, after all, I had done something awful, hadn't I?

I dressed in civilian clothes the next morning and hid as I had been told to do. They called for me and looked through the building for a long time, and I began to be afraid that they might actually find me ... and then what would I do? How could I explain? They finally left. I went outside and caught the bus. I had my Bible with me. I held onto it, got off the bus at the right stop, and made my way to the doctor's office.

His office was a tiny hole-in-the-wall. The receptionist behind the tiny desk in her tiny space was an older lady with dyed red hair and dark heavy makeup. I filled out the form she handed me. My mouth was dry. I was afraid.

The examining room was extremely small and sparse. There was barely enough room for the examination table. I took off my clothes as instructed and followed directions to assume the necessary pose. I was in survival mode. I was hanging on by a thread. I'm sure my face betrayed my anguish because the doctor actually stopped momentarily when he entered and spoke kindly to me. He told me what he would be looking for, asked me questions about my general health, and then gently began his exam. There may have been someone else in the room during the exam—I think it's standard procedure for a woman to be in attendance when a male doctor does this type of procedure—but I don't remember anyone else. The room was so small it seems unlikely. I did not wonder about this at the time. I did not want any witnesses to my shame.

When he was finished, he asked me to sit up on the end of the table. In the kindest voice, he told me that, yes, I was pregnant. He told me that he could see and feel all the indications of a healthy pregnancy of approximately three months' duration. He told me that he would be reporting his findings to Major Fisher. I never gave my permission for this. It was something they arranged between the two of them. He also told me that he would verify his visual examination with a urinalysis. When the results of that test came in, he would mail the results to me and to Major Fisher as he had been instructed.

He then turned toward the door to leave. Hesitating with his hand on the knob, he came back and asked me how I was feeling about all this. I could not answer. There was nothing in me to answer. I was hollow of feeling. I was hollow of words. I was a shell. I could not look at him. I could not answer.

He told me that there was nothing for me to be ashamed of. He told me that I had everything to live for—I was young and strong, I would have a healthy baby, and then I would get on with my life. He asked me a few softly probing questions ... trying to determine if I was suicidal, I think. I had not thought about that. I was sorry he brought it up.

In a few days, I received the chemical report. Pregnant.

Ironically, the pregnancy did not last. In the most paradoxical of twists to this story, a spontaneous abortion ended the pregnancy. I slipped on the concrete steps leading out of the dorm. I lost my footing and fell down about six steps—bouncing from step to step on my buttocks. When I stopped at the bottom, I was in severe pain and my diaphragm was in spasms. I could not catch my breath. The pain in my back was excruciating. I was eventually able to get my breath, but I was barely able to walk.

I made my way to the medical office and reported what had happened. The officer on duty asked me a few questions and then said it didn't look like I had broken anything. Maybe I should just go to my room and lie down for a while. I went to my room and lay down on my bed. I don't remember much about the rest of that day, but during that night, I had severe cramping.

I endured the cramps as long as I could, and then I haltingly made my way to the bathroom. There was a huge discharge when I sat on the toilet. I remember being afraid one of my roommates would come in and find me, so I immediately flushed. For some time, I stayed in that position, flushing the discharge periodically. When the worst was over, I rolled up a towel and put it between my legs and went back to bed.

I was not able to get up the next morning. Major Fisher eventually came to check on me when she was told I had not gone to my classes. I told her I had my period during the night. By that time I was relieved it was over. The baby thing was gone. Whatever else happened, at least I did not have to have John's baby. I was thankful for that. Major Fisher asked me if I was doing okay. I told her I thought I was. She said that I should take my meals in my room that day—she would tell someone in the kitchen to prepare trays for me. She told me again that I was to observe absolute secrecy about the pregnancy. And she told me I would be advised soon about the plans that were being formulated for my future. And then she left. She expressed no real concern for what I had gone through alone during the night. She never offered any kind of help or medical follow-up. She just turned and left …

The next day I was very sore and weak, but I made myself get up and go to meals and class. I bled for a few days, and then it stopped. That, at least, was over. No one ever asked about the miscarriage. I never brought it up. I knew by this time that I was on my way out. I had no illusions about them allowing me to stay just because I was no longer pregnant. I had made allegations that could lead to a scandal. I was a threat to their equanimity. I had to be gotten rid of. If they had asked me, I would have told them that they did not have to worry. I did not want a scandal. I wanted to be an officer. No one asked me.

Major Fisher kept close track of me. I went about my daily routine on autopilot. I don't think I was switching. In looking back on this period, I believe I was so hyper-vigilant that there was no room for switching. My alters were as dazed and vacant as I was. We had allowed ourselves to believe that all of the bad was behind us. We were wrong.

I remember things that happened during what was to be my last week in training. I do not know the exact chronology, but that really doesn't matter. What matters is that they be recorded here. I began this story to tell the truth. It seems important to tell the whole truth.

The Tribunal: At some point during that last week, a tribunal was arranged. It was convened in a conference room near the training school principal's office. Sitting around the table were four or maybe six men. Colonels, commissioners, lieutenant commissioners—every one of them holding some high office. I don't remember being introduced to them. But I could see the brass on their uniforms. Their faces were closed.

They asked me questions about my allegations against Captain Hart. I answered their questions. I stared at my hands in my lap and I answered. There was no one in that room representing me. No one expressed any concern about my physical, emotional, psychological, or spiritual wellbeing. No one asked a question that would indicate that I was anything other than an obstacle to be gotten around. I was never offered help of any kind.

About 30 minutes into the meeting, John came charging into the room. There was immediate confusion and consternation.

John came into the room hurling insults at me. He had pictures of each member of his family in his hands. He threw the pictures down in front of me and yelled, "Do you see what you're doing? Look at them. You're ruining their lives." I saw the pictures of Peggy, Pauline, Jackie, Donny, and Robin. I saw the pictures of people I never intended to hurt. I never looked at him.

He said all the things he told me he would say if I ever told about our relationship. He said I was a liar and that I just had a grudge against him and wanted to ruin him. He said I had tried to have an inappropriate relationship with him, but he had rebuffed me. He said that was the motive behind my allegations. He adamantly affirmed his innocence and called on everyone there to acknowledge all the good work he was doing in Salinas. The meeting ended. That was the last time I ever saw John. I do not know if they believed him. I was never told anything.

During that last week—when they were "making a plan for me"—I would sneak out of my room late at night and make my way into the chapel. I would kneel at the altar and pray. I don't know what I was expecting. I was so alone. I was without hope. I was afraid.

One night, Major Fisher discovered me there—at the altar in the chapel, praying. She asked me to come up to her room. She lived in an apartment in the administrative wing above her office. I remember following her into a cozy room. She fixed us a cup of tea. I drank my tea. She said very little, but I had the feeling she was trying to be kind. She had her orders, she had to be obedient to her superior officers, she had to carry out the plan, whatever that turned out to be. But I think, in that moment, in her apartment, she was trying to be kind.

It was now the middle of December, and the pace at training school was escalating toward Christmas. Final exams were over, the semester ended, everyone was now fully involved in the Christmas campaign. With people coming and going at odd hours on various and sundry assignments, with no set schedule, I did not feel so conspicuous. Everyone was looking forward to the Christmas break, and I just kept my head above water as best I could and waited for whatever would be next in their designs for me.

The Plan: The meeting finally happened. I was called to the principal's office. His name was Colonel Larsen. He was certainly not a beloved figure—he had little to do with individual cadets. He was a rigid and demanding officer. I do not remember him ever smiling or participating in any informal activity. He was aloof.

When I arrived at his office, there were three people present: Colonel Larsen, Major Fisher, and a representative from the territorial office—I don't remember his name. I was told the following:

1. I was being sent to the Southwest Division office in Phoenix to be secretary to the Divisional Youth Secretary, Major Lincoln Upton.
2. I was to call my family and tell them that I was accepting an assignment outside the training school at the request of superior officers. I was not to say anything about the reason for this transfer. I was to tell no one about the relationship with John.
3. I was to immediately pack my belongings and put my bags under my bed. I was told to do this secretly.
4. That night, in the middle of the night, I was to take my bags with me and report to a doorway that led out onto the street.
5. I would be met there by a driver. The driver would take me to Colonel Larsen's home.
6. The next morning I was to board a plane and fly to Phoenix where I would be met by Major Upton.
7. And I was told that if I did all of this exactly as instructed, I would be allowed to come back to training after my session mates graduated and were ordained in June of 1965. If I was good—if I played by their rules and protected the organization—I could come back to training. I listened to that promise. It signified the only bright spot I could hold onto. I silently vowed to make it come true. I could still do it.

The Separation: That night I did exactly as I was told. No one saw me leave. There were no goodbyes. I disappeared from the scene. I don't know what the cadets were told the next day when I was gone. In a few short months, I had gone from being the fastest rising star in the constellation to disappearing into a black hole.

I was seen as tainted and I was expelled. I was a liability.

Everything that was done from the moment I told Major Fisher about my corps officer forcing me to have sex and eventually impregnating me was done to conceal what had happened and to protect the organization. I was sent away and told to tell no one. I never received so much as a kind word. I was thrown away.

Throughout the whole process of my expulsion, I was never able to tell my truth. They were not interested. I never had a counselor to listen, to offer succor. No one ever said that John's behavior with me was wrong. No one ever apologized for the harm done me. In an organization ostensibly representing God, I was treated in the most brutal, unforgiving way imaginable. No one in the world—no worldly person—has ever harmed me as dispassionately and thoroughly as these "godly" people did.

There was no place for truth. There certainly was no place for grace.

And the story was not over.

CHAPTER 33

The Salvation Army's Reaction to Reported Clergy Sexual Abuse

"For the time will come when they will not endure the sound doctrine; but, having itching ears, will heap to themselves teachers after their own lusts; and will turn away their ears from truth …"

II Timothy 4:3-4 ASV

WHILE UNDER CAPTAIN JOHN HART'S DIRECT CONTROL IN SALINAS, I was first raped and then coerced into an ongoing relationship of sexual abuse perpetrated by Captain John Hart, ordained clergy of the Salvation Army, over my expressed objections to such relationship.

I felt powerless to extricate myself from the relationship. Captain John Hart was my corps officer; he was much larger than I was physically; he told me that I would not be believed if I tried to tell anyone, because of the position he held within the Salvation Army; he told me God wanted him to do it; he threatened to tell my mother that I had initiated the relationship; and he threatened me and my family with physical violence. These threats were ongoing and became more frequent as the illicit relationship continued.

I suffered all of the physical, emotional, psychological, and spiritual ramifications of this abusive relationship, while maintaining a full-time job, regular volunteer positions within the corps, and connections within my family. I suffered enormous stress, anxiety, fear, guilt, and shame.

A psychological syndrome—Dissociative Identity Disorder—which was in a state of remission, was reactivated and exacerbated by the sexual acting out of a man in a position of power over me—reenacting childhood trauma by my father. Dissociating became routine as a coping mechanism during sexual encounters and as a way of maintaining normal activities between sexual encounters. Suicide became an ever-present danger as a possible way out of the morass of emotional, psychological, physical, sexual and spiritual abuse.

I told no one of the ongoing sexual predation by Captain John Hart because of the threats made by him. I was totally alone in all of it.

When I found myself pregnant with Captain John Hart's child, I finally decided I must tell the truth. The idea of unburdening myself of this secret was compelling. I was no longer in his direct control. I was a cadet in the Salvation Army's training school. I had fulfilled every responsibility and requirement of the training regimen in an exemplary fashion. Surely this would be a safe place to tell the truth.

When I told the truth—who the father of my child was—the reaction of rejection and isolation was immediate.

I found no one willing to listen to the tragedy of my story—no one wanted to know the how, why, when. They knew all they wanted to know—an officer and a parishioner had been involved in a sexual relationship. The parishioner must be isolated, silenced, and sent away.

The burden of silence—initiated by Captain John Hart—was immediately reiterated by the officials I spoke to at training school. The truth could not be told.

I was required to submit myself to further trauma in the form of an intimate medical examination in the coldest, most barbaric circumstance: required to hide myself within the campus and then find the doctor's office on my own, advocate for myself as best I could in a totally foreign situation (i.e. a doctor I had never met before, a dank, small office, no information on what would happen), and find my way back to school in the state of shock engendered by the examination itself and the knowledge that I was, indeed, three months pregnant.

Ironically, in the sterile medical environment, I received the only kindness which would be offered to me—from the doctor who was a stranger, yet looked at me with compassion. No one in the Salvation Army offered me any form of kindness, compassion, or support.

I was required to obey the edict of silence and go about the daily routines of training school as though nothing were amiss so that my fellow cadets and the life of the training school would not be disrupted.

I lost my footing and fell down a flight of stairs on the Salvation Army campus, injured my back, suffered excruciating pain and cramping, and then experienced a spontaneous miscarriage alone in my dorm room—it did not occur to me to ask for help. Based on the treatment I had thus far received, I had no reason to believe there would be any help.

When I reported the miscarriage to the Women's Chief Side Officer, I was offered no medical help. I did not even realize I should have received medical care.

I was instructed to make a phone call to my family telling them I was being assigned to Phoenix, Arizona. I was instructed not to tell my family the reason for this reassignment.

I was required to secretly pack my belongings and wait alone in the darkness for someone to pick me up and take me to the training school principal's house.

I was taken to an airport as early as practicable the next morning and put on a plane destined for yet another trauma by yet another officially ordained clergy of the Salvation Army.

As an aside—I have no way of knowing this for sure—the way my "case" was handled seems to lend itself to the assumption that this was a routine, standard procedure. The immediate reaction by the Army to silence me, control my actions, institute every possible means of damage control, and then send me away with the continuing order that I tell no one was self-serving to the extreme.

It was all so clearly and neatly orchestrated. They circled the wagons and tossed me outside the circle. Had there been others? Was this standard procedure? Was the Salvation Army routinely harboring sexual predators and muzzling and discarding victims as a way of maintaining their standing as a philanthropic, God-centered organization of goodness, holiness, and mercy for the disadvantaged and marginalized?

I know of no way this can be proved in my particular case. But among the reasons for my finally telling my story now is the fact that I believe, without a doubt, that there were others—perhaps many others. I believe—and I will tell you in due course why I believe this—there were others throughout the organization. Even though I obeyed the order for silence, eventually, I received phone calls of support from some of my session mates from training. They knew things they were willing to confide to me, in spite of the Army's effort to muzzle and silence

According to these informants, the sexual predation within the organization in California at the time I was cast out was from the top-down—the territorial lieutenant commissioner, the Divisional Youth Secretary, corps officers. When these clandestine phone calls came, at least I finally knew I was not the only one. There was a sisterhood of us. Sadly, in this one respect at least, I was no longer alone.

CHAPTER 34

Joining the Upton Family in Phoenix

"Out of the frying pan and into the fire."
                                            An Old Adage

YOU WILL RECALL CAPTAIN AND MRS. UPTON FROM MY EXPERIENCE AT Redwood Glen Camp near Santa Cruz, California. At that time, Captain and Mrs. Upton were the Divisional Youth Secretaries for the Northern California Division of the Salvation Army. When I was sent out of training, they had been promoted to the rank of major and were stationed in Phoenix, Arizona as Divisional Youth Secretaries for the Southwest Division. I had mixed feelings about seeing them again.

I had been told that Major and Mrs. Upton were aware of the reason I was being sent to Phoenix. What would they think of me? Would they be as cold and uncaring as the officers at training school had been? I was to be Major Upton's secretary—a job which would have seemed wonderful under other circumstances. Now I was tainted by scandal and was being sent to the Southwest as part of my discipline for the harm I had done to the Salvation Army. I had no idea what to expect.

Major Upton met me when my plane landed. He was friendly and welcoming. He remembered me fondly from his tenure in Northern California. And nothing—not one word—was said about the reason for my assignment to him. He chuckled as he told me that he was thrilled to have me working for him—he remembered how good I had been at everything asked of me at camp. And he told me that he was hopeless without a good secretary. He told me that he and Mrs. Upton preferred that I use their first names rather than their official titles—so it would be Linc and Jean from that time forward. His kindness took the bite out of the anxiety I felt.

Without fanfare, Linc told me that he and Jean just wanted to help me establish myself in my new surroundings. He told me I would be staying with them until we could find an apartment in an appropriate location. I would be given part-time use of a vehicle for use in connection with my job, but I would not be taking it home with me at night, so he wanted to find a location within walking distance of the office.

The Uptons lived in a beautiful house in a quiet residential area. Jean Upton accepted me without question. She showed me to my room—actually, their daughter Christine's room, which I would be sharing. Christine was 16 and absolutely charming. She welcomed me without reservation. I was quiet and withdrawn. She did not seem to mind. Later on, as a relationship was built with their family, I began attending high school basketball games with Christine and her brother, Doug, who was a couple of years younger than she. They were both wholesome, good kids.

Within the family setting, Linc and Jean were kindly attentive to me in the same way they were attentive to Christine and Doug. They were an obviously affectionate family. Christine was very much like her dad—the same outgoing, engaging personality. Doug was more like his mom—a little more pensive and quiet. There was also a great big, shaggy, exuberant sheepdog named Sheba. A family. I did not react to this family as I had to John's, though. I was too spent and wasted. I did not have the energy it would take to covet their loving connectedness. I was just there. I never thought I was a part of what they had.

The day after I arrived, Linc asked me if I was feeling all right. He said I looked wan and when he checked my forehead, he said he thought I was feverish. I had not felt physically well since the miscarriage—there had been intermittent cramping and sporadic bleeding. Linc wanted me to see a doctor who was a friend of the family, and he actually made the call for me and was able to get me an appointment that afternoon. I do not remember the appointment. I have one faint memory of the doctor himself, but I remember no specifics about that appointment or the course of treatment that followed. He did put me on a regimen of antibiotics because there was an infection, and at some point, there was a procedure to clear my uterus of the remnants of the pregnancy. I remember none of it.

There was also the issue of the back injury from the fall I took at training school. I had been suffering muscle spasms and moments of extreme, debilitating pain since the accident. Linc made sure that I received treatment for that problem too. I remember that I saw a physical therapist for a period of time for electrical stimulation therapy, and I took a muscle relaxant and pain medication until the symptoms subsided.

When I met Sherry, the young woman whose place I would be taking at the office, she told me that she was moving out of the area to be married. She had only worked for Linc for a few months—filling in temporarily when his previous secretary, Jan Black (not her real name—see note at end of chapter), left to enter training school. Sherry said I could take over her apartment if I wanted—it was in an ideal location, about a 20 minute walk from the office. The apartment was furnished, and she was not interested in taking anything with her except her personal effects. This was a real windfall for me. I came to Phoenix with literally no money. Her kindness meant I had the necessities—kitchen equipment and linens. She was leaving in a week. Before she left, she gave me the training I needed to do my job at the office, and she introduced me to the apartment manager, facilitating my having a place to live.

Jan Black had been one of my better friends in training. I knew she had come into training from Phoenix, and I was aware she had been Linc's secretary. We had an interesting relationship at training, Jan and I. There was a "knowing" that we shared. When we were together studying or just hanging out, personal issues would come up and then be abruptly pulled back. We avoided looking each other in the eye. All the time that I was fighting to keep things hidden, Jan was hiding something too. I felt it.

A few days after I moved into my own apartment, Jan arrived back in Phoenix for her Christmas break. Jan and I were the same age—she was a pretty blond with blue eyes. She was small, but she was full of vitality and was mentally quick. When she walked into the office, Jan was immediately embraced by everyone—they were all excited to see her and to hear about training school. There was a definite feeling of a homecoming, and invitations were extended to keep her busy during her time in Phoenix.

Jan's family of origin lived in Southern California, but she was not close to any of them. She had been fully involved with the Army in Phoenix for several years and viewed the Uptons as her family. They seemed to return these feelings, and they happily welcomed her into the household for the duration of her break. I did not know what Jan knew about my reassignment to Phoenix, so I was ill at ease with her. We never spent any time alone together during that break, but six months later we would.

Moving away from the Uptons, I was relieved to have my own space and some privacy. I was also very lonely. I had never lived alone in my life. The apartment was okay, and I felt lucky to have it, but it was in an older building and it was dreary. My salary left nothing to the imagination—I had absolutely no discretionary income. So I settled in as best I could. I worked a regular 9:00 to 5:00 at the divisional office, and I began, tentatively, to attend the Phoenix Citadel Corps. I wanted to do everything I could to stay connected, because I was counting on the promise that I would eventually be able to return to training.

I remember nothing of that Christmas in Phoenix in 1963. I had no family. I had yet to make friends. The Uptons were busy with Jan and other family members who visited from out of town. I'm okay with not remembering that Christmas—it was my first Christmas without my family. It had to have been a sad time for many, many reasons.

There was no one my age at the office—all of the other women were 40 to 60 years old. Several of these older women were kind to me, but there was nothing more than a minimal business relationship. I was immediately comfortable with the tasks my job entailed, and I worked hard. I certainly carried my own weight, and I was happy to pitch in when help was needed in another department. Linc was an affable boss, giving me plenty of leeway to use my skills in planning events and publishing the division newsletter. We were also busy putting together all the building blocks for the upcoming summer camp season. Camp O'Wood was located in the mountains outside Tucson in Oracle Junction. I attended service club meetings with Linc to solicit support for this program for disadvantaged youth. I was a unanimous hit on these occasions—again, using the people skills that came very naturally to me. Anticipating an entire summer working with Linc and Jean away at camp gave me something to look forward to.

As far as worship was concerned, it was never the same for me after the mess at training school. I felt no connection to God. I felt God hated me the same way the Salvation Army did. I attended worship, and I was available to do small leadership duties when called upon. I traveled with Linc and Jean when they visited the corps under their jurisdiction in Arizona, New Mexico, and Nevada.

Linc had been a fighter pilot during World War II—a highly decorated one. He loved to fly and had his own four-passenger plane, which he used routinely for his work. It was a natural in this part of the country where towns were small and spread across great distances. As least two Sundays a month, we flew to corps in rural areas to participate in worship and encourage the youth programs. I had never flown in a small plane before, and Linc was happy to initiate me. When I flew with them, Jean gladly gave me the copilot seat.

We would leave Phoenix early on Sunday morning and fly to

some small landing field in the middle of nowhere; the corps officer would pick us up, and when we got to the corps, we would lead their worship service. Linc routinely asked me to do the children's sermon. He and Jean enjoyed my easy ability to entertain and teach, and Jean was happy to have someone else do the part she would have been expected to do. Linc did the preaching—he was easygoing and uplifting. He was an encourager and used gentle humor to bring his point home. I never felt beat up after one of his sermons.

I was still very lonely. In spite of the time at work and time spent with Linc and Jean, I had way too much time on my hands. I know now that I was depressed, but I did not know that then. I wondered constantly about John, Peggy and their children. What had happened with them? I did not know if John ever realized I was pregnant. I wanted him to know the reason I told—I would never have told except for the pregnancy.

I felt responsible for damage done to John's family. And my fear of John grew. He had promised that he would harm my family. Would he actually do this? I could not tell my family anything because I was told not to tell. The Salvation Army was aware of his threats, but they never brought up the idea that there might actually be danger. Their only thought had been the possibility of damage to their reputation. No other issue was addressed.

Jan left to go back to training right after the first of the year. A few days after her departure, Linc and I were working on a large project together at the office. We were putting together a flowchart of camp responsibilities. Looking up from what we were doing, Linc asked me to come upstairs with him. On the second story of the office building, the public relations manager had a small office, and the remainder of the space was used for storage

I followed Linc up the stairs, he unlocked the door to the large storage room, we walked in, and he closed and locked the door behind him. Linc opened his arms and enfolded me in the kindest, gentlest embrace. He was much taller than I was—I'm barely five feet tall, he was probably six foot two. He kissed the top of my head. His embrace was not in any way sexual. It was warm and kind and sheltering. He asked me how I was doing. I had no real answer for him. At that exact moment, I was savoring the feeling of being taken care of. I nestled in his arms, he held me like a father might.

Linc asked me to look up at him. He again asked me how I was doing. I remember exactly what I said to him: "It just feels good to be close to someone again." He told me that he wanted to take care of me if I would let him. Then he laughed, pulled me closer and snuggled me into his chest. Being touched, held, embraced was an elixir for my longing, broken heart. Here was kindness. Did I know then what the price for that kindness might be? On some level, perhaps I did.

Post-traumatic Stress Disorder is a commonly accepted diagnosis now. The name itself says it all. The stress that remains after major trauma. Symptoms include anxiety, fear, flashbacks, nightmares, suicidal ideation, sleep disturbances—I had them all. To be offered one small moment of respite was priceless. Linc's words and his holding me without sexual overtones was a balm, a salve. I was as vulnerable as it is possible to be. I accepted the comfort he offered.

Author's Note: Regarding Jan Black: In this book, I have used actual names in every instance *except* for the person I name as "Jan Black." This is not her real name. I chose to protect this person's identity because she, like me, was a victim of sexual abuse. You will read more about her in this narrative. I did not feel it was my right to out her.

CHAPTER 35

Intimate Knowledge

"Sex, in and out of the forbidden zone, can become the adult medium through which a woman continues to play out the childhood scenario of healing those around her."

Sex in the Forbidden Zone by Peter Rutter, M.D.

O NE OF THE DUTIES I HAD ASSUMED SINCE COMING TO PHOENIX WAS "tavern collections." This activity had to be the worst possible assignment for a young woman. I dressed in full Salvation Army uniform—including bonnet and white gloves. I had a driver who took me on a prescribed route of taverns and bars in the area. These were not "night clubs." These were smelly, stagnant dives. The route would begin at 7:00 on Saturday evening and last until midnight. I went into each establishment and offered the Salvation Army's *War Cry* in exchange for a donation. The younger and prettier the Salvation Army "lassie," the better the donations. I hated tavern collections, but I did not want to say no when I was trying so hard to buy my way back into training. Like everything else I did, my collections were good. I smiled and answered politely and took their donations. But I could hardly wait for the evening to be over so I could go home and take a shower.

When we finished our route, the driver had to take the money back to the office and put it in a night deposit box to be accounted for on Monday morning. The Saturday night after Linc's embrace in the upstairs storage room, my driver and I came back to the office to drop off the money and found Linc in his office. He called to me. I remember standing in the doorway of his office. He was sitting behind his desk and he smiled warmly at me. He motioned me to come in. He asked me if I was tired. I was a little embarrassed—I felt soiled with tobacco smoke and all the other pungent smells of the dives I had been through that evening. I told him I just wanted to get home and shower. Continuing to smile, he looked at me and asked, "Can I come over and give you a back rub? I know I could put you to sleep."

I remember feeling ambivalent. This was nothing like the physical bullying which I endured with John. I felt the pressure of Linc's rank and his position as my boss. I liked Linc and I did not want to hurt his feelings. This was another aspect of relationships with "father" figures. Linc was old enough to be my father. He had cuddled me like a father might. He had been good and kind to me. He was openly appreciative. I did not want to disappoint him or hurt his feelings. Looking down, not meeting his eyes, I said, "I guess so."

I will openly admit that once Linc began showing more than an employer-employee or father-daughter interest in me, I was beyond caring. The comfort of his arms was everything. I just wanted to be his "little girl." I did not want him to leave me. I was broken, alone, desperate for acceptance and love.

When I told Linc, "I guess so," his face lit up. He told me that he would give me 30 minutes to get home and shower and then he would come over. He told me to listen for him because he did not want to wake anyone else in the building. He asked me what I wanted him to bring with him—I must be hungry. I told him I wanted tacos.

I did listen for Linc. I showered, washed my hair, and put on my long flannel night gown and a robe and slippers. It was a cold night, and I turned up the heat in the apartment. I remember being a little concerned because the apartment was not spotless—Sherry had not been a good housekeeper, and I hadn't had the heart to give the space the deep cleaning it needed. I sat on the couch with my legs pulled up under me and listened for Linc.

He arrived a little later than he had thought he might because he had to look for my tacos. When I let him in, he bent over me and smelled my hair and then pecked me on the cheek—again, like a father might.

He put the tacos on the coffee table, and then he sat down beside me on the sofa. He did not bully or rush. He was gentle. He looked at me and said, "Eat your tacos, Bunny. You've had a long day." I was too nervous to eat. I looked down at my hands in my lap. "Can I eat my tacos after you leave?" I asked. He smiled and gently took my hand and pulled me onto his lap. He said, "They're yours. You can do anything you want with them."

I can still remember how wonderful it felt to sit on Linc's lap. He was a big man—tall and strong—with dark wavy hair. He was always immaculately groomed. He was handsome in a way John had never been. And his eyes always held some mischief. He was caring and handsome and fun. When he snuggled me on his lap, there was no sexual touching. This would be true throughout our relationship. When the sex happened, it was always in bed. For me, when he held me on his lap, it was about comfort and caring and being special and being taken care of. Just like Daddy.

And so this was a different rape entirely. Linc *knew* about the relationship with John. He was aware of my depleted physical and emotional condition when I arrived in Phoenix. He was a bright man. Being bright, he methodically took advantage of all the horrible events which led up to my being sent out of training. He was a different kind of predator—he was smarter, even kinder in a way—but he was a predator nonetheless. He looked for the vulnerability and then struck. Rape of a different kind perhaps, but coldblooded, premeditated victimization of the weak and vulnerable. Rape is rape.

Linc took my right foot in his hand and looked at it. He said,

"You have the tiniest feet. You are the cutest little bundle I've ever seen." Other than kissing the top of my head or holding my foot or running his fingers through my hair, Linc seemed to enjoy the closeness as much as I did.

Should Linc have been preying on my vulnerability? Should he have used his position over me to go beyond our professional relationship? Should he have used my deep sense of loss to further his own goal of a sexual relationship? Should he have ignored the boundaries that his office as clergy imposed on him?

Linc's methods were different, but the end result was the same.

That first evening in my apartment, Linc and I sat on the couch for a long time. He talked to me. While he was holding me, he told me stories about other parts of his life—funny, touching, loving stories. Sitting on his lap, listening to his voice, I was again with the father who loved me and told me stories. Every fiber of my being connected with the daddy I had lost so many years before. The deep connection with Linc in this particular setting, of course, was in large part generated by my split-off child parts, who were indiscriminate in their hope for the good father.

When he gently lifted me up and off his lap, he did not say a word. He just took my hand in his and led me toward the bedroom. He unbuttoned my robe and helped me step out of it; he pulled the covers back, sat me on the edge of the bed and then indicated that I should lie down. When I lay down, he pulled the blankets up to my chin and tucked me in.

Linc slowly undressed. He continued to talk to me. He did not seem to be in any hurry. When he crawled into bed beside me, he pulled me to him and snuggled me against his bare chest. He whispered to me—telling me how special I was, how beautiful. He did not grope me or tear at my night gown. He remained quietly engrossed in my nearness. Just like Daddy.

When Linc's interest became overtly sexual—when fondling and removing my night gown and panties began, I dissociated. Because of the work done in therapy, I now know this is exactly what I did when my father was sexual with me. I dissociated. All of the little moments leading up to the actual beginning of the sexual acting out could be rationalized. When the sexual foreplay began, I dissociated. This was the way I maintained the fantasy of having a father who loved me. Because of the dramatic similarities between my father's victimization and Linc's behavior with me, there was a familiarity that helped compartmentalize, for the moment, the harm he did. I never said no to my father or to Linc. I was a "good little girl" and did what I was told.

When I was again aware, I was lying next to Linc, cradled within his arms. Just like Daddy. He was looking at me with bemused satisfaction. "You are a darling one," he said. "How did I get so lucky?"

CHAPTER 36

Who Was Lincoln Upton?

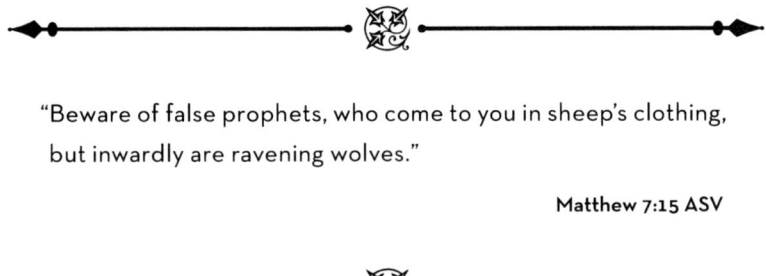

"Beware of false prophets, who come to you in sheep's clothing, but inwardly are ravening wolves."

Matthew 7:15 ASV

LINC WAS CHARMING. HE WAS OUTGOING AND GENEROUS—WELCOMING everyone. He was perfectly suited to his responsibilities as a pastor, leader, and motivator. He was an exuberant prankster—pulling practical jokes at the office, at home, and even at public events within the community. And he was perfect as a camp director—mixing recreation, fun, fellowship, and spiritual teaching. He was universally loved and admired.

Did all these traits help him when his platonic interest in young women in his environment became predatory? I remember how I felt about Linc when I knew him in Northern California—especially at camp, but also when he visited the Salinas Corps. I felt a natural pull to be near him—his enthusiasm was contagious. He was the fun religious person—the one who made God seem accessible and interesting.

I think all of Linc's positive and attractive physical and personality traits made it very easy for him to engage young women in exactly the way he engaged me. He was first friendly, welcoming, and helpful in a rather general way—facilitating doctor appointments and helping me find an apartment. There was the gentle guidance and the appreciation for my abilities at the office and when we visited other corps. This led to the warm and caring non-sexual touching. By the time the actual sexual activity took place, there was no resistance. It's like the old story about the frog in the pot. The frog is thrown into a pot of cold water—this feels good, almost like home. When the temperature of the water is slowly and gently raised, the frog has been lulled into carelessness, and before he knows it, he has been cooked.

Because I was suffering from Post-traumatic Stress Disorder, I was an easy target for Linc's type of predation. The thing I yearned for, the cuddling, always happened before sex. That was the biggest part of the time we spent together. The cuddling, caressing, and holding could go on for more than an hour. And it was not fondling—it was not sexual in nature. This part of those times together seemed totally innocent and lovely. He whispered endearments. The endearments themselves were things a loving father might say to a beloved daughter. His voice was soothing, calming, intimate. Just like Daddy. I loved listening. I said little when we were together. I never felt I had to speak. I felt that I could just soak up his attentions—like someone who has gone without for a long time, I was parched for the kind of attention he showed me during this blessed fatherly time. And when foreplay began, I dissociated. Just like with Daddy.

After that first time, Linc usually brought liquor with him. He never asked me to drink with him. In fact, it's interesting for me to remember that he thought drinking would not be "good for me." Having sex—on the other hand—was not proscribed. Drinking was. Linc often brought me little gifts when he came. I looked forward to his giftwrapped trinkets.

My father gave me a gift once—a golden locket. He sent it to me for my birthday when I was in fifth grade. Out of nowhere came a gift from my father. My mother begrudged me receiving a gift from him—he owed her everything. What right did I have to his gift? I felt odd about that gift from my father. I wanted it and was ashamed of it, too.

Las Vegas was in Linc's territory, and he visited that corps often. Jean did not like to go to Las Vegas, so Linc made that trip alone. He said it worked out well because he liked to visit the casinos. I was no longer naïve about the sex, but I was astonished that a Salvation Army officer drank liquor and went to shows in Las Vegas. You would have to be inside the organization to realize just how taboo these things were. In the Salvation Army, women did not wear makeup, total abstinence was required, and movies were even frowned upon. Worldliness in any form was to be eschewed. Yet Linc was sitting there telling me how beautiful the women's bodies were when they were performing on swings in the nude.

He went on to explain that there is nothing shameful about the female body—that it is the most beautiful thing that God created. He was absolutely serious about this, and as paradoxical as it may seem, I found this more confusing than his having sex with me. How could he be God's servant and yet be so caught up in this world that I had been taught was of the devil? Who was right? Did he know more about God's mind than the church he was supposed to be serving?

Linc talked about taking me to Las Vegas with him. He said he would love for us to stay together in a beautiful hotel suite. He said there was a whole world of things he wanted to introduce me to, to teach me. He said that to him loving God meant loving all of God's creation—especially the female body, which was God's crowning achievement, given to man for his appreciation and enjoyment. I remember him saying, "It's beautiful, Bunny. There is nothing more beautiful. I adore your beautiful, little body." His eyes would mist over as he was saying this. He truly believed every word he was saying.

Again, the sex was authorized by God.

CHAPTER 37

My Complicity

"The cultural messages encouraging passivity, the personal wounds from her family that have shown her there is no protective boundary, the hope that someone will treat her differently, all come together as an overwhelming flood at the moment the man touches her. This paralysis can last for minutes, hours, days, and sometimes years. In the meantime, the man has proceeded with his sexual scenario."

Sex in the Forbidden Zone by Peter Rutter, M.D.

WHEN I STARTED THIS BOOK, IT WAS TO RECORD THE BETRAYAL I FELT in the relationship with Captain John Hart and the brutality of the Salvation Army's handling of me when that relationship came to light. In that first draft of the book, I did not even mention Major Lincoln Upton. I needed to believe that Linc was somehow different. I know now that his methods were different, but his motives were the same as every other predator—the taking of something forbidden for his own satisfaction without any thought for the life of the prey.

Once again, I think it's fair to mention all of the other factors that made me vulnerable to Linc's advances:

My disgrace and isolation from everything and everyone I knew when I was sent out of training in San Francisco to Phoenix—a foreign country as far as I was concerned: I had rarely been more than 100 miles away from the town where I was born—I had never been out of the state of California. I had never been on an airplane in my life.

My weakened physical condition: I was reeling from the aftereffects of a miscarriage and an injury to my back. I did not know how to advocate for myself, even to obtain minimal health care.

My underlying psychological condition—Dissociative Identity Disorder—compounded by Post-traumatic Stress Disorder and depression: I was living moment by moment in a state of mental anguish that necessitated switching personality states in order to just get by. I was doing what the Salvation Army itself told me to do—at the risk of my own health and safety, I was following orders. I slept little and thoughts of suicide were my companions during night terrors.

At the base of all this was the irony that the place of healing became the place of greatest harm. John Hart, the Salvation Army as an institution, and then Lincoln Upton could have been my saving grace. As a child, I had endured a litany of abuse. Church should have been my haven—and for some years it was. But when church became the place of danger, the foundation of my life was taken away from me. The place where I had found sanctuary became a prison. My body and soul were in torment during the relationship with John. When I thought I had escaped that, the Salvation Army, itself, discarded me. And then there was Linc. How could I be expected to renounce his advances? Was I, at that time, in that weakened state, supposed to be the "adult" who educated him? Who taught him how to behave?

And yet it has always been difficult for me to blame Linc—I think I needed to believe that someone loved me. Someone, out of all those people in those blue uniforms with the brass buttons and epaulets, someone loved me. Of course, he did not. That is not how love works. We can look up the word love in the dictionary, in the Bible, in M. Scott Peck's masterwork, *The Road Less Traveled*, and we will see that love does not take advantage, does not seek its own way, does not exploit. But I did not know that then. I thought he loved me.

It may be that this insidious type of betrayal is worse that the more obvious brutality used by John. Linc cloaked himself in an aura of goodness and benevolence—tenderness even—in order to do that which was evil.

And so if I was complicit in the relationship with Linc, it was because of my excess of neediness, my brokenhearted disillusionment, my willingness to pay any price for a moment of kindness. I accepted the deal he offered.

This much I know: I never sought a sexual relationship with Linc. It became the price I paid for what I did seek: kindness, gentleness, succor for my physical and psychological wounds. To have one, I accepted the other. At the time, it felt like survival. I yearned for the closeness and connection Linc represented in a world that—for me—had become unfathomably cruel. Those moments of tenderness gave me a reason to live. At that time, there were not a lot of those. I held on to them as though my life depended on them. The relationship with Linc was what the Salvation Army offered me. Who was I to refuse?

CHAPTER 38

What About Mother?

"'Damned if I have to put up with this.' For whatever reason, the parent places the raging infant into the crib to 'settle him down.' That infant has been abandoned again. S/he is clearly registering and learning the meaning of abandonment, fear of which will shadow the rest of childhood and become lined with an inevitable sense of impotency."

Magical Child by Joseph Chilton Pearce

I SPOKE WITH MY MOTHER REGULARLY BY PHONE WHILE I LIVED IN PHOENIX. I was guarded in how much I told her about my life. I told her only what she insisted on knowing—what I did during the day, how involved I was at the corps, did I know when I would be coming back to training school. I hated these conversations because they renewed the shame I felt in the dissembling that was now a way of life. And I was very lonely—I especially missed my brothers.

When Mother called to tell me that Pete was getting married, I jumped at the chance of going home for his wedding. Mother was paying my airfare, and it would have seemed preposterous not to go. I knew I would have to be careful—my mother could not know how miserable I was in Phoenix, and the Salvation Army could not know I was returning to Salinas. But I looked forward to being back in the familiar.

Pete's wedding was small and intimate. It was hard for me to see him and his new wife so happy when my heart was full of dark secrets. I wished for Pete and me to be the best friends we had been during our teen years—we double dated and shared many of the same friends then. But I had changed so drastically, I knew we could never be those relatively carefree kids again.

When I got up on the Sunday morning after Pete's wedding, I knew I had to put on my Salvation Army uniform and pretend that I was going to church. I knew that if I did not do this, my mother would wonder what was going on—supposedly, I was just in a temporary assignment in Phoenix. She still believed me to be a cadet, and I did not disabuse her of that idea. She gave me permission to use her car, and as I went out the front door, I remembered the corps in Watsonville—about 30 miles away. I decided that perhaps I could go there. It was a very small corps, and I hoped I would not be recognized or noticed.

When I arrived for church at the Watsonville corps, the service had already begun. I sat toward the back of the building and joined in the familiar routines. When the service ended, I quickly stood up to make my way to the door to leave. The corps officer's wife—I do not remember their names—came up to me. I did not know what to expect, but I knew I could not ignore her and rush out the door without making a scene. My mouth was dry. I stood frozen in place. I braced myself for whatever onslaught might come.

She came up to me, reached out to take one of my hands in both of hers, and looked me full in the face. She said, "Bunny, we know what happened to you. We just want you to know you can worship with us anytime. No matter what they told us to do, we answer to God, not to them. You are welcome here." And then she hugged me tightly to her, released me, and walked away.

Of all the people I've ever known in the Salvation Army,

she—and her husband by extension—were probably the most grace filled. They did not judge or ask for an explanation. They just did the simple compassionate thing that, perhaps, Jesus would have done. They did not throw me out. They invited me in.

I dreaded the return to Phoenix. The relationship with Linc was becoming more and more uncomfortable. I knew the sex, the secrecy, his sneaking behind Jean's back was wrong. But he, similar in this way to John, became more bold and careless about his coming and going from my apartment as time went on. I wondered what my neighbors might think. He was now coming any time he felt like it—many times, during the day. He would invent reasons for us to go places together. I was confused and ill at ease. On one hand, we had a professional relationship at work; on another hand, we had a clandestine sexual relationship outside work, and now we were spending time together as though we were just good friends? By this time, I dreaded seeing Linc also.

I returned to Phoenix. Life went on. Work went on. I spent time with Linc and Jean's family. I volunteered at the corps. And Linc continued to call on me.

CHAPTER 39

The Uptons Leave for Portland

"When it occurs in the forbidden zone with a man who has a responsibility not to let it happen, a woman inevitably leaves the sexual relationship with more damage than when she entered it."

Sex in the Forbidden Zone by Peter Rutter, M.D.

Within a month or two after I came back from Pete's wedding, Linc and Jean received orders that they were being transferred to the Northwest Division Headquarters in Portland. I believe this was a promotion to divisional commander. When Linc told me, there was an avalanche of mixed feelings. The sexual part of our relationship was difficult for me to be sure—and that had escalated recently—but Linc was the only "friend" I had in Phoenix. What would life be like without him? Without his family? I knew no one else. There were many acquaintances, but no friends.

I helped Linc make the arrangements for his move. We tied up all of the loose ends at the office. Plans for camp had been solidified, and everything else was completely up to date. Linc was good at his job—not a procrastinator—and I was good at mine. The office was ready for whoever was next. He told me who would be replacing him. I would be secretary to Captain and Mrs. David Riley, who had four children aged six to twelve—two boys and two girls. I felt anxious about losing the Uptons and queasy about gaining an unknown quantity in the Rileys. What did they know about me? What would he expect from me?

After we wrapped everything up at the office on his last Friday in Phoenix, Linc asked me to get in the car and go for a ride with him. We stopped at a jewelry store. He parked and told me he would be back in a few minutes. When he came back, he had a beautifully giftwrapped box. Handing it to me, he asked me to unwrap it. Inside was a stunning jade pendant on a gold chain. He told me something about the meaning of jade—I'm not sure I was listening even then, and I remember nothing of it now. I liked the gift, but I felt wrong receiving it. It was so cliché—the "kept" woman who gets the token jewelry gift when the man smilingly moves on to whatever is next in his life. Leaving human wreckage in his wake.

That afternoon, Linc and I spent a long time together in my apartment. I knew it was the last time, and I was sad. By this time, I was just so tired of being tossed to and fro—never knowing what to expect, never given a choice. I felt lost and alone already. Linc was excited about his new assignment. He said all the right things. I was special. He would miss me. But I believe I had known all along that I was just the person who was handy at the moment. I needed his attention, but I never thought I was more to him than an extracurricular activity. He enjoyed the time we spent together for one reason. I for another.

I remember a little more about that last time we were in bed together. I was on top this time. I think this was the first and only time I was in that position with him. He was totally entranced—he was not touching my breasts, but he was telling me how beautiful they were. He actually said, "Bunny, you are so beautiful." After the sex was over, I lay on top of him for a long time and he held me tenderly. Just like Daddy did.

Linc and his family left the next morning. I took them to the train station. They were making a vacation of the trip to Portland—enjoying the train ride. I shipped Sheba to them a few days later.

Linc and I would see each other only once more—about six months later.

CHAPTER 40

Auntie Rita of the Morality Police

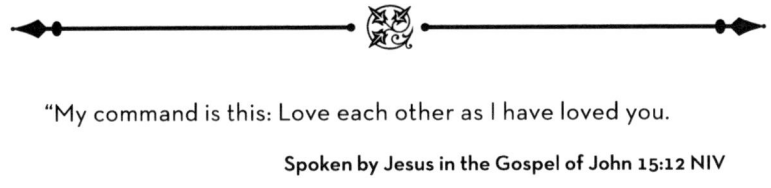

"My command is this: Love each other as I have loved you."

Spoken by Jesus in the Gospel of John 15:12 NIV

I RECEIVED A PHONE CALL FROM AUNTIE RITA—THE CORPS SERGEANT Major at the Salinas Corps. The moment I heard her voice, I knew this was no friendly call. There was no, "How are you doing, Bunny? We miss you. Are you getting along okay? Can I help in any way?" Without preamble, Auntie Rita said, "If you don't tell your mother what you did, I will."

I did not ask Auntie Rita how she knew. Had John told her? Had the Salvation Army told the corps after telling me to tell no one? I do not know.

What Auntie Rita told me was this: She wanted to hear the story from my lips, in person, in front of my mother. If I did not arrange for this to happen, she was going to confront my mother herself. I don't think Auntie Rita had much more than barely met my mother. Auntie Rita often picked me up for church during my teen years, and I was present at family celebrations for her nieces. But I don't remember her having any reason to know my mother. Mother never went to church—not even the last Sunday when there was a goodbye celebration before I left for training school.

I don't remember much of what I said to Auntie Rita that day on the phone. I know I told her I would do what she asked. Did she know that what she was demanding was putting me in harm's way yet again? Did she realize just how abusive my mother had always been? Did she realize that this was the very worst punishment she could have devised? I don't know what she knew or imagined. On the phone, she sounded as though she were enjoying herself. There was the sound of the person who has the upper hand in some grievance and enjoys going for the proverbial jugular vein—knowing the weaker party is at her mercy. Yes, she was enjoying herself.

I had been told not to go near the corps in Salinas and not to initiate any contact with members of the corps. I never hesitated about what Auntie Rita was asking, though, because she was obviously a woman on a mission. That much was evident from the tone of her voice and the threats she was making.

Auntie Rita? I had grown up with Sharon and Karen, her nieces. She had always been my aunt by extension. She was a person I looked up to by way of her relationship to my best friends and by way of her position in the corps. Why would she be so intent on my abasement? Didn't she remember all the good I had done in the corps? Wasn't she my friend? And what about the love that Jesus preached? Didn't that matter at all? It is strange for me to ask these questions—all these years later. She was delighted to forget everything my actions had stood for for 20 years. In her enthusiasm for the titillating, she chose to see only the scarlet letter the Salvation Army had stitched on my bodice.

I took a few days off from work—explaining there was a family emergency. I called my mother and told her I was coming home for a short visit to take care of some business for the Army. Colonel Neubold—the divisional commander—offered to give me a ride to the airport. My mother picked me up at the airport in San Francisco.

Before my mother pulled away from the parking place at the airport, I told her why I had to come home. I told her about John Hart. I told her that was why I had been sent to Phoenix. I did not tell her about a pregnancy. Of course, I did not mention anything about Linc. I told her Rita Muther had called me and threatened to tell my mother about the whole sordid mess if I didn't. I told her that we had to invite Rita to the house so I could tell her in front of Mother. I can't remember what exactly I told her, how I worded it. I do remember her response.

First, she said, "Why didn't you tell me? I could have told you that old men always want that from young girls." I had not expected that. She could have helped? I still cannot fathom that. But that's what she said first.

And then she said all the things I would have expected. "What were you thinking? How could you put me in such a humiliating position? How will I ever live this down? My daughter screwing the preacher? So now you've done it. You have ruined a good man."

That last refrain—"You have ruined a good man."—would stand her in good stead for the rest of her life. She said that exact thing to me shortly before she died at age 87 in 1999. I asked her why she would bring that up again—over and over again. She said, "If one of your sons had done something that bad, wouldn't you think it was your job to remind him of his sin?" I answered, "No, Mother, I would think it was my job to defend him against someone who took advantage of him and to love him more completely because of what he had been through." She looked at me with disgust and shook her head.

When we got to Mother's house, I called Rita Muther. She came right over. I remember her sitting on the sofa in my mother's living room. She was a fat woman. She held her purse firmly in her lap. Her fleshy legs bulged off the edge of the sofa. She stared at me with a bemused expression. Mother was sitting opposite her. I was sitting off to the side. I could not tell you exactly what I said, but I'm sure I did not blame anyone but myself. By this time, I believed what everyone else believed—I must have done it. Everyone said so, so it must be true. I know I said as little as I thought I could get by with. Something like, "It's true. John Hart and I had an affair." When she was satisfied that I had admitted the truth—had confessed the sin I had committed against God and the Salvation Army, Rita Muther smiled. She actually smiled. She said, "I knew it. I knew it all the time. I saw how you acted around him. I knew what was going on. This does not surprise me at all. You will have to bear the results of your sin." Then she got up and left.

Where is love when we need it most? Where is the effort to know and understand? Where is kindness? I found none with this woman. She was too full of righteous indignation. She was thrilled with her power to humiliate and humble. No room for love.

I asked mother if she was going to tell my brothers. She said, "Of course not. Do you think I want to spread my shame any farther than I have to? There's no reason for them to know how far you've fallen. Just keep your mouth shut." This I was more than happy to do. I did not want Buzz or Pete to know. That much I could agree with. Neither of them ever knew.

But there was more during that awful visit home.

Peggy Hart called me at my mother's house. She was furious. Over the phone, she yelled at me that she was going to sue me for alienation of affections.

What more could possibly go wrong?

Luckily, I kept my wits about me enough to remember the man for whom I had worked for the year before I went to training school. Andy Church was a junior partner at the Law Offices of Abramson and Bolz. When I became his secretary, he was just out of law school, joining the firm that his uncle had founded a generation earlier. Andy and I had a great relationship. As the newest member of the firm, he handled the personal law for the owners of the large agricultural companies the firm represented. He was newly married, bright, ambitious, and needed someone who could keep up and help him prove himself at the firm. I did that for the year I worked for him. Andy appreciated me, and the senior partners soon learned that I was accurate, efficient, and an excellent typist.

When I told Andy and then Mr. Abramson that I was leaving because I was entering training school to work in the Salvation

Army, they were both disappointed to lose me. John later told me that the firm had set up a fund to pay my tuition at training school. They had done it anonymously. I was touched by Andy's thoughtfulness and by Mr. Abramson's generosity.

After the call from Peggy, I called Andy and told him I was in town for a short visit. "Could I come by the office and see you," I asked. I told him I wanted to say hello and I had a legal question for him. He was delighted to hear from me.

Andy told others that I was coming by the office, so there was the flurry of enthusiastic greetings and hugs. Then Andy asked me into his office so we could get caught up.

I sat down opposite Andy and briefly told him about John Hart. Again, I don't remember exactly what I said. I just remember Andy looking at me with true sorrow and sympathy and saying, "I am so sorry, Bunny. What happened to you is classic. It happens to the good girls who are too naïve to know what's going on until it's too late. Predators like him aren't attracted to women their own age or to women from whom they could buy sex. This type wants the young innocent. I'm so sorry."

I told Andy about the call from Peggy and her threat to sue me. Andy said, "Just give me her phone number, Bunny. I will make one phone call, and I guarantee you that will be the end of it."

It was the end of it. I never heard from Peggy again.

But I did hear from Donny. I mentioned his phone call earlier in the book. In spite of what was going on in his own home and in the corps, he remembered who I was to him and to the others I loved and mentored. He was so dear and so sweet in his total belief in me. He never entertained any doubt.

And Andy. I am not sure what Andy's religious philosophy might have been. We never talked about it. But, in a pinch, he was the epitome of the good neighbor that Jesus talked about in the Parable of the Good Samaritan—the one who did not ask for explanations and did not blame the victim, but bound up his wounds and made sure he was taken care of. Andy did that for me. Maybe it matters more who a person is deep at the center of his being—not what religious philosophy he espouses. Those in the Salvation

Army openly espoused religion—preached it loud and long—but in their attitude and actions toward me, they were like the priest and Levite in the parable who spurned the injured man and, with disgust, passed by on the other side of the road so as not to be contaminated by his obvious complicity in his own dire situation. They were religious, but they were not good.

In Andy, there was the effort to take an extra step, to demonstrate love.

CHAPTER 41

The Emotional Toll

"Frankel (1976), in his seminal work *Hypnosis: Trance as a Coping Mechanism*, outlines the evidence that dissociative/hypnotic mechanisms play an important role in dealing with day-to-day stress as well as protecting an individual against catastrophic trauma."

Diagnosis and Treatment of Multiple Personality Disorder by Frank W. Putnam, M.D.

EVEN NOW, IT IS DIFFICULT FOR ME TO SORT THROUGH THE MINEFIELD OF emotional upheaval that was occasioned during that visit home.

I was aware for the first time of the fallout of vitriol that awaited me among people who had been my support system as I was growing up in the Salinas Corps of the Salvation Army. I was never again willingly in the presence of any one of that cadre.

I was viciously attacked by Peggy—the person I most regretted hurting. Somehow, in my disoriented state, I thought Peggy would understand and forgive. It now sounds too naïve to be true, but I expected Peggy to somehow see my side of the story. I thought I would have an opportunity to explain. I had not yet fully comprehended the depth of my loss—Peggy and the four Hart children had been the core of my newly experienced sense of family. Loss of all of them—each one a treasured friend—felt like an amputation of some vital part of myself. I found it hard to breathe in this new atmosphere devoid of the oxygen they had been to me.

My mother had been given the "gift" of something she could hold against me for the rest of her life. For her, the knowledge of the nature of my relationship with John validated her opinion of me and gave her the moral high ground to look down on me as the depraved female she actually needed me to be. She never wavered in that opinion. I spent the rest of my life with her trying to change her mind. It took a mountain of therapy for me to finally realize—about six months before her death—that I could separate from her. My husband, my two sons, and I had built her a lovely studio apartment adjacent to our beautiful home—complete with Jacuzzi tub, full kitchen, vaulted ceilings, private entrance, and chauffeur transportation at her beck and call—only to have her decry me to her visiting nurses, and to family assembled for a wedding, as the one person who made her life a living hell. In the John Hart travesty, the Salvation Army gave my mother the gift of the righteous indignation that would fuel her hatred of me for the remainder of her life.

During this visit, I do not remember seeing my brothers. While I was staying at my mother's house, I managed to be away from home as much as possible. She did not even protest. And I retreated into dissociation. It was a way of getting through moment by moment. Different alters could handle different situations and no one personality had to take all the burden of the assaults that came at us randomly. It could have been totally overwhelming. That is one of the key benefits of dissociation—dispersing the trauma among many.

As I prepared myself to return to Phoenix, I dreaded returning to what was now an emotional wasteland for me. While I knew I could not remain in Salinas, my anchor in Phoenix was gone. Linc and his family had left for Portland. The whole reason I was willing to allow Linc sexual access to me was so that I would have someone to be close to there. And I was still laboring under the mistaken idea that there had been something meaningful about the relationship with Linc. As previously stated, I think this was a rationalization so that I could maintain some sort of equilibrium in the midst of yet another betrayal by a spiritual mentor. Jean's low key acceptance of me and her appreciation of me as a promising speaker and leader mattered also. And I enjoyed Christine's friendship. As uncomfortable as I was about the sex that Linc initiated as the price of my attachment to him and his family, his family was the only thing I found to attach to in Phoenix. I had no other friends. I had no other anchor.

Captain and Mrs. David Riley were a part of what awaited me in Phoenix—no anchor there, but no predator either.

CHAPTER 42

Help Located at an Address Near Me

"No act is more unnatural, and hence more human, than the act of entering psychotherapy."

The Road Less Traveled by M. Scott Peck, M.D.

The first day after my return to Phoenix, I came out of a period of dissociation realizing that suicidal ideation had progressed to actual planning. If you have never been that depressed, hopeless, isolated, it is hard to explain the phenomenon. For me, it was a bottomless chasm of despair. The whole fabric of my life had been decimated—there was now no place where I was valued. On the contrary, I was seen as a liability in my own home, in the corps I had been a part of all my life, and in the institutional Salvation Army.

Any connection to a God who loved and forgave was destroyed also—I now felt the constant fear of punishment my mother delighted in predicting, and this on the heels of the mistreatment by those who I thought of as God's messengers on earth—the Salvation Army.

My plan was simple. I used public transportation routinely to get around Phoenix. That morning I found myself standing on a street corner with the firm intent of jumping in front of the next bus that came along. When I came completely out of the dissociative state, I calmly thought about the plan. I was not horrified. It seemed logical. I had no fear of the pain involved. It was the end result that beckoned and winked at me enticingly. I would be okay. I would no longer be suffering. I did not think about hell. As far as I was concerned, I was already there. Anything would be better than the torment I felt in trying to hang on another moment. For what? More moments of the same torment? I just felt finished.

As I stood there, I clearly saw myself leaping in front of the bus; I saw the moment of impact; I saw myself as a rag doll being tossed high in the air and then coming to rest under the wheels of the bus. There was no fear. There was only anticipation of the surcease I longed for.

A woman standing nearby came up to me and asked, "Are you okay? Do you need directions? Can I help you?"

The trance was broken. I told her I was okay, and then I turned and began to walk away. It was at this moment that I was shaken. I wasn't sure my legs would hold me. I realized just how close I had come to making the ultimate decision from which there is no turning back. At that moment, I wondered if I could find another way—a way that did not include any of those who had despised and rejected me. I knew I was powerless to change the Salvation Army's mind. I knew my mother saw nothing redeemable in me. Where could I find help?

When I arrived home, I picked up my phonebook and looked under psychiatrists/psychologists. I found a listing for a Jack Z. Elias, Ph.D., whose office was located in an area with which I was familiar. I dialed the number and made an appointment to see Dr. Elias the following Wednesday morning—four days hence. Could I get through those four days? I visualized talking to someone who was not a part of the world I felt mired in—surely a therapist would be able to help me stop my repetitive, self-destructive behavior with older men. That is the way I characterized my problem. I just had a hard time saying no to someone older than I was. It never occurred to me that those older men should not have put me in a position to have to defend myself against their advances.

The first time I met with Dr. Elias, he asked me how I happened to call him—who had referred me? I told him I called him because I knew how to get to his office. He was aghast. He told me that was not the way to choose a therapist—how did I know he was accredited? How did I know anything about his qualifications? He wrote some phone numbers on a slip of paper and handed it to me. He asked me to call them—the state licensing board and the professional organization of which he was a fellow—before our next meeting. I took the piece of paper, but I knew I was not going to do anything with it. I had made it this far. This had to work. I had no energy or motivation to look further.

When Dr. Elias asked what prompted me to seek the help of a therapist, I told him about the episode on the street corner. I did not tell him anything about my amnesiac episodes. While I knew that I "checked out" at times, I thought of that as a survival technique, not a problem. Dissociation had spared me much. I had no reason to want to give that up. But I told him about being on the street corner and planning my own death in minute detail. I told him about the woman who came up to me and the fear that I might not be able to step back from that brink if I was to get that close again.

Dr. Elias did not dramatically react to what I was saying. As a true therapist, he asked me to go on—tell him everything I could remember about the events directly leading up to the episode. At that point, I mentioned to him that I had been sexually involved with two older men, and I felt helpless to prevent such repeat occurrences. I told him I had no such problem with boys my own age. He said that we could definitely work on that if I was willing to enter into a contract with him regarding my suicidal acting out.

I remember Dr. Elias leaning across his desk, looking at me intently, and asking, "Do you think you can do that, Bunny? Do you think you can honestly enter into an agreement that you will not harm yourself between now and our next appointment?" I remember that I had a difficult time meeting his eyes. I looked at my hands in my lap. He put a pad of paper and a pen in front of me. He said, "If we are to work together, there has to be trust. You can trust me, Bunny, to always act in your best interest in my role as a therapist. I need to be able to trust you to keep your end of the bargain—do yourself no harm—because I believe that is also in your best interest. Can we agree on those two things?"

I told him I thought we could.

He asked me to write a simple statement saying that I would not harm myself between that meeting and our next meeting one week later. I did as he asked. It was a very powerful moment. When I signed my name to that statement, I felt like I was in this with someone else—I was not totally alone. And this person had guaranteed that he would always act in my best interests. The words themselves and the sincerity with which he said them kindled some small hope deep within me. For the next week, I remembered his words, and I remembered the promise I had made.

When I saw Dr. Elias one week later, he asked me to tell him about the relationships with older men that concerned me. I explained the context of the relationships—they were both ministers in my church. Both of them were people I admired and looked up to before the sex began. I just did not know how to stop the sex from happening.

I believe therapists have a responsibility to remain dispassionate and objective. But when Dr. Elias heard that the two men of whom I was speaking were my ministers, he came upright in his chair and said words I will always remember, "They were your ministers? They were your ministers, both of them? They were in the wrong, Bunny, to introduce any hint of sexual overtone, let alone sexual acting out, into the relationship. That was *their* responsibility, not yours. Do you hear what I am saying? What happened in those relationships was in no way your fault. We will talk about this further, but I am telling you now that you have been badly betrayed. I believe I can help you, but first I must say that these two men are the criminals. You are innocent of wrongdoing."

Andy had said something similar. Donny had affirmed his belief in me. But they both knew me—they were my close friends—and maybe that colored their perception. Here was a man—a professional therapist—who had no vested interest in humoring or placating me. He was stating categorically that I was innocent of wrongdoing. I did not know him well. He did not yet know me well. But he did not hesitate or qualify his comments in the least. He was adamant. I know I did not actually believe him at the time—it's probably never that simple, except, perhaps, in the movies—but his words gave me the hook I needed to hope. Could I believe what he was saying, in spite of what the church said, in spite of what my mother believed about me? At that moment, I only knew I wanted to try.

At the end of that session, Dr. Elias asked me to renew my promise to not harm myself. For many months, this was the way each meeting ended. I know that the relationship with Dr. Elias saved my life. I had absolutely nothing else going for me. He became my lifeline. He told me the truth even when I wasn't ready to believe him. As the details of the two relationships came out over the course of my therapy with him, he never once waffled on his initial assessment: They were to blame. What they did was an egregious violation of professional ethics, and their behavior was without any possible redeeming quality. They were just wrong.

I paid the fees for my therapy with Dr. Elias. I had to scrimp on everything else in order to do this. And there was never a question in my mind about the value of this partnership. There was something essential in finding someone, finally, who had no ulterior motive, who did what he said he would do—acted always in my best interest.

My therapy with Dr. Elias lasted until the day before I left Phoenix. His concern went beyond the physical distance created by my move. He told me before I left that I was not finished. He was very concerned that I continue therapy. I listened but was not sure. I was leaving, wasn't I? I was separating from the organization that caused the harm, wasn't I? I just wanted to leave everything behind me. When I had relocated, I received a very professional—and very caring—letter from Dr. Elias. In it he encouraged me to continue my therapy by contacting someone in my area—and he included the contact information for several qualified therapists. I did not follow his advice then, but what he said was true. Eventually, I realized I was far from finished.

CHAPTER 43

Captain and Mrs. Riley

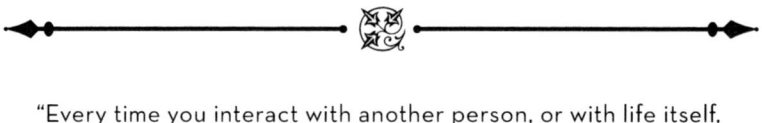

"Every time you interact with another person, or with life itself, you either create love or destroy love ..."

Miracles Are Guaranteed by Bill Ferguson

Captain and Mrs. Riley were okay. There was not much there to admire, but there was nothing to fear either. I had never seen or heard of them before their assignment to Phoenix. Captain Riley, as I saw him, was a loud buffoon—so full of himself he rarely listened to anyone's voice but his own. He told me he had an agenda which would put him on the fast track to higher office in the Salvation Army, and he admitted that was the focus of every action he took. He was concerned that I be able to keep up with his agenda, and I believe I did that. He rushed around the office, disrupted projects often, and darted from task to task with regularity. I found nothing likeable about him, and I found that my opinion was shared by others in the office.

Mrs. Riley was first and foremost a mother. With four children under twelve, that's where she wanted to spend her time. She was nice enough to me, but there was never any relationship beyond surface niceties. I was a guest in their home a time or two—once when I was very ill with the flu and Captain Riley insisted that I stay at their home until the worst of the illness was over. This was a kind gesture on both their parts, but his bossy insistence that I relocate when all I wanted was to be left alone was grating. In this example, as in every other, he brooked no dissent. Eventually, I did what he said.

On a few occasions, I babysat for them. I experienced their three older children as much like their father—bossy and belligerent with an air of entitlement. Doug, their youngest attached himself to me with tenacity, and his obvious need for closeness resonated deeply. Doug and I spent many hours together—him just sitting beside me or nestled on my lap. He was nothing like anyone else in his family, and I willingly became his touchstone of quiet and security in the midst of the activity generated by people with whom he had little in common.

One incident in my work with Captain Riley stands out as indicative of who and what he was.

The corps officers in Flagstaff, Arizona, Captain and Mrs. Jack Prescott, were a fun and engaging young couple. Because Linc was so into flying, Jack became intrigued, took flying lessons, and obtained his license to operate propeller-driven, small aircraft. I rode with him once during the summer I spent at Camp O'Wood in the mountains outside Tucson, near Oracle Junction. Jack had flown up to camp and was thrilled with his newfound skill. When he offered to give a couple of the other officers a ride in the plane, he asked me to go along. I thought nothing of it because I had flown in and out of that same landing strip with Linc on numerous occasions. But Jack was not Linc. I felt uncomfortable throughout that short flight because I sensed that Jack had none of the assurance Linc naturally brought into the cockpit with him. When we were safely back on land, I knew I would never want to fly with him again.

Early one Saturday in late fall, Jack took off from Flagstaff with Phoenix being his destination. Flying with him—as a special treat arranged by their mother—were two teenage sisters from the Flagstaff Corps. I knew the girls from my season as camp secretary during that preceding summer. They were both full of youthful exuberance and always ready for an adventure. Jack had not had his license for long, and flying across the mountains in Arizona can be unpredictable. When the plane did not show up at the appointed time, an alert went out, and within hours a search was organized. I watched the news at a friend's house that afternoon. Recreating Jack's flight plan, the searchers spotted the wreckage from the air in a rugged canyon in the mountains between Flagstaff and Phoenix. When rescuers arrived on the scene, there was very little that could be identified other than the fuselage—everything else has been demolished on impact. Jack's body was recovered, and eventually, what could be located of the remains of the sisters was placed in a single coffin.

Captain Riley was asked to speak at the girls' funeral in his official capacity as the division officer overseeing all youth work. I did not go to the funeral—I worked that day to cover for Captain Riley's absence. When he came back to the office after the funeral, he described the part he played.

"When I stood up, I didn't use the mic and I didn't need notes. I recited the girls' histories in the Salvation Army. I talked about all the contributions they had made at Camp O'Wood during the summer. Then I told everyone that the girls had been 'Promoted to Glory' and so the tables had been turned, and they were now my superior officers." All this was said in a gleeful, self-aggrandizing way. He was relishing every moment of the retelling. And then he finished, "When I wrapped up my speech, I walked over to the casket, stood at full military attention, and gave my best Salvation Army salute. You should have seen me. You'd better believe there wasn't a dry eye in the house!" He said this with delight, and then beaming broadly, he walked into his office. It was *all* about him He did not even bother to pretend. He paraded his shallowness for everyone to see.

That summer at Camp O'Wood was a mixed bag for me. I felt like the odd man out. I was ill at ease in my relationship with the

Rileys, and because they did not put me forward in any way, others were prone to overlook me also. I did my job and was rarely asked to participate in any other way. I never took part in the campfire events that had been my forte at Redwood Glen Camp. I stayed in the background and waited. For what, I did not know.

Doug—the youngest Riley—sought me out continually. He was younger than the other kids at camp, and rather than be in a group he wasn't suited for, he chose to hang out in the office with me. His mother did not mind, and he was never a bother. There were huge thunderstorms with sheet lightning in those mountains—typically at night. Doug would leave his parents' cabin and find me—in the office if I was working late—or in my cabin. For whatever reason, he felt safe with me.

During the few days between camp sessions, Captain Riley and I went back to the office in Phoenix to take care of other business. And I continued to see Dr. Elias. I never missed an appointment. In the midst of all the activity at camp and back in Phoenix, my meetings with him were the one thing that consistently grounded me in working my way out of the enigma my life had become. I was trying to maintain a bond with the Salvation Army so that I could one day go back to training—while the Army was using me and endeavoring to keep absolute control over where I went and what I said so that they did not have to deal with the inconvenient truth I represented. It took a while for me to see clearly just how self-serving this arrangement was for the Salvation Army.

There were two events that helped me gain that insight. The first one involved Jan Black.

CHAPTER 44

Another Victim

Predator: one who lives by plundering and robbing
Victim: someone plundered, killed, destroyed, or sacrificed
Friend: an ally, supporter, or sympathizer

Webster's New World Dictionary

During the spring break from training school, Jan Black was back in Arizona. I believe she had been assigned to the corps in Tucson. One day at the office, Captain Riley brought up Jan's name and asked me if I had known her while I was in training. I, of course, said I had. With a bemused look on his face, he went on to say that he had been called in to consult with other Salvation Army personnel on an incident that Jan reported.

Captain Riley said that Jan claimed she had been raped by a stranger who attacked her one day when she was driving on a desert road outside Tucson. According to Captain Riley, her story was garbled and inconsistent. He said she did not appear particularly upset, but was not able to give any clear information about her assailant—how he gained access to her inside her car, exactly what he had done to her, what he looked like. And she refused to submit to a physical examination. He said that at one point she just sat mute for a prolonged period of time. She then stated that her assailant had bitten her on both thighs and on her buttocks. Still, she was not willing to be examined—even by a female.

Captain Riley said he believed she had made the whole thing up. I sat and listened but said little. I had not seen Jan during that break, and I hadn't had any contact with her since the previous Christmas break when she was in Phoenix—spending most of her time with the Uptons. Since I had little respect for Captain Riley, I was not sure I was receiving accurate information. How much should I believe? Frankly, I knew he was not above presenting negative information about others in any context simply in an effort to make himself look more important.

I was troubled by his story. I was uneasy, because in spite of my wish not to know, the story resonated at some level where secrets are hidden and memories are locked away. There was something about the allusion to unbidden sexual activity that reminded me of those moments when Jan and I connected at training school. Moments when we recognized ourselves in each other and immediately retreated from things that could not be spoken. I knew, without knowing why, that Jan was in trouble.

In July, Jan came to visit me at camp. She had gained a lot of weight. Not all over. Just in her abdomen. It was the middle of a scorching hot summer day, and I was sweaty and miserable. My small cabin was like an oven, and I had returned just long enough to replace my sweaty clothes with fresh ones. I heard a knock, opened the door, and there was Jan.

On this glaringly hot day, she was dressed in her dark blue Salvation Army dress uniform complete with bonnet and gloves. Her A-line uniform skirt was voluminous and her tunic was loosely draped over a bulging stomach. I tried not to see what I knew I was seeing. I denied the possibility. I was hurt for Jan and for myself. I was seeing in the flesh what I had experienced in training—farther along, but the same experience. I made no comment. I was stricken for Jan, but I immediately knew I did not want to be any part of another problem like this. I am not proud of how I reacted to Jan. For a lifetime I have wished that I had been a better friend to this friend with whom I had everything in common. On that hot day in July, at Camp O'Wood, I was not a friend to her.

The minute the door was closed, Jan burst into tears and said, "Bunny, I have to tell you what Linc did to me."

I watched her cry. I did not touch her. I did not speak kindly. I did not reach out in any way. I said only, "Jan, don't tell me. Don't tell anyone. I know what happens to people who tell." That's exactly what I said. No comforting words. I had no time to prepare for this moment. And the first and only thing that came out of my mouth, ironically, were the words used on me by John Hart and then by the Salvation Army leadership. "Don't tell." I think I wanted to save Jan from my own fate. I think I wanted there to be some other way for her. What was I thinking? She had come to me in desperation, needing to tell someone—just as I had needed to tell those months before. I failed her. I knew that. And yet I meant what I said too. To me, telling had only made it worse. I had not figured out that Jan *had* to tell. There was no choice. I could have been the one who listened.

Jan regained her composure, and without a word, she turned and went back out the door. I never saw her again.

The story of the rape in the desert several months earlier made some sense now. I believe it was an effort to come up with an explanation for the pregnancy she—by that time—knew existed. She could not submit to an exam because it would only prove that she was pregnant—and would not show any evidence of a recent sexual assault. That had happened in December when Jan was on Christmas break, spending all her time with the Uptons. Linc in particular.

The next time I was back in Phoenix, Rita—one of the women in the office with whom Jan had been particularly close—called me aside and asked me if I had seen Jan. I was noncommittal. She went on to tell me that Jan had come to visit her a week before. And then Rita said, "Bunny, she's six months pregnant. Believe me, I should know. I have three kids. Jan is pregnant." She talked a little more and then she said, "I asked her if she wanted to tell me anything and she said no, she was fine. What in the world got into her? She was always a nice girl. Now what's she going to do?" Again, I was heartsick. Jan had chosen to come to me. She would have talked to me if I had allowed it. But I was also relieved. I was still suffering from the shock of my own encounter with sexual predation by both John and Linc and of being cast out. I had not yet begun to consider the profound injustice of the Salvation Army's treatment of me and the depth of the wounds I would carry for a lifetime. I did not yet have it in me to reach out and take in more hurt, anguish, or destruction. I had no capacity for it.

And, belatedly, I realized just how much of a predator Linc was. This was not my first reaction. But a week after I saw Jan, after Rita had talked to me, it began to sink in. Not just me. Jan. Not just John. Linc. How many were there of them? How many others were there of us? It began to sink in when I allowed it to. This was a disease, a cancer. If there were two of us in such close proximity, just how far and wide did it go?

CHAPTER 45

The Lieutenant Commissioner Comes Calling

"Judge not that ye be not judged. For with what judgment ye judge, ye shall be judged."

Spoken by Jesus in the Gospel of Matthew 7:1-2 ASV

THE SECOND INCIDENT THAT OPENED MY EYES TO HOW SELF-SERVING the Army's actions toward me had been involved the territorial lieutenant commissioner—the second in command in the seven western states, Alaska, and Hawaii. Colonel Parkins (I am not sure of the spelling of his name—please see note at the end of this chapter.) came to see me in Phoenix shortly after the camping season was over. Captain and Mrs. Riley and I were newly back in Phoenix. I remember Colonel Parkins' arrival. It was an unusual occasion. People usually went to see them—the upper echelon—when necessary. They did not usually come this far out of their own bailiwick. It did not occur to me that this unusual occasion was on my account.

I knew well who Colonel Parkins was. He had been the emcee who called me back up to take my bows when I spoke at the welcome banquet. He had gone out of his way to make contact with me at gatherings after that. He made determined eye contact when I was participating in any program on stage. I remember one time when I was singing with the training school chorus. Colonel Parkins was seated with the other dignitaries in the front row. He repeatedly made direct eye contact, smiled at me broadly, and nodded his head at me. His interest in me was obvious. I was flattered.

But when I was called into the divisional commander's office for a private conversation with Colonel Parkins, there was no broad smile and certainly no nod of approval.

Colonel Parkins was seated behind the desk. He asked me to sit down in the chair across the desk from him. I sat with my heart pounding; I had no idea what this might be about, and I was extremely nervous. Whatever he had to say to me, I wanted to be ready to answer, but my mouth was dry, and I felt like I could barely breathe. It was just the two of us in the room. I entertained some fanciful idea that he remembered me and was there to encourage me. Could it be that I was going to be allowed to go back to training?

His brow knit with concern, Colonel Parkins went right to his mission. He told me that he had been asked to come to Phoenix and talk to me because a decision had been made regarding my future. He leaned forward with his arms on the desk and looked at me intently.

"Bunny, you will not be coming back to training. Not this year, not next year, not ever. This was the decision of the council that met recently to discuss your case. You see, Bunny, the Salvation Army is for good people. That term no longer applies to you."

With that, he sat back in his chair, relaxed, and looked at me with a collegial expression on his face. "I'm sure you can understand and appreciate our position, Bunny. After all, what would the public think if people like you were allowed to represent the Army? We have to consider the expectations of the public we serve." And then he smiled at me.

I had not cried during all of the horrible tribunal at training school. I had sucked in all of the heartache. I had remained dry-eyed. I hid in their building. I kept my midnight rendezvous. I flew on the plane they arranged. I went away. I did my job in Phoenix. I told no one. I did everything they asked with minute care. And I sucked it in and never cried.

Now I cried. With great heaving sobs, I cried. I begged. "Please, Colonel Parkins, they said if I did everything they told me to do, I could go back to training. They promised! I've done everything. Honest I have. I've done it all." I choked all this out between sobs. I twisted in my chair in absolute terror. This could not be happening. Now what would I do? Where could I go? How would I explain this to my mother? I had told her that the assignment in Phoenix was temporary because that's what I was told. That's what I believed.

Colonel Parkins was looking at me calmly. "I know this is a lot for you to take in. That's why I was asked to come personally to tell you. I know it's hard now, but I'm sure you will come to realize that we really had no choice."

I stood up and made my way blindly out of the office.

Author's Note: As earlier stated, I have used actual names throughout this narrative—with one exception previously noted. In the case of Colonel Parkins, I am not sure of exactly how his name was spelled but am confident that this is a close approximation.

CHAPTER 46

Considering Change

"It is also clear that the further one travels on the journey of life, the more births one will experience, and therefore, the more deaths—the more joy and the more pain."

The Road Less Traveled by M. Scott Peck, M.D.

My life in Phoenix changed dramatically after Colonel Parkins' assessment of my moral state—unfit to serve. I now knew there was no future of any kind for me in the Salvation Army. I had no friends in Phoenix. I lived in a dumpy little apartment.

I began to eat gluttonously. I stopped at a small market on the way home from work every day and bought a cake or a pie and other junk food—candy, chips, soda. I went home and ate all of it. Whole cakes. Whole pies. I ate until it was impossible to eat more.

I had never slept well. Now I didn't sleep at all. I know the common perception is that when someone says they aren't sleeping, they just mean they aren't sleeping a lot. I was wide awake all night long. I exercised to make myself tired. I visited the library and checked out books to read so I would get sleepy. Many nights, I didn't sleep at all. My nights were full of dread and anxiety. I was fearful in a new, searing way.

I became suspicious of all the other women at work. How much did they know about me? What were they saying behind my back? In spite of the fact that I was not sleeping, I was never tired during the day. I worked hard. I found new ways to expand my job. I stayed in frenzied activity all day. I was sure people were spying on me, so I was determined to give them nothing to report on.

From the day Colonel Parkins talked to me, I never went near the Phoenix Citadel Corps or any other Salvation Army church building again. I did not worship there. I stayed as far away as I could. No one ever visited, called, or asked why. The only contact I now had with the Salvation Army was my 9:00 to 5:00 job. I hated it, but it never occurred to me to look for another job. I believe I was too depleted to think about another change. And I felt I had something to prove. I would do my job. I would be good at it. They could not define who I was within my job. I was good at it, and I became even better.

I began to think I might find God somewhere else. Maybe then I could sleep. Maybe then I could stop eating. I began to attend a Nazarene Church near my apartment. It was dark and foreboding inside, and the rituals of worship were different from anything I had previously experienced. I had never taken communion. I did not understand the process. People went forward to receive communion at the altar. I tried to watch what others were doing, but I did not get it right. The priest looked at me quizzically and then passed by me.

The Nazarene Church was huge and cavernous, but there were few worshipers, and no one ever spoke to me after service. Again, I was alone. I felt abandoned, even in the company of others, even in the house of God.

Ellen, one of the women who worked in the accounting department, began to ask me to join her to go swimming or to a movie. She was probably 45 years old. One of the other women warned me that I should not accept her invitations. In very cloaked language, she told me that Ellen was odd, and it would not be good for me to encourage her. As was my usual inclination, I did not want to hurt anyone's feelings, so I went swimming with Ellen one time. I was extremely uncomfortable. Ellen *was* odd. She hovered over me and had no respect for personal space. She may have been good intentioned, but I was relieved when the evening was over and I could go home. I never went anywhere with her again. Just another thing to be uneasy about.

I continued to see Dr. Elias. That was the one positive connection I had, and I now depended on that relationship for the support I found nowhere else. Dr. Elias was a plump man in his sixties. He was kind without being cloying. He was never too friendly or intrusive. He remained placid, unflappable, and gentle. In spite of all this, therapy was not easy for me. I was still afraid to tell him too much. And whereas Dr. Elias knew the basics about my relationships with John and Linc, I did not mention them by name—referring to them merely as "my ministers" or in other general terms. And I never mentioned the name of the Salvation Army. Even in the confidential therapist-patient relationship, and in spite of all that had happened to distance me from the organization, I still felt compelled to keep the Salvation Army's command to "tell no one." Nor did I tell him anything about my relationship with my mother. I saw my therapy with Dr. Elias as being totally about my inability to protect myself from sexual intrusion from men old enough to be my father. I was not ready to look deeper into the dynamics within my family of origin. And I definitely was not ready to break the code of silence imposed on me by the Salvation Army. All of that would come much later.

Dr. Elias and I talked about my eating and about my not sleeping. When I told him that I exercised for hours after work so I would get tired and want to sleep, he told me that I should try to unwind, that exercising close to bedtime might be counterproductive. When we talked about food, he suggested that all the sugar was a substitute for love and connection. Could I possibly conceive of leaving the unsatisfactory job?

I longed for my appointments with Dr. Elias each week, but I was inexperienced in merited trust and intimacy of any kind. In spite of the care he took, I was afraid that the relationship with him depended on some kind of "correct" behavior on my part. I disclosed little new information. Dr. Elias remained patient and consistently present. In his every action and word, he kept his promise to always act in my best interest. I believe his constancy and his ability to stay present without pushing made it possible for me to stay involved with him. I believe that saved my life. Each time I reaffirmed my part of the contract at the end of our sessions, I felt I had a reason to live until the next appointment.

Dr. Elias asked me about dreams. He routinely asked if I had any dreams to report. Since I was not sleeping, I was not dreaming either. Finally, one day I had a dream to tell him about, and it felt like a great victory. I had actually slept. It seemed too wonderful to be true. That dream seemed to be a turning point of some kind. It did open me up to the idea that I could consider a change. Maybe I could go home. That was what I longed for now. I just wanted the familiar. No matter how brutal home was at times, it was still home, and I needed a home, any home. I detested everything about the life I was leading in Phoenix. Except for Dr. Elias, there was absolutely nothing and no one there for me. I hated the office; I hated the little market where I bought my trashy food; I hated my dingy little apartment. I hated the strange women I worked with. I was still doing a good job for Captain Riley, but since the conversation with Colonel Parkins, I had even less respect for everything Captain Riley stood for—the pomposity, the self-congratulatory verbiage that came out of his mouth, the chuckle at someone else's expense. It all disgusted me now. I had no reason to care, now that I knew I would not be allowed to go back to training. Ever.

I began to contemplate change.

CHAPTER 47

The Last Time I Saw Linc

"For if, after they have escaped the defilements of the world through the knowledge of the Lord and Saviour Jesus Christ, they are again entangled therein and overcome, the last state is become worse with them than the first."

II Peter 2:20 ASV

On a rather overcast and gloomy Saturday afternoon in September or October, I was restlessly roaming around in my small apartment. I had not yet made up my mind to return to Salinas, but I knew that I had to do something to change the status quo—long days and longer nights with constant, nagging anxiety. Because I was seeing Dr. Elias regularly, I no longer routinely entertained the idea of suicide. But facing the fact that I had to make a change meant I also had to face the fact that returning to Salinas held problems of its own.

For some reason, I pulled back the curtain on the front door of my apartment and glanced outside. In the grassy area that faced the street, there was a man who seemed confused and lost. He looked agitated—quickly walking from door to door and then back into the grassy area in the middle of the complex. I saw his back first and was instantly aware that it was Linc. Speechless, I made no move. When he turned around and I saw his face, I saw clearly that this was, indeed, Linc.

I had moved twice since his transfer. He had somehow obtained my address, but apparently, did not have the apartment number. I watched him for a moment or two. He continued to roam around aimlessly—seeming not to know what to do next. His face was ashen, his clothes disheveled, and his eyes darted from place to place.

Without a clear plan or any idea as to the wisdom of what I was doing, I opened the door and said, "Linc?" He turned and ran over to me. I did not invite him in, but seeing me, he pushed into the apartment and closed the door behind him. He then pulled the curtain aside and looked back out the window as though he were afraid someone might be following him.

He then leaned against the door and looked down at me in what seemed like a state akin to panic. His eyes were bloodshot and his voice was strained when he spoke. I was extremely uneasy being this close to anyone representing the Salvation Army, and especially being in close proximity to Linc again. By that time, I was finished with everything and everyone associated with the Army. I felt no pull toward Linc. His unusual state merely exacerbated my general unease.

I also felt ill-prepared to have anyone see me—I was carelessly dressed in old baggy jeans and an oversized blouse. I had gained 20 pounds in the past few months, and I knew I did not look presentable. I did not want him there.

Without so much as a hello, Linc took hold of my two hands, and trying to look me in the eyes, he said, "Someone is talking about me. Is it you?" I instantly knew what Linc meant. So, the tables had somehow turned, and he was the one in trouble? He certainly looked like a person on the run from something.

I did not look him in the eye. Keeping my eyes downcast, I

quietly said, "I haven't said a word to anyone, Linc. I know what happens to people who talk."

I used the same words with him that I had used with Jan a few months earlier. "I know what happens to people who talk."

Dropping my hands, he turned, opened the door, and left. I watched him go down the sidewalk and out onto the street. He never looked back.

That was the last time I ever saw Lincoln Upton.

CHAPTER 48

Going Back to Salinas

"If children feel unloved and abandoned, they will do anything to win back the love of their parents, accepting them on any terms, no matter how much abuse they have suffered."

Sex in in Forbidden Zone by Peter Rutter, M.D.

I USE THE ABOVE QUOTE TO BEGIN THE CHAPTER ON RETURNING TO Salinas because I needed to go home—I needed to leave everything in Phoenix behind me. Phoenix had been the culmination of the abuse visited on me by the Salvation Army. One Salvation Army officer had violently sexualized the sacred relationship of pastor-congregant, another Salvation Army officer had preyed on my weakened condition to sexualize the relationship of clergy-congregant and employer-employee, and then the Salvation Army as a church had informed me that I was not "good" enough to serve God in any capacity. I was decimated when I arrived in Phoenix. As I looked forward to leaving Phoenix, my only hope was leaving behind the organization that had victimized and ostracized me. My goal now became getting away from the Salvation Army.

But as I moved in the direction of returning to Salinas, I knew I had no ally in my mother. For the rest of my life, I would continue unconsciously trying to win her approval, but on a conscious level, I knew I could expect nothing from her except what she had always been willing to give me—her caustic judgment and disapproval of everything I was. I cautiously brought this up with Dr. Elias when I began talking to him about my possible return to Salinas. But I was never able to tell him in any depth about my fear of my mother and her outright viciousness toward me. I think I needed to hide this even from myself as much as possible. In order to get away from the Salvation Army, I needed somewhere to go. For the time being, I felt that had to be back to Salinas. That was the only thing I knew to do. Except for Dr. Elias, I had no one to talk to, no one to advise me, no one to offer any alternative.

When I called my mother and asked her if she would come and get me, she agreed to do so. She did not ask questions or belabor the issue. I was thankful for that. I told her nothing about further developments in the Salvation Army. She never knew about Linc. I did not tell her about Colonel Parkins' pronouncement. I just told her I wanted to come home. I told her that I was through trying to reengage with the Army. I wanted to come home and get a job—perhaps go back to work for Andy at Abramson and Bolz. I told her I wanted to leave Phoenix.

When my mother came to get me, she brought her friend Audrey with her. I was thrilled that we would not be making the two-day trip alone together. Audrey's daughter and I had gone to school together, and Audrey had always been kind to me. I knew having her with us meant my mother would not be her outright caustic and attacking self. She could still be pompous and derogatory, but she would not use the worst weapons in her arsenal in front of others. She never had. Her worst weapons—whether physical or verbal—were used behind closed doors.

The trip was uneventful. When she first arrived in Phoenix, my mother commented on the weight I had gained but said little else about my life in Phoenix and asked no questions. I sat in the backseat of the car. Mother and Audrey chatted in the front. I was largely ignored, and for that small mercy, I was grateful.

I was apprehensive about returning to the scene of so much upheaval and unhappiness. I knew John and his family still lived in Salinas. I knew I never wanted to see anyone from the Salvation Army again. I was uneasy about what unexpected encounters might still await me. Still, I was so bountifully thankful to be leaving everything that Phoenix stood for that I was willing to risk whatever might lie ahead.

PART III

HEALING

CHAPTER 49

Salinas Again

"They then that received his word were baptized ..."

Acts 2:41 ASV

B**ACK IN SALINAS, MY BROTHERS ASKED NO QUESTIONS OF ME. AS FAR** as I know, neither of them ever knew about my relationship with John. I know they did not know about Linc. I never mentioned Linc's name until 40 years later ... when I was in therapy with the doctor who worked patiently with me through all of my Salvation Army trauma. Even when I told him about Linc, I made excuses for Linc—I held on to the idea that Linc had been kind to me, he had never been violent, he had actually helped me. It took a long time for me to realize that was exactly the attitude I had held onto about my father. Neither of them was kind, neither helped me, each was—in his own way—violent.

I had no problem finding a job in Salinas. I talked to Andy first, but there was no immediate opening at the law office. I went to work for Kingston and Company, a private loan agency and insurance brokerage. I became the girl Friday for the insurance agency. I completely reorganized the agency, instituted a new filing system, and won awards for my boss from Safeco Insurance Company. Here was a place where I could succeed. My efforts were appreciated and I began to grow in the confidence that I had made the right decision to start over. Perhaps, I thought, I could put everything behind me and make an honorable life for myself after all.

I lived in my mother's home, but managed to be absent a good deal of the time. I worked, I dated a little, and I became friends with Pete's wife—and fell head over heels in love with Pete and Diane's baby, my nephew, Jimmy. He became the light of my life.

I had been in Salinas for a few months when a friend of Buzz's asked me to go out with him. I had been aware of Doug Stevens—but only as one of Buzz's many friends. The fact that Buzz knew Doug and Doug was a member of the group that had grown up building cars and drag racing together made Doug seem safe.

We had been dating for only a few weeks when Doug asked me if I would attend church with him. This seemed to be perfect timing. I wanted to find a new spiritual home, and so his invitation even seemed providential. The Church of Christ was in a quaint old building on California Street in Salinas. Since this church uses no instrumental music, I was immediately entranced by the enthusiasm with which they sang the hymns—naturally carrying on beautiful four-part harmonies. The small building was packed on Sunday mornings, and the acoustics—so many people in such a small space—seemed to amplify and highlight the sacred words. I felt immersed in their joy.

When Doug and I became engaged, the Church of Christ minister, Brother Bussard, asked me if I would like to study the Bible with him and learn more about the history of the Church. I was happy to be asked. Having studied with him for several weeks, I asked if I could be baptized. Brother Bussard called his wife to come and assist, and I was baptized by immersion that night. I felt that God was in this new experience. It was very rule oriented—as long as I did the exact things prescribed, I was a part of the Body of Christ that was the Church. I needed this structure in order to completely separate from what I had learned in the Salvation Army, which was much more haphazard and subjective. In the Salvation Army I had experienced, rules changed as capriciously as the motives of the speakers changed. There was no safety. Abandonment happened at the whim of an organization whose self-image was their greatest currency.

When I became engaged to Doug, I told him about John. I did not know enough about physical intimacy to know if Doug would be able to tell I was not a virgin. If he could tell, would he be disappointed, feel betrayed? I was not going to take any chances on this relationship. The relationship with Doug—especially when combined with my newfound faith through the Church of Christ—seemed to validate me as a human being. I was going to be married to someone in good standing in the community—Doug was 25 years old and owned and operated a Chevron gas station. I was going to worship God at a church where the rules were laid out for all to understand. I was working for a well-liked, community-minded company that paid me well. I began to feel like an honest woman—someone who could leave the past behind. But I also believed Doug deserved to know something about that past.

I needed Doug to know about the relationship with John Hart for two reasons:

1. I was not a virgin. Back then, in the 1960s, this mattered. I believed that Doug deserved to know this, and I wanted him to know how it had happened.
2. I was still afraid of John. He had threatened to harm me if I ever told about him, and now that I again lived in close proximity to him, I believed this was possible. I had seen John when he was irrational, and I thought he was capable of violence. Would he seek me out? I had no way of knowing, but I thought Doug deserved to know about this possibility.

Doug took my disclosure in stride. I don't remember him being upset one way or the other. As in many other matters, Doug was fairly stoic. He accepted things as they were and made the most of whatever came his way. It definitely did not change his mind about wanting to marry me. And he said he was certainly not afraid of some old geezer who picked on girls half his size.

Doug and I were married at the Church of Christ on California Street in Salinas on October 24, 1965.

CHAPTER 49

The Past Comes Calling

"... Dependency may appear to be love because it is a force that causes people to fiercely attach themselves to one another. ... It works to trap and constrict rather than to liberate. Ultimately it destroys rather than builds relationships, and it destroys rather than builds people."

The Road Less Traveled by M. Scott Peck, M.D.

WITH SO MUCH TO BE THANKFUL FOR IN MY NEW LIFE, AND SINCE I was doing so many things right, I imagined—and actually fantasized—that my mother would finally approve of me. Perhaps since so many other things were "normal" in my life, my mother and I could have a normal relationship too. That was not to happen. If anything, she became more determined than ever to control and dominate me. It was as though she had to prove that her beliefs about me had been right—to believe otherwise would have toppled the foundation of her existence.

When I first showed her my engagement ring and told her that Doug had asked me to marry him, her response was, "Oh, no."

After I was married, working full-time, keeping my own house—cooking, shopping, laundry—she still demanded that I return to her house several times a week to do her ironing. She felt I owed her that. I did not know how to say no. I did what she demanded. Her harassing and belittlement did not diminish one iota. I was acting as a responsible adult—managing life on my own—and still answering to her. She was vindictive and punishing in everything she said and did toward me.

Soon after I was married, I invited my mother to go to lunch with me. I held a responsible position which required me to dress professionally. I wanted my mother to see me in this role and be proud of me. I took her to a fine restaurant—linens, beautiful flatware, unique menu. I felt like an adult who could give her mother a gift—a delicious meal in a beautiful setting. After we had placed our orders, my mother—looking at me with undisguised hatred—said, "Do you know how hard it is to sit here with you? To know that under all this pretense there is a person who did not have the sense to keep her legs together? To realize that the person you are sitting with ruined a messenger of the Lord?" Reality check. I felt like I had been punched in the stomach. No matter how hard I tried, my mother would always remind me of who and what I was—after all, I might fool others, but she was the one who knew me, really knew me.

On another occasion, I gave a large party at my house, to which, of course, my mother was invited. She was at my house a few days later when I received a note from a dear older woman who had been in attendance. The note read in part, "Thank you for inviting me to your lovely party. The day was special from start to finish. It was filled with the laughter and joy of people who truly enjoy each other. I never heard a negative word, and I never heard a child cry."

When I showed the note to my mother, she said, "They lie to you."

Of all these occasions when my mother bit at me and gnashed her teeth on me and verbally flailed me, the worst moment of all concerned the death of John Hart.

I had been married three years. Except for the times when my mother brought up the subject, I tried to eliminate all thoughts of John Hart and the Salvation Army from my consciousness.

I was at home alone one Saturday morning when the phone rang. I remember answering the phone in my bedroom. The room was fresh and clean and full of light. I took pride in my ability to keep a house. Though not fancy, it radiated life and fullness. My mother's houses had always been dark and dank and soulless. My house was different. I was different. I answered the phone while sitting on my bed in this fresh, clean room full of life and fullness.

My mother had just gotten off work. She said, "I want you to know what you did to me last night. John Hart was brought into the emergency room dead on arrival. Dead, Bunny, dead! Do you hear me? Dead. And the woman who was with him at the time was hysterical. She wasn't hurt when the car he was driving went out of control and hit a tree. She was sobbing hysterically, and she yelled to everyone within earshot, 'He's dead because some girl lied about him and ruined his life. She lied about him. I loved him and he was going to marry me. Now he's dead and it's all because of her. He never got over what she did to him.' Do you know how that felt, Bunny, to be there with this poor woman and know that the person she's talking about, this ruiner, was my own daughter? Do you know what it's like to never be able to escape the damage you've caused?"

As I sat there on my bed listening to my mother, I was empty. There was no feeling. There was only emptiness. Of all the things I had imagined about John in the past five years, I had not imagined this scenario. He had lived the rest of his life blaming me. Blaming me. He died blaming me. Had he so totally deluded himself that he actually believed I lied? I still don't know what he believed. The one thing that was apparent was that he never realized what he did to me was wrong. He never took responsibility for his own actions—even to himself. He raped me, told me God wanted him to do it, threatened me, impregnated me, left me isolated in the aftermath of his sin and lasciviousness, and he blamed me.

And in his delusion, he had reaffirmed everything my mother believed about me. Even in his death, he laid the blame for the mess his life had become at my feet. And she not only believed what he said, she took it as a personal reproach on her, as a burden she must carry—just being related to me was her cross to bear. Again, John Hart—even in death—and the Salvation Army had given my mother the gift of vindication. She had been right all along—I was to blame. For everything. For all her losses and disappointments. For all of the debauchery and depravity that John had chosen for himself and visited on me. I was to blame for it all.

CHAPTER 51

Voices From Out of the Past

"All the forbidden sexual liaisons took place in an atmosphere of enforced silence, which was observed not only by the men and women who became involved but also by witnesses who did nothing to stop it."

Sex in the Forbidden Zone by Peter Rutter, M.D.

Sometime in the mid-1970s I received a phone call. When I answered the phone, the caller reminded me he and his wife had been session mates of mine when I was at training school. After a moment, I was able to place them. He told me that they were now the corps officers in Salinas. I was extremely awkward during this part of the conversation. I was not sure why he might be calling, and I felt ill at ease because I had been told not to be in touch with anyone in the Salinas Corps. Now, here was an officer of that corps calling me. I wanted no part of it. That had to be kept in my past. By this time, I had two young children and had made a new life for myself within my family, my community, and my church. When I heard this voice from my past, my first thought was that everything I had worked for and accomplished could come crashing down around me. Any contact from the Salvation Army took me back to that feeling of shame and fear. What could they do to me now?

After a brief interval of small talk, though, the caller said, "Bunny, we know what happened to you, and we feel like it was very wrong." I still had nothing to say to him. How much did he know? Was he really on my side? And how did he know what happened? I had been told no one would know. I did not want to talk to him. My reaction to his bringing up "what happened" was embarrassment and confusion.

The caller then told me something else—something he said I had a "right to know." He said that Colonel Parkins—the man who came to Phoenix to tell me the Salvation Army was for good people—had been found to be a womanizer and a philanderer of the worst kind. He said, "He had women everywhere—inside and outside the Salvation Army. Women he seduced and women he paid for sex. The man was rotten to the core, Bunny." For a moment I had no reaction. And then all I felt was sad. I did not even feel angry at the hypocrisy, the lies, the holier-than-thou attitude. I just felt sad. This brought home the realization that sexual predation was rampant within this organization—my corps officer, the Divisional Youth Secretary I worked under, and the lieutenant commissioner of the Western Territory, who had judged me as not worthy of the term "good."

If he told me how Colonel Parkins' double life had come to light, I don't remember it. He did remind me that Colonel Parkins' wife had been an invalid for years, and he apparently used this as an excuse for his behavior—"It's not my fault because I had to find sexual satisfaction some place." The caller sounded deeply upset by this perfidy at high levels in the organization he was serving. He sounded troubled. Maybe his phone call to me was a way of defusing the shame he felt on behalf of all of those who had been misled by yet another Salvation Army officer.

I don't remember how the conversation with him ended. I just remember that I wanted no further contact from or connection to this organization. I knew the caller and his wife to be good people, and it was kind of him to think of me—to call me and let me know they thought I had been wronged. But the information about Colonel Parkins just made me sad and sick. I knew enough to not want to know more.

Around that same time, Jan Black called me a few times. Again, the conversations were stilted and uncomfortable. I don't remember how she found me, but apparently, someone was keeping track—the first caller and then Jan calling me after I was married and had taken my husband's last name. The shame imposed on me by the Salvation Army was the dominant emotion I felt when talking to Jan. I could not go back to that part of my life without feeling all the dark emotions attendant to my isolation and excoriation. I'm not sure Jan and I could have been friends. There was too much we both lost, too much we both regretted, too much hurt we both carried with us.

Jan may have been trying to be a friend when she called me. She may have been capable of that. I was not. I could not be her friend. I still hated everything she innocently reminded me of—the person I was when I was cast out, the secrets I was keeping, the pain that was always just below the surface. For me, there had to be absolute separation from anything and everything attendant to what I saw as my ultimate downfall and disgrace. I could not look at the past. All my worst demons peopled that past.

CHAPTER 52

Two Beautiful Boys

"When we take an extra step or walk an extra mile, we do so in opposition to the inertia of laziness or the resistance of fear. Extension of ourselves or moving out against the inertia of laziness, we call work. Moving out in the face of fear we call courage. Love, then, is a form of work or a form of courage. ... Love is always either work or courage. If an act is not one of work or courage, then it is not an act of love. There are no exceptions."

The Road Less Traveled by M. Scott Peck, M.D.

Doug and I had two sons. Douglas was born in February of 1969. Jason was born in October of 1970. I knew the reason for my existence was to raise my children with love and break the chain of abuse, hatred, and tyranny that my mother had visited on my brothers and me. I never had any doubt that I could do this. I loved my sons immediately and never had to make an effort to treat them with all of the delight and spontaneous joy they engendered in me.

The home I had created was nothing like the home my mother lived in. The life I lived was nothing like the life my mother lived. I never had any doubt that I could be a different kind of mother than she had been. Mother was as hateful and full of bitterness toward me while I was mothering the boys as she had ever been. She told me no one could stand my children. Not true. She berated me for soothing them when they cried—I was spoiling them. She told me repeatedly over the years when I was being the very best parent I could be, "One day they will hate you." Thanks, Mother, for the kind words of wisdom and encouragement.

While I thought I wanted a daughter when my second son was born, I soon found that raising two boys was the job for which I had been born. The house that Doug and I purchased soon after we were married was located on just under an acre of land in Prunedale, a rural community eight miles north of Salinas. We did not own a television until the boys were near middle school age, so they grew up imagining and building and role playing with a pack of eight other little boys who lived nearby. They played army and knights and cowboys in the unimproved pastures behind us and built forts and tree houses in the oak groves.

I had a good friend who had two boys the same ages as Douglas and Jason, and she and I took our boys camping, hiking, and swimming. We visited amusement parks, zoos, nature preserves, the ocean, and the forest. We attended the Church of Christ in Prunedale, and the church provided a large extended family that cared about them and nurtured their spiritual growth. I taught Sunday school and helped organize and teach Vacation Bible School.

Doug and I, with our two sons, were a family in a much different sense than my family of origin.

But—and this is a big "but," difficult even now for me to write about—when the boys were between seven and nine years old, some old ghosts came back to haunt me. Douglas was changing from an engaging little boy to a bigger boy with much more male characteristics. I began to feel an aversion to my own child. I struggled with this, trying to figure out what was going on. I began to avoid physical contact of any kind. What was bothering me was the very natural phase that Douglas was going through—identifying in a pseudo-romantic way with the parent of the opposite sex. Even though intellectually I knew what was happening, I could not tolerate it. All kinds of alarms were going off subconsciously. When I realized I needed some help sorting this out, I made an appointment with the boys' pediatrician.

Dr. McArthur and I had a wonderful, ongoing relationship of mutual trust and admiration. I had been a charter member of the Childbirth Education League in Salinas, and Dr. McArthur was on our advisory board at a time when conscious childbirth and breastfeeding of infants were pretty much nonexistent. Dr. McArthur affirmed the health and happiness of my boys and actually told me that Jason should win the "Breastfed Baby of the Year Award" in his practice. He was, of course, using hyperbole. There was no such award, but that just exemplifies how affirming he was of my skills as a mother. He watched my boys grow and thrive, and he knew I loved my role as their mother.

When I met with Dr. McArthur to go over what was troubling me, I told him, "Douglas loves me too much." Dr. McArthur looked at me in his smiling, grandfatherly way and said, "He's a smart boy. There's a lot there to love." I appreciated Dr. McArthur's kindness, but it did not help with the deeper issues I was feeling. He gave me the name of a counselor who he said might be helpful if I felt like I needed to talk with someone. As soon as I got home, I called Joe Gulla, M.S.W.

I met with Joe once a week for a couple of months. When I next talked to Dr. McArthur, he told me, "I got a follow-up letter from Joe Gulla, and I'll be honest with you, it was almost like reading a love letter. That's how much he thought of you." What Joe and I had talked about was the obvious—my parenting tactics, the boys' social skills, and their school performance. Joe told me he could see nothing amiss. I told him nothing about my history with my mother, sexual abuse by my father, or the rape and abuse by two clergy. I wanted answers—a quick fix. I did not want to talk about things that were dark, troubling, forbidden.

Eventually, I called Joe and made another appointment. I wanted so badly to be a good mother, and something inside was blocking me. As badly as I wanted to make things right on my own, I was unable to do so. I would be more honest this time when I went to Joe for counseling.

During that additional appointment with Joe, the story of John Hart came out. It was like projectile vomiting. It just flowed out of me like a stream of garbage that I could no longer keep a lid on. It had fermented without my being aware, and was now coloring the relationship I had with my sons. That appointment with Joe was the beginning of a downward spiral that saw me in therapy with five different doctors, a patient on two different locked psychiatric units, and a tormented mother who could not touch her own children for fear of harming them in the way she had been harmed. And throughout this spiral, I never mentioned the name of the Salvation Army. I had been commanded to "tell no one," and I was still following—without question—that commandment. I never told anyone the name of the organization. I used general terms—"minister," "church," "clergy." I never broke the commandment to "tell no one."

This lasted approximately three years. I ran miles every day, ate little, slept less, took medication, visited psychiatrists, dissociated, and tried with everything that was in me to be a good enough mother to the boys I loved more than life itself and yet could not bring myself to touch. My touch would bring them harm. The sexualization of relationships of trust—first by my dad and then by John Hart and Lincoln Upton—had so skewed my idea of appropriate touch that I lived with the stark terror of ruining my children. Inside me, there were dissociated parts that agreed with the Salvation Army's assessment that I was not good. Add to all of this my mother's continual, ever-present condemnation of everything I was, and you have a maelstrom that, once loosed, was impossible to contain. I was sure that I could do great harm to my boys just by association. This was the legacy that my father, Captain John Hart, Major Lincoln Upton, and the Salvation Army left with me. My relationship with John Hart was always the "presenting issue" when I began therapy with yet another doctor or was committed to a hospital yet again. I believe this was because John was the person on whom I placed all my hopes of a "good father" in the safe and sacred space of the church to which I clung throughout my difficult childhood. Because he destroyed that safe place by intruding into my very body and soul, his was the most brutal betrayal of all.

Starting with Joe Gulla and progressing through four psychiatrists—Dennis Evans, M.D., Stansel Johnson, M.D., George Milne, M.D., and Michael Libowitz, M.D.—I talked and talked. But I never told any of them about my dissociative fugues. I tried to tell. I told them about hearing voices, about doing things I did not want to do, about being in a place and not knowing how I got there. I wanted someone to know, but on the other hand, I could not bring myself to tell. I was afraid they would lock me up and never let me go home.

One morning, I came out of a prolonged period of dissociation. I woke up and realized I had wasted three precious years of the limited time I had to be a parent to Douglas and Jason. I knew I had to do it on my own. I had found nothing to help me in the psychiatric world. I remembered my vow from years before when I was a small child myself: "When I am big, I will never hurt someone who is small." I knew I had never physically abused my children, but I also knew that I had not been emotionally available to them for some time. I made up my mind that I would put everything else aside—I *had* to—in order to do the job my boys needed me to do—be their mother.

Wherever that kind of strength comes from, I reached down and found what I had to have. I apologized to Douglas over and over. It was he who had been hurt most deeply by my inability to be present for him during those three years. I think we came out of it with a relationship that bore many scars. He changed a lot. I have regretted the time lost with him more than any other ramification of the damage done by John Hart and the Salvation Army. Damage to myself was something I could internalize and deal with. Damage to my son was something I could not undo. It remains the biggest regret of my life.

When I sucked in my own doubts and hurts and reentered

the arena of parenting, the boys were ten and twelve years old. I wanted to make up for everything left undone for those three years. I took up the reins I had dropped as parent volunteer at school, at church, and within the wider community.

The boys grew.

Both Douglas and Jason found excellent teacher mentors during their high school years at North Monterey County High School. I had thought that it might be good for me to back off from my very active role in their school life when they were both in high school. Jason came home one day and asked me, "Mom, why aren't you involved with us at school anymore?"

I answered, "I thought maybe you guys would like me to back off a little now that you are in high school."

Jason looked at me with a puzzled expression on his face and said, "You're the mom everyone wants. Why would we want you to back off?" My sweet Jason.

I became chair of the School Site Council, vice chair of the District Advisory Council, and a member of the Long Range Planning Committee. I did it all—worked full-time in our family business, volunteered at church and at school—and tried to make up for all of the things I regretted in my own past by making the boys' present as good for them as it could possibly be. It was not perfect. I paid a price. I lost precious time with them when I feared that I was not the mother they deserved. But, above all and through all, I loved them and perhaps they knew that.

I treasure some of the mementos the boys gave me in the way of notes and cards.

From Douglas about the time he graduated from high school:

Hi there Mom,
    I am so lucky to have a mother like you. I would like to thank you for all the attention you still manage to devote to me amongst all the junk you are involved in. I spend a lot of time torturing you, but it is just my way of showing that I still care. I ... um ... uh ... I guess I love you. Douglas

From Douglas on the occasion of a recent Mother's Day that I spent with him:

> Thanks for everything you did for me on this visit. Much more than I could of expected!! Most importantly, thank you for being my mother. The most unique person I know and love.
> P.S. This card is good for 10 Mother's Days!
> P.P.S. I will deny all knowledge of ever giving you a card. Douglas

Douglas is witty and kind. He is true and honest. I look at him and know all is not lost. He is good.

A Mother's Day card from Jason when he was in high school:

> You've always been behind me, Mom,
> No matter what I did.

And then in his own handwriting:

> It's true, Mom!
> You deserve the best Mother's Day ever!
> I love you, Mom. Jason

I also want to share a letter Jason wrote me after a recent phone conversation wherein I told him that I had been receiving flowers from someone who signed the card only as "An Admirer." At the time, I explained to Jason that I was surprised and delighted by the first delivery. When a subsequent beautiful bouquet arrived, I felt a little uneasy and was sharing these feelings with Jason.

A week or so later, I received the following from him:

> July 13, 2013
> Re: Why not?
>
> Mom:
> You know what, well there is no reason you shouldn't receive flowers. I have thought a lot about some lovely

person sending you random flowers. 'Random' being a misnomer, because the flowers arrive to a person who has spent much of her life serving others. Sometimes equally anonymously! Right? So I see it as your turn to receive the goodness. We do not always understand where the goodness in our lives comes from (or why), but enjoy it and love it we must do. God asks that of us. How can we refuse that request?

I entirely and will always be in love with my mom and in awe of all Bunny has and continues to do in her life and in the lives of the many people who touch her life. Love you Mom. Jason

I know I could not ask for more. Looking at these mementos—and there are many others—I feel that we have come through a lot together. And if there are things that were lost along the way, I have to let go of that. Regrets? Yes. Joy in what we still have? You bet.

Douglas and Jason are now productive, self-supporting adults who are good and honest and a credit to themselves and to those with whom they share their lives. One of them still lives in Salinas, the other lives in New York City, and I live on the Oregon Coast. In all the ways that matter, we are very close.

There was that rough patch. And there have been other moments when things were not perfect. But Mother was wrong. They do not hate me.

CHAPTER 53

Did You Know You Were My Hero?

"See what you lost when you left this world ..."

Sweet Old World lyrics by Lucinda Williams*

B UZZ DIED BY HIS OWN HAND ON JUNE 4, 1991.
My mantra as an adult had been, "Buzz made it, so I can make it."

All of a sudden, Buzz had not made it. Without him, how could I make it?

My world imploded. Nothing made sense. Buzz had done everything right. He was my hero. He had shown me the way. He had his own business—Midway Engine Rebuilders. Doug and I owned and operated Valley Automotive. We bought engines from him. He referred mechanical work to us. I was proud every time I saw him. My big brother.

---

* Williams, Lucinda, *Sweet Old World*. 1992 by Warner/Chappell Music, Inc. Audio CD.

Here is the eulogy that I wrote for his funeral:

Who was Dave Umbaugh?

Beneath the sometimes gruff exterior was the heart of a man who rescued cats and made room in his life for a homeless mutt named Doobie.

Known by his nephews as "Uncle Fuzz" because of the full beard he always wore, he was adored when they were little, and as they grew up, he was revered for his skill at making cars go fast—a talent any teenage nephew would value. But whether it was tickling them when they were little or building an engine for them when they were not so little anymore, he always had time.

The one and only love of his life was Sheryl. Her quiet and patient personality was the perfect match for his more noisy and less patient outlook on life.

Known affectionately as "June-Bug," his daughter, Debbie, was the light of his life. He was a part of every slumber party, and the pancakes he made for her friends the next morning were legendary.

He was a devoted son. When his mother needed a larger car to take her friends to doctor appointments and grocery shopping, he bought the car and brought it to her.

Dave attacked life with almost ferocious zeal. When he ran, he ran marathons. When he biked, he rode double centuries—covering 200 miles in one day. When he listened to music, it was loud. He loved all kinds of music, traveling wherever necessary to hear good music played well.

And this zeal carried over into his vocation. His reputation as a builder of high-performance engines was second to none. He had a natural talent and a bent for perfection. His craft was more than the way he made his living. He was a perfectionist, and his product went beyond utility to almost an art form.

Who was Dave Umbaugh? He was many people. He

loved deeply. He was the young man who, with his friend Clarence Mendes, built Pontiac race cars that won drag racing titles all over California. He was the father who proudly supported his daughter's efforts at field hockey and came to her sorority initiation at Fresno State. He was the uncle who showed up at soccer games played in the rain. He was the son who quietly left a dozen roses on the front steps for his mother to find when she came home.

So many good things. So much to offer. So much given.

We will miss you, Dave.

After Buzz died, I found out that he suffered all the major symptoms of depression and Post-traumatic Stress Disorder that I had battled all my life. He kept it within the four walls of the beautiful home he provided for his family. He never sought help. In some ways, Buzz may have taken on some of the characteristics of the parent who raised him. As a small child, I saw what mother was and vowed to never be like her. Buzz was the textbook case of violence begetting violence. Eventually, he used that violence against himself. Buzz did not make it.

I struggled along for about a year after Buzz died. I was again working in the insurance industry—running the Personal Lines Department in the large independent agency that had evolved from the two-person office I had worked in 25 years earlier. I loved my work, had a dedicated staff and a loyal clientele. But I was dissociating again, and I was having a very difficult time putting aside my own suicidal ideation, which now took on the added dimension of my actually putting "kits" together with all of the items necessary to mimic Buzz's suicide. I hid all this very well in the office and even at home, but under the outward façade, I was not doing well.

I remembered Doctor Evans from one of my hospitalizations 15 years earlier. When I called him shortly after Buzz's death, it was ostensibly to find help for Buzz's daughter Debbie. Douglas had kept close tabs on Debbie after her father's death and came home late one night to tell me, "Mom, we have to go get Debbie.

She's in bad shape." We got in the car and went to the house Sheryl and Debbie shared. I asked Sheryl if she thought it would be good for Debbie to stay with us for a while. She welcomed the idea. She knew Debbie needed help, but did not know what to do. By this point, Debbie was barely communicating with her.

Debbie lived with us for the better part of a year. She and Douglas had always been close, and it was good for me to have her there with us. Debbie and I bonded over our common grief. We went shopping. We talked for hours. We shared a lot—both of us were artists, both of us were writers, both of us missed Buzz. When her mother began dating, Debbie saw it as a betrayal. Debbie could not replace her father. I could not replace my brother. But husbands were different: There could be another husband. Debbie felt like she had already lost her dad, and now she was losing her mom. During that time, she saw Dr. Evans regularly. Slowly, she improved. A few months into her therapy, I asked her if she thought it would be okay for me to talk to Dr. Evans also. Since she was okay with the idea, I called and made an appointment to see Dr. Evans "to help Debbie."

Thus began a therapy that would last 15 years. I saw Dr. Evans three times a week every week for all of those 15 years. Buzz's death led, eventually, to me finding my life. Not a perfect trade, for sure. I miss him. Now that I have my life so richly and so fully, I miss him. I wish he could have found what I found. A simple life. Filled with joy.

CHAPTER 54

A Beginning

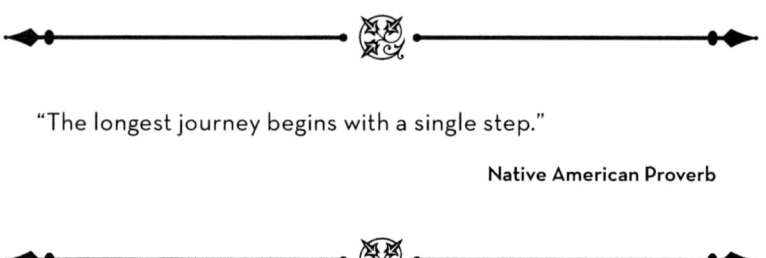

"The longest journey begins with a single step."

Native American Proverb

Dr. Evans' physical appearance had changed dramatically in the 10 years since I last saw him. He had gone from GQ—every hair in place, three-piece suit—to "hippie" casual. He had long, gray hair pulled back in a ponytail, and his fine-boned face looked weathered and no longer boyish. I was glad, actually. When he had been my physician on the psychiatric unit at Community Hospital of the Monterey Peninsula, I was intimidated by his almost-pretty, good looks. I liked him better the way he was now—I was much more comfortable with this person who looked as though he had lived some. I certainly knew I had.

I am an amateur sketcher, illustrator, and cartoonist. I was gratified that Dr. Evans had kept the cartoon I drew for him years before. When I saw it in his comfortably rumpled, rather haphazard consulting office, he pointed out that it had faded—some of the lines were barely distinguishable. With his permission, I took it home with me and re-inked it. It felt like a connection that mattered. Because he had kept the cartoon that I drew, it seemed that something of me had lingered in his space also.

For the first few weeks, Dr. Evans asked questions about what I had been doing since our relationship ended those years ago. He asked if I still wrote my column for the local weekly newspaper, if I was still a runner—things that indicated to me that he remembered me. And in a positive light.

At first, much of our talk centered on Buzz's death and the impact it had on the family—especially Debbie. Within a short period of time, though, we were talking about how Buzz's death had affected me. I remember telling him that I believed my mother was responsible for his death. Dr. Evans pointed out that when we are adults, we become responsible for our own lives. "Otherwise," he stated, "you would have to give your mother credit for everything you've become and everything you've done with your life. I don't think she deserves that."

When we began talking—frankly and openly—about my family of origin, especially my mother, I was tortured with guilt. I remember asking Dr. Evans, "Do you think my mother can hear what I'm saying about her?" It was at times like this, in those first months with Dr. Evans, that I became hyper vigilant—determined to cloak the symptoms I was afraid to approach again in this therapeutic setting. While I was not fully aware of where this tendency toward "magical thinking" was coming from, I knew that talking about "voices" and rapidly changing emotional states had gotten me nowhere before.

I had made up my mind that I would never try to explain my dissociative episodes to anyone again—I felt like I had tried to bring this out when I was in the hospital 10 years before, and at that time, no one was listening. I did not want to try again—I wanted to keep that part of myself hidden. I wanted to feel better—talk things out—but I did not want to sacrifice my innermost self on the altar of "feeling okay." There had to be a middle ground—something that would get me back to the place where I could function well enough—not perfectly, just well enough.

When we had been meeting for maybe six months, Dr. Evans mused that he was looking through his old files in an effort to find my previous records. He said he never threw any of his patient files away, but they were stored in various places. Stating that he could remember some of what we talked about before, but that he was puzzled and mystified and unable to put some of the pieces together, he said that something from that past therapy "kept nagging at him." I was not particularly interested, nor was I concerned about anything he might find in those old records. He had been my psychiatrist, overseeing hospital care and medication, but my talk therapist had been Joe Gulla, the social worker.

In my therapy with Joe, the relationship with John Hart became the centerpiece. I finally had someone who would listen—for the first time in my life, here was someone who would hear my truth. I talked and talked—rehashing the basics of the story over and over, never disclosing the name of the organization. And I never got beyond what the Salvation Army—and my mother—had told me. Because I continued to accept the blame they placed on me, I never realized how wrong John had been; I never forgave myself for what I saw as my complicity in allowing the continued liaisons; I regretted the harm to his family, for which I felt responsible.

Joe did not have the background necessary to understand and go deeper into my core issues, and Dr. Evans, as his adviser for my therapy, recommended that Joe terminate my treatment unless he (Joe) was willing to put in the time necessary to equip himself for the challenges my case presented. This was not something that Joe felt he could do, and—over my objections—therapy was terminated. Because Dr. Evans was, at that time, taking a sabbatical from his practice, I was referred to Michael Libowitz, M.D. Dr. Libowitz was a disaster for me. It was at this juncture that I decided to make it on my own—at which I was fairly successful until Buzz died.

I remembered the therapy with Joe as heartbreaking. I wanted so badly to overcome all the things that were holding me back psychologically, but Joe seemed to minimize everything I brought to him.

"You've got so much going for you." "You're healthier than I am." "I'm not convinced of the value of long term therapy." The more he tried to send me away, the tighter I held on. I had made an emotional investment in this one person hearing me. Leaving him felt like a defeat. Eventually—with Dr. Evans' encouragement—Joe refused to see me further. Now, ten years later, I did not want to replicate with Dr. Evans any of that confusion and heartache. Soon after I started seeing Dr. Evans this time, I told him, "I don't ever want to go through with anyone again what I went through with Joe."

Dr. Evans was thoughtful about his response to my concern. He said, "You may not have to. The relationship with me may be entirely different." He was talking about the transference phenomenon that takes place in many situations and that is a natural for the psychotherapy venue. I knew I had invested Joe with all of the hurt of previous relationships—mother, father, John, church—and leaving him was tantamount to experiencing all of those losses all over again. And that is exactly what it felt like when he terminated me. I never wanted to go through that again. Ever.

CHAPTER 55

Boundaries

"The therapist draws these feelings out of clients because of the power he has either to reinjure his patients or to relate to them in a way that will free them from wounds of the past. Many laws defining professional malpractice recognize the life-and-death power that the transference phenomenon grants the therapist and therefore place an extra responsibility on the therapist not to abuse the transference."

Sex in the Forbidden Zone by Peter Rutter, M.D.

R EALIZING MY HESITATION BECAUSE OF PAST INJURIES IN RELATIONSHIPS of unequal power, Dr. Evans assured me from the beginning that he had "bulletproof boundaries." He stated that he would always act in his patients' best interests. He recommended Dr. Rutter's book to me, saying that he fully subscribed to Dr. Rutter's idea of accountability on the part of the therapist/doctor/clergy/teacher in relationships where a man holds the greater power over a woman in his care.

I read the book. It was gratifying to realize that a renowned clinician who did not know me affirmed the fact that the relationships with John and Linc were *their* responsibility. Still, I remained stuck. "If he knew me, he would see that it was my fault. I have the power to ruin good men." The Salvation Army's attitude and my mother's words still held an entrenched place in my thinking.

Dr. Evans' consulting office was large. He sat in an overstuffed chair and the patient typically sat on a sofa facing him. There was a lot of extra space behind his chair. I had a very difficult time sitting still during our sessions. I would get up and roam the office—looking at things on his shelves, poring over certificates and pictures framed on the walls. Dr. Evans was not perturbed by this, but did point out that it was difficult for him to do his job when he could not see me. In spite of this, I continued to roam. I sometimes sat with my back against the wall behind him. I felt safe, somehow, in his presence, but invisible to him.

During this introductory period, I told Dr. Evans that I had developed no attachment to him during our previous therapy relationship. This was not true. The attachment—transference—with Joe Gulla had been much stronger, but I had attached to Dr. Evans, too. But it was important to me now for him to know that he was not important to me. I needed to pretend that I did not "need" him, that I could leave therapy at any time. I needed to believe this because every previous relationship of this nature had ended badly for me—with my dad, with John and Linc, and with Joe Gulla. There had been other, less intense relationships in which I had been successful—Captain and Mrs. Irby, teachers—but none of them knew the "truth" about me. I needed to have a plan of escape if the truth proved too much for Dr. Evans. I could not tell him everything until I knew I—and my truth—would be safe with him.

Dr. Evans' boundaries never faltered. I pushed and tested and argued and tried my best to elicit rejection from him. It did not come. He remained constant throughout.

Eventually, I told Dr. Evans about John Hart. In order to be sure that he would not denounce me, I actually lied to him about my age at the time of the first sexual encounter with John. I told him I was 16. I had already decided that if he knew I was 20 at the time, he would say that I had asked for the relationship and was equally responsible for it—that it was a relationship between two consenting adults. I was taking no chances. I would be truthful, but not too truthful. I told him only the barest facts of the relationship—no details, placing no blame, minimizing the extent to which my life had been changed. I said that John had been my "minister" in my "church." I did not say "The Salvation Army." The commandment to "tell no one" was still the most important thing—more important than my own health, more important than freeing myself from misplaced guilt and blame. I remember very little about that first session when we talked about John. I remember that Dr. Evans did not reject me—did not say I had "ruined a good man." In fact, I remember him saying, "Bunny, that goes beyond sexual abuse. That is spiritual abuse of the most heinous kind." Later, Dr. Evans also brought in the idea that when the clergy-congregant relationship is sexualized, it is a form of incest.

That first session about John was, yet again, a test—could I finally make Dr. Evans admit that he didn't want to work with me? Dr. Evans was nonplussed. He seemed able to absorb the tests without effort. But the tests did not stop. And he did not change.

Sometimes, however, Dr. Evans found it necessary to let me know there were rules for *both* of us in this therapy relationship. When I told him that I had lied to him about my age at the time the relationship with John began, Dr. Evans was furious. I sat there stunned on the sofa across from him. He was really angry. "Why would you lie to me?" he asked. "How can we have any kind of honest relationship if one of us is lying?" I told him I was afraid he would blame me if he knew I was not a minor when the relationship took place. He said, "Bunny, wouldn't you rather know if that's the way I think? What good would it do if you had to lie to me to gain my support for your process in therapy? Do you really think you would gain anything if you have to come here and lie?"

I felt chastised and embarrassed. And I felt relieved. Apparently, this person did not have to be protected from me. I could actually tell him my truth. He *wanted* my truth. Dr. Evans never wavered about whose responsibility the harm was—before I told him the details, before he knew that John forced himself on me and then threatened me, before I told him I was lied to and expelled from the church, long before he knew anything about Linc—he believed me and, perhaps more importantly, he believed in me.

CHAPTER 56

Finally, a Diagnosis That Makes Sense

"The patient will be experiencing a number of concerns and fears at this moment. Foremost, in my experience, is the fear that this development will somehow change or terminate the therapy and that the therapist will abandon the patient as have so many other important people in his or her life."

Diagnosis and Treatment of Multiple Personality Disorder by Frank W. Putnam, M.D

"Do you still hear the voices?"

It was a Friday session. On Mondays and Wednesdays I met with Dr. Evans at his office in Pacific Grove on the Monterey Peninsula. On Fridays he was in his office in Salinas. With very little preamble that Friday, Dr. Evans looked at me and asked that question, "Do you still hear the voices?"

My heart sank. *Uh oh*, I thought, *he knows*.

"I wasn't ever going to talk about that again," I replied.

"And why is that?" Dr. Evans prodded.

"Because I told both you and Joe about the voices years ago, and neither one of you seemed to believe me," I said.

Dr. Evans continued, "I finally found your old records and read my notes about the voices and other manifestations of a disorder I now recognize, although it never occurred to me at the time."

I sat on the sofa in that sunny little space on a shady side street just off the main business district in Salinas with my heart literally in my throat. I leaned over, dropped my head, and stared at my shoes. Something important was about to happen—I could feel it. Did it bode well or ill for me? I imagined that it would be something I did not want to hear, did not want to deal with.

"I think you have Dissociative Identity Disorder, Bunny."

"What does that mean, exactly?" I asked, still looking down at my feet.

"The name of the disorder was recently changed from Multiple Personality Disorder, and it means that the patient has split-off personality parts that operate within the same body but have a largely separate consciousness," he stated.

The first thing I asked was, "Does this mean I have to go to a different therapist? Are you going to send me to someone else now that you know what's wrong with me?"

"No," he said.

No? Had I heard correctly? At this point, I looked directly at Dr. Evans with a puzzled expression on my face. He was smiling at me. A very big smile. "You mean I won't have to go away?" I asked.

"No," answered Dr. Evans, "this is an area in which I have significant training and experience. It's actually an area in which I now specialize."

In this short exchange with Dr. Evans, another huge secret came to light. This burden would no longer have to be born alone. He did not see me as a freak or a bother to be gotten rid of. He would stay. I would stay. I was not going to lose this time.

Dr. Evans actually seemed relieved and optimistic about his discovery. He had known something was trying to present itself to him. Now he knew what that was. He went on to explain to me that in 1982—during that first therapy experience—Dissociative Identity Disorder was largely misunderstood and diagnosis was difficult and rare. There was little information and very little training. This had all changed in the past 10 years, and Dr. Evans had availed himself of training by the best qualified physicians in the field. He felt he was equal to the task.

Hearing the actual diagnosis was still difficult for me. I was enormously relieved on one hand, but I was entering unknown territory. What would happen during therapy for this specific disorder? Would I go through some process which would so change me that I would be unrecognizable to myself? To my family? What would others think of me? Did I tell anyone or keep it a secret? There were myriad questions. I left that session relieved and encouraged and scared to death.

I soon told Douglas and Jason about the diagnosis. They were now young adults, and they knew I had been having problems since Buzz's death. They knew I was in therapy, and I was anxious that they be included in this new information that—while daunting—seemed to promise hope for real resolution.

I remember that Jason was out in the yard when I decided to tell him. Coming up beside him I said, "Jase, Dr. Evans believes that I have Multiple Personality Disorder." His response—without hesitation—was, "That explains a lot, Mom." Jason was referring to the many times as they were growing up when I actually played with the boys. I instigated food fights and toilet papering episodes—not at all like most adults. It made sense to him that there were younger parts driving some of this behavior, and he had no problem with it at all.

Douglas became very supportive of the child alters as my therapy progressed—we went to animated films together, and occasionally, when we were shopping, he noticed that a toy caught my eye. Without saying a word, he would purchase the item and say, "Here, Mom, this is for your little creatures."

Soon after I told them about my MPD/DID, Douglas and Jason expressed a desire to meet with Dr. Evans. I facilitated this. It was reassuring to know that they were interested. I had no problem with them being involved—they were the best part of my life. I trusted them implicitly.

Their acceptance of my unusual makeup and their belief in me never flagged.

CHAPTER 57

Everyone's Invited

"The personality system will be watching closely to see how the therapist responds. This is another aspect of the cautionary tale—testing. In therapy with multiples, *everything* is a test. Their need to test the therapist over and over, to determine whether he or she can be trusted with their secrets, is one of the reasons why multiples are among the most difficult of all psychiatric patients to treat."

Diagnosis and Treatment of Multiple Personality Disorder by Frank W. Putnam, M.D.

THE FIRST MEETING AFTER DR. EVANS AND I DISCUSSED THE DIAGNOSIS, we talked in generalities about DID. I was still unsure about what ramifications there might be to actually putting a name to something I had been secretive about all my life. There was an intermittent feeling of relief and even exhilaration—finally, somebody understands! But there was also the feeling that someone was going to try to "undo" me. The people inside had been my companions, defenders, and comforters for as far back as I could remember. I did not want to lose them.

Within a couple of sessions, however, different alters were competing for time in the therapeutic setting. The first one who made an entrance was Josie. She is the tough African-American woman who acted as a gatekeeper. I found myself outside Dr. Evans' office one afternoon—I knew I was supposed to have an appointment at 4:15 and it was now 5:30. I went back to his office and told him I thought I had missed our session. He was in a somewhat agitated state and said, "Someone kept your appointment, Bunny. Believe me, someone was here." I found out later that it was Josie—testing Dr. Evans to see if he was safe before any of the others came out. She spent the 45 minute session verbally attacking Dr. Evans and accusing him of all sorts of miscues during our previous work with him. I'm sure now that she was trying to find out if it was okay for all the alters to tell their truth without fear of rejection or reprisals. This was the beginning of all sorts of acting out and testing, which included:

- Curtis stealing the sign with Dr. Evans' name on it off the front of the office building—over and over again.
- Extensive drinking just before sessions as a way of self-medicating.
- After sessions, hiding in the flower beds outside Dr. Evans' office—sometimes for hours—to watch him drive away.
- Calling Dr. Evans at all hours of the night because we could not leave the area near his office and go home.
- Showing up at the dojo where Dr. Evans taught Aikido in the evenings—leaving notes on his car so he would talk to us when he came out.
- Curtis bringing hunting knives to session over and over again—these were "borrowed" from Douglas' collection.
- Kevin writing cryptic notes and mailing them to Dr. Evans—sometimes including newspaper articles about sexual predation of all kinds.
- A female alter (perhaps Bunny Too) cutting herself when frustrated or under stress.

- Exploratory suicidal acting out—accumulating the equipment needed to suicide the way Buzz had.

I was also answering personal ads and meeting men—something I had never done. There was an enormous pressure to act on feelings put aside and repressed into some of the alter personalities. Many of the alters did not like Doug and wanted the opportunity to explore relationships with other men. And the kid parts—especially Kevin—just wanted a lap to sit on. We were demonstrating risky behavior, but their needs were compelling and hard to deflect now that they had been invited out into the world. I remember calmly telling Dr. Evans about this, and at the time, I saw absolutely nothing wrong with it. I met with total strangers, disc jockeys from the local radio station I listened to, tow truck drivers known from business relationships at the auto shop, dentists, and policemen. Looking back on this behavior, it seems very inappropriate and even dangerous, but at the time, it satisfied some deep need.

Throughout this initial phase, each alter brought forth not only fragments of his or her individual experience of John, but deep-seated ambivalence about disclosing what it had been their responsibility to conceal. Dissociation is built around a complicated method of hiding truth—both within the system, as a protective device, and from the outside world, for fear of reprisals. Each time there was a scrap of disclosure, there was the attendant fear and the feelings of disloyalty—to the system and to John. They had no clear idea of what this new milieu might hold for them.

During all of this internal upheaval, I was working full-time and carrying on all other normal activities. I needed very little sleep. I was agitated and hyperactive—handling multiple challenges and inviting more people and activity into my life as a way of screening myself from the reorientation that was going on inside. I switched from alter to alter frequently. It was as though they were making up for lost time now that Dr. Evans was exhibiting an active interest in each of them.

In order to try to establish safety for the total personality system, Dr. Evans and I came up with guidelines:

At the end of each session, he did a hypnotic exercise which he called "centering." In this exercise, he helped us go to a quiet place inside to rest—especially the child alters—and then requested that I—the host personality—come forward to drive safely and take care of all necessary business until our next meeting with him. This enabled me to get up and leave his office, get in my car and drive home—without staying in the shrubbery near his office to watch him leave. The centering exercise also helped forestall the child alters' need for an adult male to hold them.

Dr. Evans gave me his pager number so that I could reach him directly on an as-needed basis, without going through his answering service. I had been calling his service regularly from a public phone (before cellular phones) and trying to get them to put me through to him so I could break the trance I was in and go home.

He allowed us to take a book of his home with us—a medical book about the cardiovascular system. We carried this around with us in the car for years, and I still keep it on my bookshelves to remind me of the work we've done. Appropriately, we have always called it "Dr. Evans' Heart Book."

Dr. Evans allowed us to have transitional objects in his office—a baby doll for Phyllis Ann and Claudia, a teddy bear and crayons for Kevin.

As I reflect back on this tumultuous period during the first few years of his work with my alters, I see Dr. Evans as carefully navigating a minefield of ongoing challenges while remaining largely unflappable. He maintained his poise and his ability to accommodate input from myriad points of view while seeming well-grounded and calm throughout. At the time, we took all of his involvement for granted. It took years for me to realize just how far he extended himself for me and for all my alters—we soaked up his attentions as though his energy and his ability to accommodate were inexhaustible.

Dr. Evans' professionalism throughout can be viewed from the vantage point of Dr. Putnam's thoughts on "Establishing the Therapeutic Alliance": "Caring for the patient is demonstrated by respect for each of the alters. All should be considered equally important, and the therapist should be careful not to develop favorites. Caring is also expressed by setting limits on dangerous or destructive behaviors. The therapist will be repeatedly tested for his or her willingness to stop inappropriate or dangerous actions on the part of one or more alters …"

Art became a way of expressing in a more concrete way what the alter personalities were experiencing emotionally with Dr. Evans on the outside and with each other internally. I continued to sketch and draw throughout my therapy. All of the pictures were driven by different parts of my personality system, and they all expressed elements of the ebb and flow of trust and attachment within our system and within the relationship with Dr. Evans. Dr. Evans allowed us to hang all of the pictures on the wall in his office until fairly late in the therapy, when he moved into a much smaller space and there was not enough room for all of them. We had to choose one that we wanted to hang on the wall, and all the others went into Dr. Evans' chart for us.

The most important first step in therapy with a patient who dissociates is achieving stabilization within the system. Dr. Evans worked tirelessly toward this goal, but as each alter brought forth even tiny exploratory bits of the relationship with John, destabilization ensued over and over. There was the urge—the need—to disclose, and the dictum to hide—to tell no one. The pain of disclosing and the shame of not being obedient to the command for silence was the conflict that intensified every minute of interaction with Dr. Evans.

In every possible way, Dr. Evans was supportive and inclusive to all parts of the personality system and to the unique story each brought forward. Yet he maintained firm boundaries so that we were never confused about what was appropriate in the therapy relationship, and by modeling boundaries for us—something no one had done before—we came to understand and utilize this means of perceiving our separateness from the world at large. We had never felt our own personal congruity and our own right to freedom from intrusion by others whose agendas were motivated by selfish appropriation of parts of ourselves—body, mind, spirit—for their own use.

CHAPTER 58

Object Constancy

"Yet, in fact, it's when we face the darkness squarely in the eye—in ourselves and in the world—that we begin at last to see the light. And that is the alchemy of personal transformation. In the midst of the deepest, darkest night, when we feel most humbled by life, the faint shadow of our wings begins to appear."

The Gift of Change by Marianne Williamson

OBJECT CONSTANCY IS A DEVELOPMENTAL STAGE A CHILD TYPICALLY achieves between nine and twelve months. The child learns that an object exists even though she can no longer see it. As an example, imagine a child realizing for the first time that a favorite toy exists even though it is hidden under a blanket. The child will try to remove the blanket to reveal the toy underneath. The child's previous assumption had been that if the toy was out of sight, it did not exist. This developmental stage, once achieved, is then transferred to everything in the child's environment. The child learns about order and continuity in her world—people who leave will come back. There are things that can be depended upon.

Many of my child alters never achieved object constancy. They believed that people who were out of sight no longer existed. They also believed that once they were no longer in the presence of an important person, they themselves no longer existed for that person. This posed many challenges during our therapy with Dr. Evans. As he became more and more important to the child alters, they had a more and more difficult time leaving his presence. They lacked the ability to internalize his existence as ongoing even when they could not see him. They also believed that once we were out of his sight, we no longer existed for him.

Thus, the urge to be in contact with him every day—sometimes numerous times in a single day.

We called him. Having his pager number, we would page him at all hours of the day and night. He called us back. He did not get angry. He made himself available to us.

We faxed him.

We wrote him letters—especially Kevin—but others also.

We emailed him.

We drove by his office just to look at his car—evidence that he existed.

And we missed him terribly between sessions. We calculated how many hours there were in a week. We met with him approximately three hours each week. That left an enormous number of hours when we were alone. By now, for the child alters, not being in Dr. Evans' presence meant being alone. He alone knew them, recognized them, encouraged them—in essence, he parented them. They were hungry for everything he represented. They were trying to satisfy the need for bonding that eventually leads to autonomy.

It took years for object constancy to be achieved. The process was extremely difficult and caused much suffering. Every time we left Dr. Evans' office, we felt orphaned. The feeling was that we existed nowhere except in his office. In actual fact, the child alters had experienced no loving commitment on the part of an adult in this powerful position over them.

The feeling of disconnect drove the desire to leave evidence of ourselves in his office—the pictures we drew for him, little gifts we made for him, the dolls and toys and evidence of our accomplishments outside our therapy. When we won awards at work or won speech contests at Toastmasters or received notes of thanks or congratulations for some civic accomplishment, we brought them to him. His opinion of us was the only one that mattered.

Every bit of this was a way of ameliorating the feeling that he would forget us. I dealt with these feelings constantly. "We'd better call him. We haven't seen him for so many hours. We don't know where he is. Is he gone?"

Dr. Evans was patient and facilitated as much contact as seemed necessary to enable us to internalize the idea of his continued existence even when we could not see him. He called us when he was on a pilgrimage to Taizé, France. Later, when we made that same pilgrimage, he allowed us to call him. He allowed us to take away evidence of his existence—the heart book is one example.

As another way of affirming his ongoing presence for us and his commitment to our growth and progress, Dr. Evans signed "contracts" which I typed up and brought to session with me. You will find copies of these contracts at the end of this chapter.

The contract dated September 3, 1999 deals with fears of abandonment. By signing this document, Dr. Evans was committing to his role as our therapist for as long as he was practicing in the Salinas area. The contract also acknowledges the dynamics the child alters are pursuing in looking for the good parent, and it alludes to an eventual outcome of God being the good parent. This was something Dr. Evans maintained throughout. I'm not sure that we ever achieved this type of internal recognition of God as the trustworthy parent—such was the damage done in the relationships with John, Linc, and the Salvation Army.

The contract signed May 31, 2000 was signed when all parts of my personality system were trying to allow the idea that love is not a sinful, bad thing. Exploring the idea that it was safe to love Dr. Evans was a necessary first step on the path to experiencing love without also feeling hurt and fear. The love we were feeling for Dr. Evans was reminiscent of the love we felt for John before the relationship became sexual. In both cases, the child alters were engaged in the transference of their deepest longings to a powerful father figure who held the potential for healing of old wounds. John proved the antithesis of the healer. We were hesitant to try again. This contract was a movement in the direction of exploring the possibility of healing.

The contract dated June 23, 2000 deals with a period of time when Dr. Evans would be unavailable for our regularly scheduled appointments. Canceled appointments were always difficult for us—we depended on the stability of predictable actions on the part of Dr. Evans. By signing this contract, he affirmed that his relationship as our therapist was ongoing, even when he was out of sight for a period of time.

Each of these contracts was an effort to build trust. When I typed up these documents, it was always seen as a test by the child personalities—will he sign it? Each time a gesture of commitment was requested and a positive response was forthcoming, it was cause for celebration for the kid parts. A simple piece of paper with the invaluable expression of caring and constancy. Priceless.

In *The Road Less Traveled*, M. Scott Peck defines *love* thus: "The will to extend one's self for the purpose of nurturing one's own or another's spiritual growth." When Dr. Evans and I discussed this definition, he said that he agreed but expanded the definition to include other types of growth. Dr. Evans' definition was, "Love is the will to extend one's self for another's physical, emotional, psychological, or spiritual growth." When we finally talked about love, I asked Dr. Evans if he loved us—my entire self, including the alter personalities—in the sense that Peck described love. Without a second of hesitation, Dr. Evans said, "Absolutely." That helped.

And yet it would take time—a lot of time—for us to accept this attitude of caring, inclusive acceptance that was at such odds with the scars left behind by those who used us and then maintained that it was "God's will." Allowing the new kind of love that Dr. Evans represented to become a part of how we related to ourselves and to the world was profoundly challenging.

In every contact—even when he had to chide or correct or enforce reasonable boundaries—Dr. Evans modeled Peck's definition of love. He extended himself for us repeatedly over a period of 15 years. He had to have had moments when he doubted, but he never gave up on us or on himself.

> To: Bunny Stevens
>
> From: Doctor Evans
>
> I realize that you are working on some issues which are difficult and are causing you great pain--during sessions and also in between sessions when sometimes you are bound to feel alone. For this reason, I make you the following promise:
>
> "As long as I am practicing in this geographical area, I will be available to you in my role as your therapist. I know that right now the issues that are causing great distress have to do with the 'hole' you feel because you have no father/mother and never did have a nurturing parent. Much of your life's energy has been spent looking for a substitute father. . I can never fill that role for you, although I understand the feelings that generate your desire for just that: me as your parent. The role that I hold as your therapist can have some of the aspects of a good parent, and I am not offended that you feel the drive to install me in that 'hole' in your interior life. I feel that God is the only one who can fill that 'hole,' but I am willing to work with you as a visible 'place holder' until such time as you are able to accept the fact of the invisible."
>
> Signed: _D. Evans MD_   Date: _9/3/99_
> Doctor Evans

To: Bunny Stevens

From: Doctor Evans

I realize that you are working on some issues which are difficult and are causing you great pain--during sessions and also in between sessions when sometimes you are bound to feel alone. For this reason, I make you the following promise:

"As long as I am practicing in this geographical area, I will be available to you in my role as your therapist. I know that right now the issues that are causing great distress have to do with the 'hole' you feel because you have no father/mother and never did have a nurturing parent. Much of your life's energy has been spent looking for a substitute father. I can never fill that role for you, although I understand the feelings that generate your desire for just that: me as your parent. The role that I hold as your therapist can have some of the aspects of a good parent, and I am not offended that you feel the drive to install me in that 'hole' in your interior life. I feel that God is the only one who can fill that 'hole,' but I am willing to work with you as a visible 'place holder' until such time as you are able to accept the fact of the invisible."

> To: Bunny Stevens
>
> From: Doctor Evans
>
> Date: May 31, 2000
>
> I, Doctor Evans, promise that I will never, under any circumstances, for any reason whatsoever, punish Bunny Stevens or any part of her personality system for loving me.
>
> Signed: _D. Evans, MD_   Date: 5/31/00
> Doctor Evans

To: Bunny Stevens

From: Doctor Evans

Date: May 31, 2000

I, Doctor Evans, promise that I will never, under any circumstances, for any reason whatsoever, punish Bunny Stevens or any part of her personality system for loving me.

To: Bunny Stevens

From: Doctor Evans

Date: June 23, 2000

I, Doctor Evans, will be on vacation from this date through July 10th. During that time, I will be out of the country. My intent is to come back. I will be gone for a while. But my intent is to come back. It is not my intent now, nor has it ever been, to abandon Bunny Stevens or to abandon the work I am doing with Bunny. My intent is to come back on July 10th. Bunny Stevens has an appointment to see me on Wednesday, July 12th, 2000, at 4:15 p.m. My intent is to keep that appointment.

Signed: _D. Evans MD_
Doctor Evans

Date: 6/23/00

To: Bunny Stevens

From: Doctor Evans

Date: June 23, 2000

I, Doctor Evans, will be on vacation from this date through July 10th. During that time, I will be out of the country. My intent is to come back. I will be gone for a while. But my intent is to come back. It is not my intent now, nor has it ever been, to abandon Bunny Stevens or to abandon the work I am doing with Bunny. My intent is to come back on July 10th. Bunny Stevens has an appointment to see me on Wednesday, July 12th, 2000, at 4:15 p.m. My intent is to keep that appointment.

CHAPTER 59

Transference Issues

"In multiples, a major source of transference reactions is simply the uncovering and eliciting during the course of therapy of alter personalities who embody past trauma. The therapist's gender or mere presence is often all that is required for his or her inclusion into a highly emotional transference reaction."

*Diagnosis & Treatment of
Multiple Personality Disorder* by Frank W.

By the time Dr. Evans had met with the majority of my alter personalities, there was a growing awareness of the powerful position he held in our lives. We began to feel enmeshed with him—we obsessed about every minute nuance of his reaction to us. We wanted to be always near him, to have him fill the vacant space within us for the unlimitedly available parent.

And we feared the developing dependence and the feelings of love attendant thereto.

I remember being afraid to bring up the word "love" with Dr. Evans. I remember one phone conversation where I posed hypothetical questions trying to determine what his response might be. He said, "Bunny, if the time ever comes when you are uncomfortable with any feelings you have toward me, we can talk about it. It's not unusual for all kinds of feelings to be activated in therapy." I remember thinking, *That doesn't make sense. If I said the wrong thing to him, he would send me away. I can't admit I feel the same way about him as I did toward John. Love is a sin. It has to be because that's what got me in trouble with John.* John had demonstrated that my love unleashes the darkest, basest actions—sexual arousal, predation, and rape. While I do not remember ever feeling sexual energy coming from Dr. Evans, there was my mother's admonition that I ruined good men. Could I bring ruin down upon Dr. Evans?

And I was afraid of love. You will remember that it was my son's innocent love for me that led to my initial emotional breakdown when he was just a youngster. How could I tolerate this emotion that seemed to have a life of its own? It came unwished for. I did not want to love because my love could harm. In particular, I never wanted to love anyone in a position of power over me again. The residual pain from the relationships with John and Linc made my meetings with Dr. Evans intolerable because feelings of high personal regard—love—were impossible to quell and they were the harbingers I most feared. There was a part of me—Charlotte, an adult alter dressed in full Salvation Army uniform—who constantly chided me about the sinfulness of love. "Flee from this evil. I know you remember where this leads," she admonished me.

And so I decided I had to leave therapy. I had to leave the place where this sinful thing—love—was manifesting itself. I struggled with a raging internal conflict—the need to leave in order to keep Dr. Evans safe and to save myself from the suffocating attachment to him and the feelings of the child alters who now saw Dr. Evans as their ally and their only reason to go on living.

On a Wednesday afternoon, I told Dr. Evans I had to stop therapy because I was experiencing feelings I could not tolerate—feelings that were evil. He encouraged me to look at what was happening in therapy. We were working toward stabilization of the personality system. Many of the alters had established ties with him. We had come up with safeguards that helped negotiate the rockier moments between sessions. He had never required anything from us except the rules instituted for the safety of all concerned. He reiterated that he had "bulletproof boundaries," and no matter what our feelings might be, he would remain exactly as he had always been—the stable, listening, supportive partner to all parts of our system. I listened with the absolute conviction that he was the devil incarnate—trying to persuade us to do something that was evil.

At the end of that Wednesday session, I was even more convinced that I must leave Dr. Evans. I was also devastated emotionally. I did not want to leave him, but I equated that to the struggle with John—being caught in something evil that I did not know how to stop or extricate myself from. I wanted to finally have what I had tried to find in John—the parent-person I had longed for all my life. And yet I knew I must leave. This time I would not be a party to the evil. I would flee. I would do the right thing. The relationship with John had made it impossible for me to conceive of a relationship of unequal power where it would be safe for me to be present, to accept the healing of all of those old wounds that the relationship with Dr. Evans was offering.

That Wednesday, we came up with a compromise—Dr. Evans asked me to keep my Friday appointment with him as scheduled, and we would talk about it further. If I felt the same way after that session, he would respect my wish to terminate therapy.

I cried throughout that Friday session. The fact that it was so difficult to leave him seemed to affirm the reason for doing so. If the relationship had been a casual one, it would have been easy to walk away. The very fact that we valued him so highly as to feel torn apart by the idea of separation merely exemplified the wrongness of the relationship. Another John legacy—lack of the ability to trust when trust was finally warranted.

Because I persisted, Dr. Evans agreed to cancel all my future appointments with him. I visualized "my" times in his book being peopled by others. Those were mine. Monday at 5:15, Wednesday and Friday at 4:15. Those belonged to me. I was giving them up.

It was wrenching to think of my name being erased. Gone. But I was convinced that was the right thing to do—I must flee this evil.

As I walked out the door that Friday afternoon, Dr. Evans said, "Good luck, Bunny. And remember, you can always come back. I'll be here."

CHAPTER 60

Without a Price to Pay

"To be an abused child is to be profoundly rejected by the people who are supposed to love and care for the child. ... I think that it would be difficult to overestimate the feelings of rejection and abandonment that these patients have experienced in childhood."

Diagnosis and Treatment of Multiple Personality Disorder by Frank W. Putnam, M.D.

I STAYED AWAY FROM DR. EVANS FOR APPROXIMATELY THREE MONTHS. During those months, I drove myself even harder at work, and I slid back into some of the self-destructive behaviors that I had been able to give up because of the therapy relationship my alters had formed with Dr. Evans. I was keeping liaisons with men—one man in particular who had proven himself unsafe. It was as though I could understand and tolerate an abusive relationship, but I had no frame of reference for the opposite—a positive relationship based on mutual respect and caring. I thought I deserved to be abused. I was drinking in secret in order to get through my days and in order to sleep at night. I was experiencing what Dr. Evans described as "hurricanes" inside. My alters—especially Curtis—were having a difficult time containing all of the anger over past betrayals, and swirling emotions overtook me—leading to episodes of high-speed, erratic driving and other efforts at dispelling inside pressures that were becoming intolerable.

I lacked the ability to see clearly just how illogical the termination of therapy was. I was convinced I had done the right thing. I thought I merely had to endure this period of excruciating pain that abandonment always precipitated. I recognized the emotions. In an odd way, they seemed normal. Attachment to Dr. Evans was the anomaly, the aberration, the manifestation of the evil within us, the thing to be avoided at all costs.

Another dynamic that drove the separation from Dr. Evans was the fear of abandonment. If I left him, he could not leave me. In spite of his placid ability to accept whatever my alters and I brought to him, I still fully expected for a time to come when he would tell us to leave. I knew this could happen at any moment—there need not be a reason or a lead-up or any notice whatsoever. He would just send us away. Arbitrarily. I expected this behavior. Somehow, I was not able to put together what was obvious—Dr. Evans never acted in any way as though we were beyond his help; he invited everyone's participation in sessions; he devised methods to keep us safe—there was nothing even remotely rejecting in anything he did. But we knew it could come. If we left him, we took away the very worst thing he could do to us. We took away abandonment. As Peck says, "Thus the child who is not loved by his parents will always assume himself or herself to be unlovable ..." There was no place in my consciousness, in my self-image, in my complex personality system for someone who behaved as Dr. Evans did. For us, he did not compute.

During this hiatus, I began a seminal drawing, which I perceived as a "ticket back into therapy" should I need it. I would draw a picture of my personality system as I then understood it. If I ever decided to see Dr. Evans again, this picture would be the price I would pay him so he would allow me back in. I assumed he would be angry and punishing because he had advised against terminating therapy and I had done it anyway. The drawing took a lot of my time and it took input from other parts of my personality system. It was the first effort at tangible cooperation. While I was the one doing the drawing, each of the alters brought forward his or her own body image. The work itself was calming and unifying. We worked together on a project that each of us held a vested interest in. It was not a competitive exercise. It was a collective acknowledgement of who we were.

I am not sure exactly why I made the phone call to reestablish contact with Dr. Evans. I do remember the first session back. It was a relief to be there. That space had become "home," a grounding place, a place of safety. While we were in session with Dr. Evans, he belonged to no one but us. Walking around his office, we realized that nothing had changed—our things were still there. He had not thrown away Kevin's drawings or notes, Larry our teddy bear was still there, the baby doll that belonged to the little girl alters still lay in her place atop a book shelf. He had not thrown us away, even when we had invited him to do just that. And he did not ask for explanations. We began where we had left off without punishment—implicit or explicit. There was no price to pay.

It was some weeks before we finished the drawing we had thought would be our ticket back. I had not finished it. It became impossible to go forward with it until we found out if we could go back without reprisals. Dr. Evans' allowing us to come back without fanfare or repercussions seemed to ease the feeling of hyper vigilance. We had given him the perfect opportunity to reject us, and he had not used it. We continued to test. He just continued to be himself. He seemed to do it without effort.

We did finish the picture. You will see it as Exhibit C in the following pages.

CHAPTER 61

Drawing on Both Sides of the Brain

"The multiple may benefit from nonverbal group therapies, such as art, music, occupational, or movement therapy (Kluft, 1984d)."

Diagnosis and Treatment of Multiple Personality Disorder by Frank W. Putnam, M.D.

ON THE FOLLOWING PAGES YOU WILL SEE SOME OF THE DRAWINGS I DID as an adjunct to the talk therapy with Joe Gulla and then Dr. Evans. I attempt here to provide a little background and clarification.

Exhibit A—This drawing was done for Joe Gulla during a period of misunderstanding and perceived rejection in that relationship. As mentioned earlier, Joe was not the right candidate for what I needed in the way of a therapist, but he was the first person with whom I connected, and I was loath to let him go. In this drawing, Joe is diagnosing Santa (me) who is confused about his identity—multiple personality? There are a number of things amiss in the environment—none of which the therapist sees. Instead, he is intent on attacking the obvious, clearly ignoring signs of disintegration all around him in the therapeutic setting. Seen in this light, this drawing clearly portrays the confusion I felt in this relationship.

Exhibit B—This was a drawing I did for Dr. Evans during that early first encounter with him when he was my hospital and medication manager. The point of this drawing, I believe, is that the patient (me) is caught in a repeating, nonproductive cycle from which she is seeking release. I had been trying to communicate what was wrong—probably not clearly enough, to be sure—and I felt doomed to remain isolated in my own multiple world until someone figured out what was driving my erstwhile self-defeating behavior.

Exhibit C—This is the drawing I did with conscious input from everyone in my personality system while we were on hiatus from therapy. You will see Bunny Too (the party girl) on the sofa with a drink in her hand. Josie (the gatekeeper) strikes a powerful pose on the arm of the sofa. Charlotte (the moral policewoman) is in the Salvation Army gear, beating the big bass drum—repent for the wrath of God is at hand! Delia (caregiver to the little ones) is standing patiently near the children. Curtis (repository of anger and reluctant champion of the younger children) is barely in the picture because he's not sure about Dr. Evans yet. Kevin (who was mute for the first couple of years of therapy) is communicating with his crayons. Phyllis Ann (representative of the sweet toddler I was when my dad left) is standing close to Dr. Evans—will you be my daddy? Claudia makes no contact with the world around her—she is lost in her imaginary world where she is safe. And that's me entering the picture—amazed to see everyone else already there.

Exhibit D—In this drawing Delia is leading Kevin and Phyllis Ann out of a dark tunnel into a world that holds the potential of light and love. Dr. Evans is represented by the lion. He is standing, awaiting the kids' arrival. Curtis is seen again as separate—sitting by himself with a belligerent expression on his face: "Not me."

Exhibit E—This picture of the child alters in a peaceable kingdom is a perception of their innocence and their growing ease with Dr. Evans, who is again represented by the lion. In this drawing

Curtis is the one who is interacting directly with Dr. Evans. He is finally participating and seems caught in a moment of wonder.

Exhibit E—This drawing was done while I was keeping vigil by my mother's bedside during the last few days of her life. She was in a coma, but the kid parts were still very much in awe of her and afraid that she could still get them. They needed the reassurance of the continuing relationship with Dr. Evans. We were not able to meet with him for the two or three weeks we spent in Modesto during Mother's final illness, death, and then her funeral. This picture was a connection for all the child parts to the one they now perceived as their parent. Again, Dr. Evans is represented by the lion who—in this picture—is soft and smiling and welcoming them to lean on him.

It seems to me that the pictures we drew for Dr. Evans gave substance to the kid parts. I am represented in the first three, but merely as a device trying to put forward their story. I think the child alters were happy to be visible. They always existed inside. They found someone who invited them out. They wanted to be seen by him.

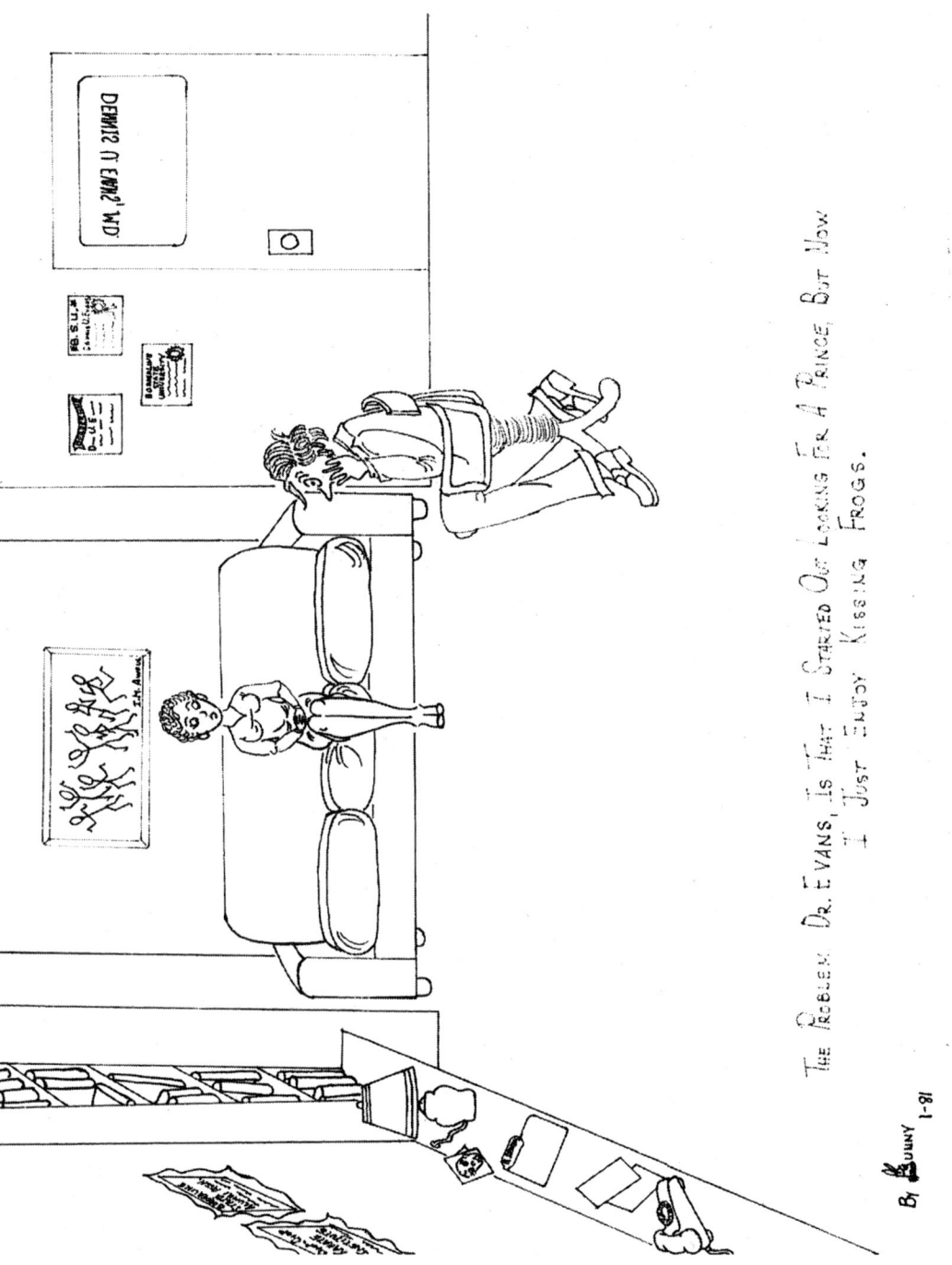

Drawing on Both Sides of the Brain | 275

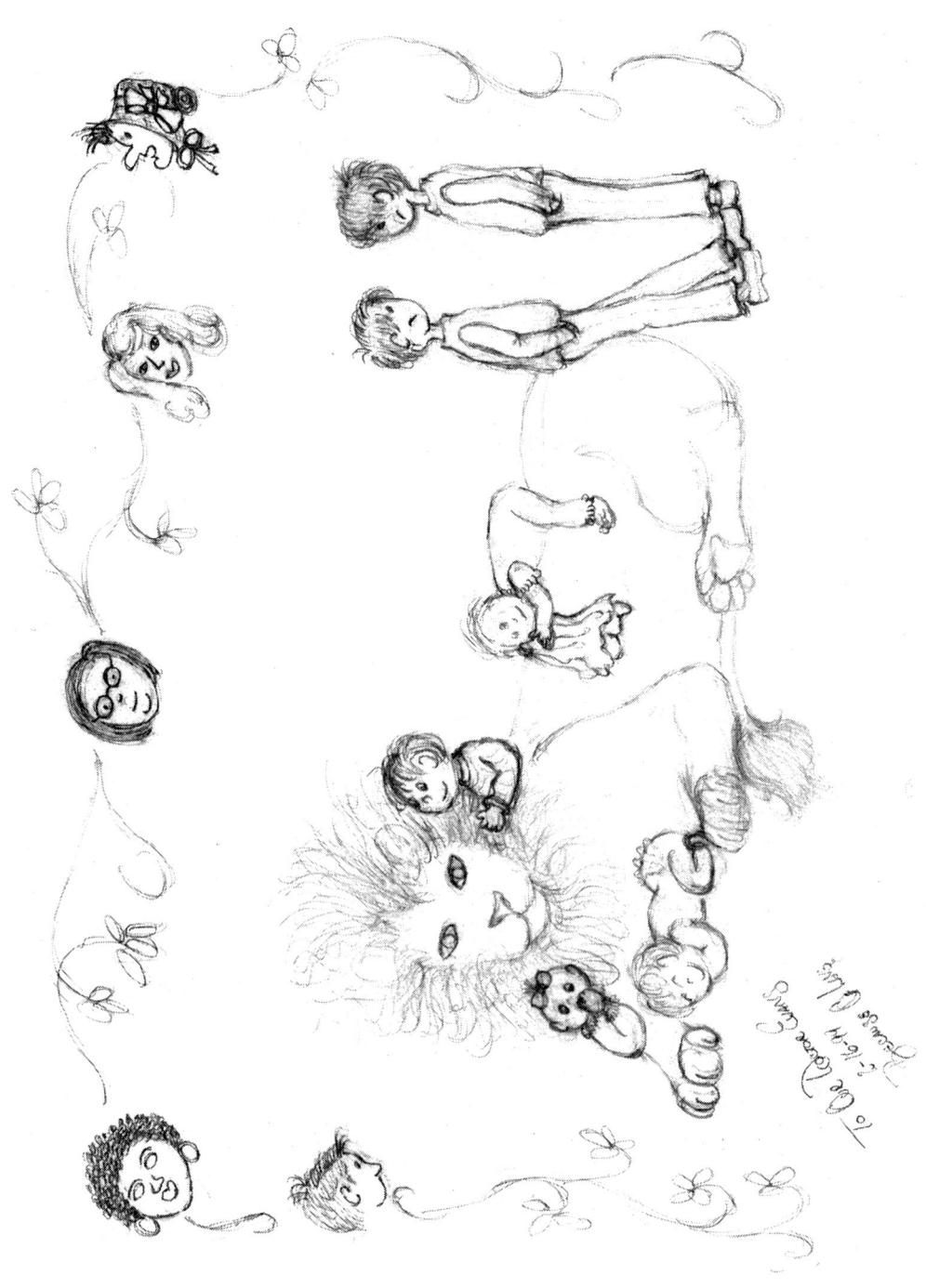

CHAPTER 62

Exorcising John

"Secrets have a power of their own that pressures the patient both to conceal and to reveal them. The therapist's efforts are best spent in creating a therapeutic climate in which the revelation of these secrets and all of their attendant trauma can safely occur."

Diagnosis & Treatment of Multiple Personality Disorder by Frank W. Putnam

As previously stated, when I first began to seek counseling—because I was experiencing difficulty in my relationship with Douglas—I inherently knew that my problems were somehow tied to the sexual abuse I suffered as a small child and then, in particular, John Hart's reenactment of that abuse within my place of respite and safety, the church. When I finally brought this subject up with Joe Gulla in 1978, the basics of the relationship with John (without mention of the organization) came pouring forth with such force that I felt lightheaded and faint. I felt sick. By the end of that appointment with Joe, I had opened a door which had been sealed because I was told to "tell no one." But no resolution was offered. Joe felt that merely speaking the words would bring about healing. He was wrong.

I deteriorated quickly. I lost 20 pounds in two weeks and was not sleeping. I could not stand to touch or be touched—by anyone. I wrote Joe a note that said, "Does it sometimes happen that the cure is worse than the disease? I'm not doing well at all." After a suicide attempt, I was admitted to the psychiatric ward of Community Hospital of the Monterey Peninsula. I remained a patient on that locked ward for 30 days.

The next three years were a series of hospitalizations and medications and interventions. I tried determinedly to "take back" what I had said about John. "It never happened," I told anyone who would listen. I was tortured by the knowledge that I had broken the code of silence and by the fear that the Salvation Army was right—it had all been my fault and I deserved everything that happened to me. I was diagnosed with a series of psychological disorders and medicated accordingly: Obsessive-compulsive Disorder, Bipolar Disorder, Borderline Personality Disorder, and Agitated Depression. I grew worse and worse. I dissociated, drank, drove wildly all night, and tried to plan an "accidental" death that would spare my children the onus of a parent's suicide.

I tried to find absolution for breaking the code of silence. I prayed to God, and I visited two psychologists attached to the Church of Christ. I visited two ministers for counseling. Telling someone about John—even though I never mentioned the name of the organization—became the sin for which there was no forgiveness. Such was my belief in the power of the Salvation Army to place blame and require obedience. It never occurred to me that they were wrong.

I took medications that drastically altered my mental state. One of them—Nardil—caused life-threatening side effects. Narcolepsy is a sudden lapse of consciousness into deep sleep. I fought this for the two years I was on this drug. Driving became agony. Nardil can also cause fatal interactions if a strict dietary regime is not adhered to exactly. After one such episode, I decided the life I was living was worse than facing the world and trying to make it on my own. At that point, I buried everything deep within myself and made the most of the time I had left to mother my sons.

After Buzz died and I began seeing Dr. Evans, I knew I would not be able to bury all of my history again. With Buzz's death, all the old debts came due. It seemed I had no place to hide now that he was gone. My mantra, "Buzz made it so I can make it," no longer made sense. I was so broken by his suicide I was willing to risk anything to finally come clean—about the way we were raised, about John and then Linc, and about the loss of the only real hero I ever had—my brother Buzz.

Dr. Evans' life partner is a Presbyterian pastor who teaches religion at a private girls' school on the Monterey Peninsula. And Dr. Evans is a deeply spiritual person. At the beginning of a session, perhaps a year into my therapy, Dr. Evans said, "From what you've told me, Bunny, you've always been a deeply spiritual person. Perhaps you need to explore a new spiritual connection." I was surprised and nonplussed by this suggestion, which seemed to come out of nowhere. And then I was angry. Who did he think he was? Why would he assume to give me *spiritual* advice? He was supposed to be a clinician, not some kind of religious guru. I told him, "Get thee behind me, Satan. I came to you for psychological help. Please just leave religion out of this. I'm not interested."

Shortly after Buzz's death, I left the Church of Christ, because their teaching was such that anyone not in their fellowship goes straight to hell when they die. I thought about all the time I had spent in that group of people who had an exclusive view of their own correctness, and I just did not want it anymore. I didn't want to be anywhere where my brother was a hell-bound sinner. I left and did not look back. I never missed them. And, strangely, I did not feel as though I had left God. I left an address on Alvin Drive in Salinas, where the teaching was that God existed only for those chosen few in that fellowship.

Because Dr. Evans often attended seminars with his partner, he told me that the teaching at San Francisco Theological Seminary was, "Thou shalt not fuck the flock." His words exactly. He said it is always the clergy's responsibility to protect the flock, not victimize it. I listened. At this point, I did not think he knew what he was talking about, but I listened.

Over the years that Dr. Evans and I dealt with the John Hart episode, more and more details came out. Eventually, with all parts of my personality system participating, we told him everything—except the name of the organization. I continued to believe that we could keep that part of the Salvation Army's commandment. We could conceal the name of the organization. But we told him everything about the sexual abuse itself. I think we needed to know that he would not betray some inner revulsion when the more intimate details came out. And, bit by bit, they did come out.

Different parts of my personality system had different stories, different opinions, different allegiances. These all had to be addressed. To the child alters, there was much confusion and over-identification with John as the good father—since he was in that position in the church, we were supposed to obey him. To other internal parts charged with moral policing, the kids who loved John were bad and sinful. This made for a complicated sorting out of all the interwoven experiences and an effort toward clarity on the issue of blame.

The day that Dr. Evans recommended *Sex in the Forbidden Zone* to me, I stopped at a book store in Pacific Grove and ordered it. When it came in a week later, I took it home and read it cover to cover. It said all the same things Dr. Evans had been saying. It was written by someone I had never met, so he had no vested interest in me personally. I tended to think that Dr. Evans was telling me it was not my fault because, after all, I was paying him, wasn't I? In spite of the fact that John raped me, threatened me, and coerced my ongoing participation, I retained the knowledge imparted by the Salvation Army that I was "no longer good." I continued to believe that if someone really knew me, they would know I was evil—as the Salvation Army had known.

Today, I still have the copy of Dr. Rutter's book that I purchased in 1994. It is tattered and dog-eared and penciled in and highlighted. But I would not part with it. It gave me some hope that there was a clinician somewhere who had done a lot of work on the subject of relationships exactly like the one John had with me. The subtitle of Dr. Rutter's book is *When Men in Power—Therapists, Doctors, Clergy, Teachers, and Others—Betray Women's Trust.* Even in the subtitle, prominently displayed on the cover of the book, the betrayer is clearly portrayed as the man in power—clergy, for example. And, for a few days, I believed him. But my belief in my own guilt was strong. It had not capitulated yet.

One afternoon at work, I glanced at the biographical information inside the back cover of Dr. Rutter's book. It stated that Dr. Rutter practiced in San Francisco. San Francisco? A mere two hours from where I was sitting at that moment? I called information, got his office number, and left a message. Dr. Rutter called me back later that afternoon. I explained that I had read his book and was interested in seeing him. Was that possible? Without hesitation, he answered in the affirmative. He was warm and welcoming from that first brief phone contact. This was before cellular phones and MapQuest and all the other convenient navigational tools, but Dr. Rutter explained the easiest way to drive to his office from my location at work. A week later, I arrived at his office for my appointment 30 minutes early. It was only a 90 minute drive. I looked at the beautiful old Victorian house on Sacramento Street in San Francisco, screwed up my courage, and walked in. Dr. Rutter's presence was calm and cerebral, and at the same time, warm and welcoming. I felt at ease with him immediately.

I met with Dr. Rutter each Monday afternoon at 5:30 for two months. He was compassionate and caring, and he was absolutely explicit about whose fault the relationship was. His book clearly documents case after case—many very similar to mine—in which the woman is first "groomed," then used sexually, sworn to secrecy, and later, blamed (even demonized) if and when the affair comes to light. He was commenting on other women's stories, and yet they were my story too. And, again, for a while, I could hear and believe. Doubts resurfaced. But each time I listened to someone in the position of power who did not victimize, but on the contrary, endeavored to build up, I came a little closer to the truth. John was guilty. I was not. No matter what the Salvation Army said.

During the course of my treatment with Dr. Evans, we consulted with other specialists, including a psychologist who facilitated a session of Eye Movement Desensitization Reprograming. This seemed to help in the area of psychiatrist-patient trust. The work she did was to reinforce the relationship of trust with Dr. Evans within my entire personality system so that a coordinated approach to healing could be found.

There were many times when I became discouraged and wanted nothing more than to just be through with the whole thing. When I periodically talked about quitting therapy again, Dr. Evans asked that we make a contract to discuss the plusses and minuses before any such decision was made. I remember him pointing out that when you are headed somewhere, the direct route—without unnecessary exits—is the fastest way to get there. Hearing this and then realizing that Dr. Evans had also invested a great deal in our recovery, I was able to stick with it.

And every once in a while, Dr. Evans would ask, "Bunny, do you think you will ever want to tell me the name of the organization?" By this time, I had a huge investment in the relationship with Dr. Evans. I wanted to be a "good" patient. But this I knew I could not do. We were doing deep work on the relationship with John. That had to be good enough—without naming the organization. *What did that matter, anyway?* I would think.

And over a period of time, imperceptibly, I inched toward the realization that I had not chosen the relationship with John, that I had not wanted it, even after I stopped my physical resistance to it, and I had dissociated in order to escape it. Because of my dissociation, my child alters bore much guilt for their compliance to John's demands. As our work progressed, Dr. Evans said that his DID patients did not differ markedly with unitary patients—everyone has repressed memories and regressed child parts. The main difference is the amnesiac barriers that the DID patient constructs to wall off traumatic information. This can make the disclosure and healing process longer, but healing is possible.

Healing. A word I did not think would ever apply to me. Sort of like that other word I was told did not apply to me: good.

I know now that people sometimes lie to protect their own reality.

My mother lied.

John lied.

Linc lied.

And the Salvation Army lied.

As each therapy session unfolded, the child parts brought forth their gut-wrenching sorrow. When we first began this therapy, there were no tears. They were sealed off with the emotions we could not acknowledge. The emotions and the tears were all the more potent because of the time spent buried in secret. We cried for the physical pain John caused. We cried for the loss of innocence. We cried for the loss of our idealism and sure knowledge of the goodness of God. We cried because there was no way to explain our story to anyone, save Dr. Evans. We wanted to explain to John's family and to Captain and Mrs. Irby. And we wanted Mother to know we were innocent. By the time we were able to approach these feelings, Mother was dead. It would have felt good to confront her—whether or not it ever changed her mind. The idea of at last sticking up for ourselves was compelling. It would never happen. Not with her at least. Belatedly, this book is our effort to stick up for ourselves to others—including the Salvation Army.

The child parts brought forth information about the sexual aspect of my relationship with my dad. I did not embrace this knowledge. When Dr. Evans confronted me with the information, I chose to believe that being in bed with my dad with no clothes on could have been innocent. Surely there was some other explanation. Entwined with the information about my dad was the story of John. Early on, Dr. Evans had maintained that sexual misconduct in the clergy-congregant relationship is tantamount to incest. Apparently, for the little girl alters, this was true. They could not separate the two.

As I struggled with the information the little girl parts disclosed about my father, I realized that they had been the ones who took the hit—were present—when John was sexual with us. I had dissociated and left them to deal with this, yet another, betrayal by a "father." As I was putting together my thoughts on this part of the book, something my mother said to me not long before she died finally made sense. During that conversation near the end of her life when she again reminded me that I had "ruined a good man," she looked at me with malevolence and said, "I could tell you something else about yourself. Something you don't know." I asked her what she was talking about. She seemed to think about it for a moment and then she said, "No, I'll go to my grave with that information." As she said this, there was again the malevolent smile that seemed to say, "Gotcha!"

Recently, when I allowed myself to revisit this conversation with Mother in the light of what she had always maintained about my guilt with John, something all of a sudden clicked into place in my mind. Perhaps it was a coming together of knowledge held in some other consciousness that I was finally willing to assimilate. In that instant, I accepted the fact that my dad had been sexual with me, and my mother knew it, and in her convoluted thinking, that proved that I held the power to ruin them both—my dad and John Hart. I had fought this realization about my dad, but all of a sudden, it was a relief to just let the truth be the truth. It was not something I had done, after all. I did not have to be afraid any longer.

When the child parts were in session with Dr. Evans, he allowed them to sit by his chair, next to his legs, and touch the hem of his trousers. This was reminiscent of the posture they remembered in the best moments of their experience with Daddy. In that posture near Dr. Evans, they were able to process the memories of their relationship with Daddy. And because Dr. Evans allowed them to be near his physical being in an appropriate manner, they were able to face the memories in the ultimately safe space afforded by this man who was steadfast in his genuine love for them.

There were times during session when words would not come. As work with the child alters began, I brought a blanket to session with me. For them, this transitional object facilitated their ability to engage difficult material and stay present in the moment. Still, there were times when all they could do was huddle under the blanket. This was particularly true when Dr. Evans was trying to help them understand they had not been "bad" when John was sexual with them. Over a long period of time, they had to explore over and over again what John had done. Even though encapsulated in an adult body, these child parts were exquisitely attuned to the pain occasioned by John's talking about God and love and then forcing on them his sexual acting out. This confusion—John's maintaining that "God wanted him to do it"—permanently damaged our concept of who and what God is. We—all parts of my personality system—still struggle with this.

When Dr. Evans and I began working with the alters, I asked him if the trauma would be gone when we were through. He said it would not be gone, but much of the emotional impact would be ameliorated—we would be able to remember without being devastated by the emotional content associated with the memories. Very gradually, this became true for us. The feelings are not gone, but we no longer feel victimized by them. We see ourselves as outside the drama of guilt and shame. The guilt and shame belong to John and Linc. And to the Salvation Army. Not to us.

CHAPTER 63

And Then Linc

"It is the 'forgotten sense of self' that leaves women unable to find the voice to say no when they are sexually invaded. This is precisely the wound that renders many women unable to defy a man who wishes to exploit the trust of the forbidden zone through sexual contact."

Sex in the Forbidden Zone **by Peter Rutter, M.D.**

WHEN I WAS TALKING TO DR. EVANS ABOUT JOHN, LINC'S NAME occasionally came up in passing, but I always affirmed to Dr. Evans that the relationship with Linc was different. Linc was nice to me. The relationship I had with Linc was special. I now know that I was so broken and without hope when I met Linc in Phoenix that I was in no condition to know what was good for me. When he asked, I mutely acquiesced.

Linc was wrong the first time he entered my apartment at one in the morning. He was wrong when he undressed me. He was wrong when he undressed and lay down beside me. He was wrong when he brought liquor to my apartment. He was wrong when he told me about his exploits in Las Vegas. He was a minister of the Gospel. What was he thinking? I did not question his motives. I easily capitulated to his needs and desires. Does that make what he did okay?

From the beginning, Dr. Evans maintained that Linc was wrong. It took longer for me to realize this. The whole realization came only during the process of writing this book. Some lies die hard.

When I began to talk about Linc in depth, I told Dr. Evans that I had known Linc when I was a teenager in Salinas. Linc flew to Salinas once and took all the youth group up flying with him—two or three at a time. Because I was already a group leader, Linc spent more time with me, and I was honored to be singled out. He was dashing and handsome, and I loved being noticed. And I told Dr. Evans about the excitement of working at camp with Linc and Jean—having other kids envy me my position close to them.

And so when I was told that I would be working for Linc in Phoenix when I left training, it seemed like this might be a bit of good news. At least I knew Linc and Jean. And my experience of them had been positive—I admired both of them.

In my work with Dr. Evans, I continued to think of the relationship with Linc as being a fair tradeoff—we each got something we needed. Since I had never explicitly said no to Linc, I did not feel like I could blame him. Dr. Evans felt that Linc was a practiced predator. And, of course, Dr. Rutter's book points out that the unequal power in the relationship makes it virtually impossible for the woman to say no.

Dr. Rutter says further, "On another level, a different danger looms: the threat of losing her connection with the man in whose presence she has come to feel some of the specialness she so deeply needs." I had lost virtually everything before I came to Phoenix—my calling, my vocation, my family, my friends—and so Linc was all I had. The specialness I felt with Linc was everything. It was the only thing.

When I realized that this book would not be complete without Linc's part of the story, I began to look again at what Dr. Evans and

I had talked about. I realized that my feelings toward Linc mirrored my feelings toward my father. I resisted until virtually the end of my 15-year therapy the knowledge that my father had been sexual with me. In much the same manner, I resisted the knowledge that Linc had not loved me at all, but had been a predator who used me to satisfy his own sexual fantasies.

He was not thinking of me—what would be good for me. He had been told about my relationship with John Hart—he knew that was why I was being sent to Phoenix. He was in a position to be a part of my healing. He could have actually mentored me and then gone to bat for me—recommending that I be readmitted to training because of the skills and gifts I demonstrated in my work with him. None of that happened. Overriding everything was Linc's lasciviousness and greed for the next sexual conquest. He thought of nothing except what he perceived as the satisfaction of his God-given right to victimize and use young women who worked with and for him. He did this in a skilled and practiced way—by the time sexual touching took place, he was totally in control.

As I worked through some of this with Dr. Evans, the story of Jan Black came to me over and over again. Because of Jan's story, I was finally able to see Linc in a more honest light. If it had been only me, I might have been able to maintain the idea that I was in some way at fault. Jan fell victim to the same spell Linc had cast on me and, conceivably, many others.

Somewhere in the midst of this work, Dr. Evans asked me, "Bunny, what do you think would happen if you told me the name of the organization? This organization betrayed you and it betrayed your friend Jan. I'm sure there were many others. What do you owe them? Why can't you just say who they are?" I had no answer. I knew I would never have an answer to that question. And I knew I would never tell.

In working through this relationship with Dr. Evans, it became apparent to me that the child part who had been most deeply invested with Linc was Kevin. Kevin was the one who always craved a lap to sit on. He was attracted to teachers and other positive male figures because he never had a dad—Kevin did not exist until after my father was gone. Kevin was the one who loved to sit on Linc's lap. He felt special there.

The sexual part of the relationship took place with Bunny Too. She was able to step in and absorb the sexual energy—thus sparing the child alters. For this reason, there was not the deep emotional scarring that took place with John. This is the part that came through to me while writing this part of the book. Because of Bunny Too, the child alters were spared the most emotionally devastating part in this relationship—the element of incest.

It was during the time spent processing the relationship with Linc that the code of silence was finally, absolutely, broken. Not on purpose. Accidentally. Unless you believe in Freudian slips.

CHAPTER 64

Naming Names at Last ...

"I was beginning to see how this kind of suppression mirrors the secrecy urged upon all sexual victims. Conversely, the breaking of silence, the defiance of the code of secrecy, has become a rallying cry ... Every speech made, every article and book written about the events and underlying dynamics of sexual exploitation render less viable the cloak of protection it has enjoyed"

Sex in the Forbidden Zone by Peter Rutter, M.D.

ON APRIL 4, 2005—13 YEARS AFTER ENTERING THERAPY WITH DR. Evans—the name of the Salvation Army was finally connected with my story. And I did not say it. I never broke the code of silence. The cloak of protection that my silence had provided for the Salvation Army was penetrated by Dr. Evans. He figured it out.

During our session on April 2, 2005, I was talking to Dr. Evans about the relationship with Linc. I mentioned the name of the camp I worked at in 1959 when Linc and Jean were the directors:

Redwood Glen Camp in the mountains outside Santa Cruz, California. I'm not sure if I had ever named the camp before, but that day I did. I never thought anything about it.

Two days later, I arrived for another session. Usually, when my sessions with Dr. Evans began, he remained silent until I initiated the conversation. When our session on April 4, 2005 began, Dr. Evans took the lead. He said, "I Googled Redwood Glen Camp when you left the other day and found out that it is a camp operated by the Salvation Army." He said nothing further. He sat and looked at me, not asking a question. Just waiting.

Panic. I sat there for an instant in a state of absolute panic. I remember looking at him with my mouth hanging open. He was gazing at me intently. When I regained the power of speech, I exploded. "What?" I said. "How dare you? How could you go behind my back and find out? What gave you the right? Who do you think you are?"

I accused him of betraying my trust. I called him the devil incarnate. I ranted and raged. I felt totally out of control. If he knew this, I was finished. And then I realized that I had revealed the truth of what he said by the vehemence of my reaction. Could I go back and deny it? All of a sudden, I was totally deflated. I had no idea what to do or say next. It had taken so much effort to keep this secret. Had I inadvertently said something that allowed him to find out? I was angry with myself; I was enraged at Dr. Evans. And I was afraid. It had been so ingrained in me to keep the secret, I had no idea what the breaking of the silence might mean. Was this, then, my ultimate sin?

I don't remember much about the remainder of that session. Dr. Evans did not return my anger with anger of his own. He allowed me to say what I needed to say without defending or justifying what he had done, and then he said, "You think it was wrong for me to look up information about the organization without your permission." Good old Dr. Evans, the master of understatement.

I agonized over the revelation. When I left that session, my emotions were in turmoil. I was still angry with Dr. Evans, and the child alters were extremely frightened. This was the final commandment—"tell no one." Would we be struck down with fire from above? As hours and then days passed, we slowly began to realize that nothing was going to happen to us. The organization that we had placed on the pedestal of omniscience and omnipresence was nothing but a bunch of really misguided people who had no power over us.

The revelation provided clarity on every issue we were struggling with. Now that this ultimate secret was out, we were able to finally talk openly and honestly. I had not realized how careful I had been to hide the identity of the organization—all the details that might have led to recognition had to be cloaked, and I remained ever-vigilant to maintain secrecy at any cost. It's interesting, also, that no alter ever came forward with this information. I believe Dr. Evans may have asked a time or two, but the answer was always, "You'll have to ask her about that."

Now I talked nonstop. I filled in all of the gaps—my family's history with the Salvation Army, the military model on which it was founded, my achievements as a Girl Guard and a Corps Cadet. What I thought would be a devastating blow to my therapy and would bring down judgment was exactly the opposite. I was now free to talk openly—naming names was immensely freeing. For the first time, I was not their hostage, their vassal, the keeper of their dirty secrets. I was telling the truth, the whole truth, *my* truth for the first time in my life! Dr. Evans knew everything about me—my dad, my mother, my brothers, John, Linc—and now he knew about the Salvation Army too. The story could now be complete.

I am still amazed at the sense of wonder I felt after getting over the first shock of Dr. Evans figuring it out. There was still work to be done. Naming the Salvation Army and disconnecting from the shame occasioned by the continued secrecy was an immense relief. It took three more years to finish the work of freeing myself from my own internal struggle with the massive emotional injuries occasioned by the organization I had been blindly loyal to for so long. But from the vantage point of full honesty and transparency in my work with Dr. Evans, I made progress in every area of my life.

I could almost feel a breath of fresh air blowing through everything I touched.

My marriage was in jeopardy because Doug and I had very different fiscal philosophies. Money management and debt had caused stress and friction throughout our marriage—we were always in a financial bind of one kind or another. In California it's very easy to run up large debts on plastic, and there were banks that loaned money to Doug on nothing more than a handshake. I was never privy to these deals—until the note came due. Finally, I realized that I could do something about that. I had the power to act in my own behalf. A lot of good things had happened in our marriage—first and foremost, our two sons—and other good things too. But at 66 years old—after 43 years of marriage—I decided I did not want to bail us out of debt again. So I filed for a divorce and moved in with a friend until the divorce was final. When I had my share of the proceeds from the sale of our home, I went on line and found a little cottage on the Oregon Coast that I could buy outright—allowing me to consider retirement.

I visited the Social Security office in Salinas and filed for my retirement benefits. I applied for Medicare. And then I quit my job. I owned my life. For the first time ever, I was acting purely on what was good for me. And I no longer looked over my shoulder expecting someone in a Salvation Army uniform to reach out and grab me. That may sound extreme, but once the secret was finally out, I realized that was what I had been doing—expecting some sort of reprisals from the group that expelled me so brutally. I still thought of them as violent and capable of harming me. When the secret was finally out, I realized that they held no power over me.

Being free of the pact of silence imposed on me by the Salvation Army made me free in every other way. Free to finally define myself in the light of who I had been and what I had chosen to do with my life—not in the light of their opinion that I was not "good." Free to finally be me, without the dark secrets I was containing within myself to protect an entity that did not earn or ever deserve my respect, let alone any type of allegiance.

In some therapies for Dissociative Identity Disorder, the goal is integration—the relaxing of all internal barriers and the dissolving of all of the personalities into the host personality. This was never my goal. Once free of the legacy of blame, guilt, shame, and self-serving secrecy left with me by the Salvation Army, I embraced all the parts of myself. During that last three years of our work together, there were several more child alters who presented themselves—Star, Rose, Phillip, and a number of infants Phillip had protected. At last, all of them were free also.

Because of Dr. Evans' inquiring mind and his attention to every detail, he diagnosed us so that we could finally work on getting beyond our trauma, and then he figured out the name of the organization in which much of our trauma had taken place. He was exactly the right person for the work we needed to do. In him, we finally had a good parent.

We still see Dr. Evans every four to six months when we visit in Salinas. Meanwhile, we—all parts of our personality system—are happy and content with each other.

My therapy with Dr. Evans ended on October 31, 2008.

My abundant life in Depoe Bay, Oregon began on November 2, 2008.

I contacted the Salvation Army on April 7, 2010.

PART IV

SEEKING JUSTICE

CHAPTER 65

Remember Me?

"Then shall he answer them, saying, 'Verily, I say unto you, inasmuch as ye did it not unto one of these least, ye did it not unto me.' And these shall go away into eternal punishment; but the righteous into eternal life."

Spoken by Jesus in the
Gospel of Matthew 25:45-46 ASV

THE ABOVE SCRIPTURE IS TAKEN FROM A PARABLE SPOKEN BY JESUS shortly before his crucifixion. In the parable, Jesus talks about the simple things that matter: a sip of water for the thirsty, a morsel of bread for the hungry, a visit to the sick or imprisoned. I love teaching this parable to children because *anyone* can do the things Jesus says are most important. You don't have to be rich or big or educated to do any of the things that Jesus calls upon his followers to do—the things he says are the *most* important. Crystal cathedrals are not the most important. Bequeathing millions to charities is not the most important. Although, I'm sure there's a place for those things too. But Jesus says the simple loving, caring, empathic things we do individually for our fellow human beings are the most important of all.

The Salvation Army did none of those things for me. The following pages contain letters written recently by myself and the responses I received from the Salvation Army. You will note that there is reference in several places about "this type of thing would not happen now." I hope that is true. For myself, Jan, and all the others I believe were routinely victimized by the Salvation Army, I hope that is true.

However, the way I have been treated by the Salvation Army *now* is indicative of the mistreatment and disrespect I received 48 years ago. In my individual, firsthand point of view, nothing has changed. And that brings us back to the above scripture. According to Jesus, those who "did it not unto one of these least ... did it not unto me. And these shall go away into eternal punishment." Wow. It seems that Jesus takes these things seriously. Alan Alda once said that we save the most important things we have to say until the last so people will remember them. If that is true, Jesus wanted us to remember just how important individual interactions with the needy, the sick, the disenfranchised and the vulnerable are.

William Booth, founder of the Salvation Army, left the Methodist Church because he felt the marginalized were underserved by the mainline religions of his time. I wonder what he would think of the organization that did not help, but cast out and scorned a woman harmed by the church he founded. In my case, the Salvation Army had become what William Booth despised most in the religious "pharisees" of his day.

And now the letters.

When I wrote the first letter, I had been out of therapy for about 18 months. I lived in a beautiful little cottage community outside Depoe Bay, Oregon—where I still live. I was thinking about the beauty in my life and all I had to be thankful for. And then in an instant of clarity, I realized there was something left undone. I wanted—and needed—to contact the Salvation Army. Until that was done, I had not completed the telling of my truth. The ones who needed to hear that truth were the ones who refused to hear it 48 years ago. Would they hear it now?

I wrote the first letter.

Bunny (Umbaugh) Stevens   Via USPS - April 7, 2010
3700 N. Highway 101 - #29
Depoe Bay, OR 97341 - (541) 764-0803

Commissioner Philip Swyers, Territory Commander
The Salvation Army
180 East Ocean Blvd.
Long Beach, CA 90802

Dear Commissioner Swyers:

    As the sexual abuse scandal in the Catholic Church continues to unfold, I can no longer resist the urge to say, "It wasn't only the Catholic Church!" I know that it existed in the Salvation Army. I was a victim of clergy sexual abuse by Captain John Hart, Corps Office in Salinas, California and then by Major Lincoln Upton, Divisional Youth Secretary in Phoenix, Arizona. John Hart raped me and then told me, "God wanted him to do it." He coerced me into a on-going sexual relationship that lasted the better part of a year. I was suicidal. I spent whole nights on my knees beside my bed, asking God to make him stop. He did not stop. He rented an apartment where he satisfied his basest sexual urges on me and told me he would harm my family if I ever told about our relationship. When I confessed the sexual relationship at the Salvation Army School for Officer Training in the fall of 1963 because I was pregnant with John Hart's child, I was summarily dismissed from training and sent to Phoenix to be secretary to Major Lincoln Upton. Major Upton picked me up at the Phoenix airport, stopped at a motel nearby and sexually assaulted me. Again I was raped. Again by a Salvation Army Officer. I was numb and in shock. I took it. I knew there was no help within the organization. Major Upton continued to avail himself of sexual satisfaction with me—bringing liquor with him when he came to my apartment in Phoenix. This relationship lasted until he was transferred to the Northwest Division about three months after I arrived in Phoenix.

    My whole life was changed by these men. It was not only sexual abuse. It was spiritual abuse as well. I am now 68 years old. I have lead a productive life in spite of what happened to me at the hands of an organization I trusted with my heart and my soul. My entire adult life has been a struggle to forget. At age 49 I finally connected with an empathic psychiatrist. Eighteen months ago, after 15 years of therapy, I have moved on. But the purpose of this letter is to ask that the organization that harbored these men "own up" to their behavior with me. I know there were others. One of my session mates ("Proclaimers of the Faith") bore Lincoln Upton's child. I cannot speak for the others. I know Colonel Parkins was the one who told me, "The Salvation Army is for good people. That term does not apply to you." I heard later that he was a sexual predator as well. How far and wide did this go? My therapy cost me more than $280,000. Laying aside the legal aspects of the statute of limitations, I am asking that you do what your predecessors did not do: own up to the tragedy precipitated on an innocent victim and reimburse me for some part of this expense. I was an idealistic young person. I was answering a call from God to be a Salvation Army officer. I was raped by my Corps Officer and then raped again by a Divisional Youth Secretary. If there are still records of the training session of 1963-1965, there will be records of the charges I brought against John Hart. Is that proof enough? Can the organization I trusted and was then cast out of because of the sins of others do the right thing? One would hope so. What would Jesus have you do?

    I have written a book about my experiences in the Salvation Army. Peter Rutter, M.D., author of Sex in the Forbidden Zone which deals with the topic of sexual abuse by men in positions of power, has read sample chapters of my book. He found it compelling, psychologically layered storytelling of the most dramatic kind of betrayal. I am attaching the first page of my book. I have not yet found a publisher. I hope the book may be published. It would prove therapeutic in the way that truth-telling always does. Is there anyone there, in the Western Headquarters of the Salvation Army, who is willing to listen to my story? That would finally, in some way, be an answer to my prayers.

    Yours very truly,

    Bunny Stevens

Enclosure: Page 1-2 of Unholy Union

Cc: Commissioner Israel L. Gaither, National Commander, The Salvation Army

Dear Commissioner Swyers:

As the sexual abuse scandal in the Catholic Church continues to unfold, I can no longer resist the urge to say, "It wasn't only the Catholic Church!" I know that it existed in the Salvation Army. I was a victim of clergy sexual abuse by Captain John Hart, Corps Office in Salinas, California and then by Major Lincoln Upton, Divisional Youth Secretary in Phoenix, Arizona. John Hart raped me and then told me, "God wanted him to do it." He coerced me into a on-going sexual relationship that lasted the better part of a year. I was suicidal. I spent whole nights of my knees beside my bed, asking God to make him stop. He did not stop. He rented an apartment where he satisfied his basest sexual urges on me and told me he would harm my family if I ever told about our relationship. When I confessed the sexual relationship at the Salvation Army School for Officer Training in the fall of 1963 because I was pregnant with John Hart's child, I was summarily dismissed from training and sent to Phoenix to be secretary to Major Lincoln Upton. Major Upton picked me up at the Phoenix airport, stopped at a motel nearby and sexually assaulted me. Again I was raped. Again by a Salvation Army Officer. I was numb and in shock. I took it. I knew there was no help within the organization. Major Upton continued to avail himself of sexual satisfaction with me—bringing liquor with him when he came to my apartment in Phoenix. This relationship lasted until he was transferred to the Northwest Division about three months after I arrived in Phoenix.

My whole life was changed by these men. It was not only sexual abuse. It was <u>spiritual</u> abuse as well. I am now 68 years old. I have lead a productive life in spite of what happened to me at the hands of an organization I trusted with my heart and my soul. My entire adult life has been a struggle to forget. At age 49 I finally connected with an empathic psychiatrist. Eighteen months ago, after 15 years of therapy, I have moved on. But the purpose of this letter is to ask that the organization that harbored these men "own up" to their behavior with me. I know there were others. One of my session mates ("Proclaimers of the Faith") bore Lincoln Upton's child. I cannot speak for the others. I know Colonel Parkins was the one who told me, "The Salvation Army is for good people. That term does not apply to you." I heard later that he was a sexual predator as well. How far and wide did this go? My therapy cost me more than $280,000. Laying aside the legal aspects of the statute of limitations, I am asking that you do what your predecessors did not do: own up to the tragedy precipitated on an innocent victim and reimburse me for some part of this expense. I was an idealistic young person. I was answering a call from God to be a Salvation Army officer. I was raped by my Corps Officer and then raped again by a Divisional Youth Secretary. If there are still records of the training session of 1963-1965, there will be records of the charges I brought against John Hart. Is that proof enough? Can the organization I trusted and was then cast out of because of the sins of others do the right thing? One would hope so. What would Jesus have you do?

I have written a book about my experiences in the Salvation Army. Peter Rutter, M.D., author of <u>Sex in the Forbidden Zone</u> which deals with the topic of sexual abuse by men in positions of power, has read sample chapters of my book. He found it compelling, psychologically layered storytelling of the most dramatic kind of betrayal. I am attaching the first page of my book. I have not yet found a publisher. I hope the book may be published. It would prove therapeutic in the way that truth-telling always does. Is there anyone there, in the Western Headquarters of the Salvation Army, who is willing to listen to my story? That would finally, in some way, be an answer to my prayers.

Yours very truly,

Bunny Stevens

Enclosure: Page 1-2 of <u>Unholy Union</u>

Cc: Commissioner Israel L. Gaither, National Commander, The Salvation Army

When I showed Dr. Evans the first letter, he asked, "What do you expect will happen?" I had to think about that. When I asked him what the Salvation Army might gain from actually acknowledging me, he said simply, "Integrity?"

When I received no response to the first letter, I wrote the second and third letters. You will see copies of those letters on the following two pages.

Bunny (Umbaugh) Stevens
3700 N. Highway 101 - #29
Depoe Bay, OR 97341
(541) 764-0803

May 25, 2010

Commissioner Philip Swyers, Territory Commander
The Salvation Army
180 East Ocean Blvd.
Long Beach, CA 90802

Dear Commissioner Swers:

On April 7, 2010, I mailed a letter to you. I am attaching a copy of that letter. I am again writing to you because I have not received a reply. I am sure this is merely an oversight on your part. As you will recall, the subject of my letter was sexual abuse suffered by me at the hands of two Salvation Army Officers—each in a position of power over me within the ranks of the Salvation Army. I had grown up in the Army and had been taught all my life that, "Your Corps Officer is over you in the Lord and must be obeyed." I believe this teaching was common at that time. Because of this very power differential, I was betrayed by those I sought to "obey in the Lord."

As the Boy Scouts of America and the Catholic Church worldwide are being forced to examine their practices and policies that allowed this type of sexual misconduct by leaders within their organizations, I am requesting that the wrongs done to me be addressed by your organization.

I am requesting the courtesy of a reply. When my psychiatrist read my first letter to you, he asked me, "What do you expect will happen?" I thought for a moment and then answered, "I'm not sure. I know I needed to write the letter. But what would they gain by actually acknowledging me?" He looked at me and replied, "Integrity." Is there yet integrity? Will you reply? Will you address the issue of suffering, time and money expended? I hope so. As I asked at the end of my previous letter, "Is there anyone there, in the Western Headquarters of the Salvation Army, who is willing to listen to my story? That would finally, in some way, be an answer to my prayers." I am waiting.

Yours very truly,

Bunny Stevens

Enclosures: Copy of previous letter
              Pages 1-2 of <u>Unholy Union</u>

Cc: Commissioner Israel L. Gaither, National Commander, The Salvation Army

Dear Commissioner Swers:

On April 7, 2010, I mailed a letter to you. I am attaching a copy of that letter. I am again writing to you because I have not received a reply. I am sure this is merely an oversight on your part. As you will recall, the subject of my letter was sexual abuse suffered by me at the hands of two Salvation Army Officers--each in a position of power over me within the ranks of the Salvation Army. I had grown up in the Army and had been taught all my life that, "Your Corps Officer is over you in the Lord and must be obeyed." I believe this teaching was common at that time. Because of this very power differential, I was betrayed by those I sought to "obey in the Lord."

As the Boy Scouts of America and the Catholic Church worldwide are being forced to examine their practices and policies that allowed this type of sexual misconduct by leaders within their organizations, I am requesting that the wrongs done to me be addressed by your organization.

I am requesting the courtesy of a reply. When my psychiatrist read my first letter to you, he asked me, "What do you expect will happen?" I thought for a moment and then answered, "I'm not sure. I Know I needed to write the letter. But what would they gain by actually acknowledging me?" He looked at me and replied, "Integrity." Is there yet integrity? Will you reply? Will you address the issue of suffering, time and money expended? I hope so. As I asked at the end of my previous letter, "Is there anyone there, in the Western Headquarters of the Salvation Army, who is willing to listen to my story? That would finally, in some way, be an answer to my prayers." I am waiting.

Yours very truly,

Bunny Stevens

Enclosures: Copy of previous letter

Pages 1-2 of <u>Unholy Union</u>

Cc: Commissioner Israel L. Gaither, National Commander, The Salvation Army

Bunny (Umbaugh) Stevens
3700 N. Highway 101 - #29
Depoe Bay, OR 97341
(541) 764-0803

July 9, 2010

Commissioner Philip Swyers, Territory Commander
The Salvation Army
180 East Ocean Blvd.
Long Beach, CA 90802

Dear Commissioner Swyers:

  This is the third time I have written to you in the hope of obtaining some consideration from the Salvation Army for crimes perpetrated on me when I was a teenager/young adult. In my previous correspondence, I included the first chapter of the book I have written which documents my treatment by the Salvation Army.

  To further illustrate the type of situation which I endured at the hands of two Salvation Army officers, I am enclosing an article from the Editorial Page of the Oregonian. It talks about the position the woman is always in when sexual crimes are committed by men in power. Please note that I have underlined the part that clearly reflects the position I was in with John Hart and Lincoln Upton in the Salvation Army. The crimes they committed are further exacerbated by your silence in the face of my cry for justice. I am a victim of clergy sexual abuse. Is it godly to ignore me?

  I am again asking for the possibility of healing through face-to-face contact with the organization that cast me out years ago. I know that I reported the assaults by John Hart to the Women's Chief Side Office and the Principal at the Salvation Army Training School in San Francisco when I realized I was pregnant with John Hart's child. The record should speak for itself still.

          Yours very truly,

          Bunny Stevens

Enclosure: "The inconvenient truth behind the Gore story"

cc: Commissioner Israel L. Gaither, National Commander, The Salvation Army

Dear Commissioner Swyers:

This is the third time I have written to you in the hope of obtaining some consideration from the Salvation Army for crimes perpetrated on me when I was a teenager/young adult. In my previous correspondence, I Included the first chapter of the book I have written which documents my treatment by the Salvation Army.

To farther illustrate the type of situation which I endured at the hands of <u>two</u> Salvation Army officers, I am enclosing an article from the Editorial Page of the Oregonian. It talks about the position the woman is always in when sexual crimes are committed by men in power. Please note that I have underlined the part that clearly reflects the position I was in with John Hart and Lincoln Upton in the Salvation Army. The crimes they committed are further exacerbated by your silence in the face of my cry for justice. I am a victim of clergy sexual abuse. Is it godly to ignore me?

I am again asking for the possibility of healing through face-to-face contact with the organization that cast me out years ago. I know that I reported the assaults by John Hart to the Women's Chief Side Office and the Principal at the Salvation Army Training School in San Francisco when I realized I was pregnant with John Hart's child. The record should speak for itself still.

Yours very truly,

Bunny Stevens

Enclosure: "The inconvenient truth behind the Gore story"

cc: Commissioner Israel L. Gaither, National Commander, The Salvation Army

In a letter dated July 6, 2010, I received a response from the Salvation Army. A copy of that letter follows this page also.

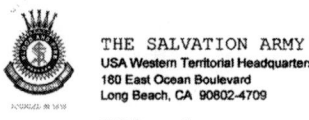

THE SALVATION ARMY
USA Western Territorial Headquarters
180 East Ocean Boulevard
Long Beach, CA 90802-4709

THQ Personnel

WILLIAM BOOTH
Founder

SHAW CLIFTON
General

JAMES M. KNAGGS
Territorial Commander

July 6, 2010

Ms. Bunny (Umbaugh) Stevens
3700 N. Highway 101 - #29
Depoe Bay, OR 97341

Dear Ms. Stevens:

I have been asked to reply to your letters to Commissioner Philip Swyers, who recently retired, and to follow up with you about the sexual abuse and other suffering you describe in your letters.

First, let me apologize for not responding sooner. We do take your letters seriously. I want to let you know that we have been actively searching our records for information about the persons and events you discuss. We also would like to speak with you to get a fuller understanding of the matters you have described to us, and I invite you to call me so that we can set up a convenient time to discuss this, my direct office phone number is 562-491-8430.

Sincerely,

Charleen Bradley

Charleen Bradley, Major
Assistant Secretary for Personnel for Officer Development

CB:HY:mtp

Fax: (562) 491-8630
Phone: (562) 491-8430

EMail: charleen.bradley@usw.salvationarmy.org

Dear Ms. Stevens:

I have been asked to reply to your letters to Commissioner Philip Swyers, who recently retired, and to follow up with you about the sexual abuse and other suffering you describe in your letters.

First, let me apologize for not responding sooner. We do take your letters seriously. I want to let you know that we have been actively searching our records for information about the persons and events you discuss. We also would like to speak with you to get a fuller understanding of the matters you have described to us, and I invite you to call me so that we can set up a convenient time to discuss this, my direct office phone number is 562-491-8430.

Sincerely,

Charleen Bradley, Major

Assistant Secretary for Personnel for Officer Development

CB:HY:mtp

Subsequent to that letter written by Ms. Bradley of the Salvation Army, we had a lengthy phone conversation. She asked questions regarding the two men I named and asked further questions to place a historical framework around the events I described. I answered every question openly and honestly. I did not hedge or dissemble. I gave names of all involved and was able to provide important dates.

In the beginning of this phone conversation, Ms. Bradley stated that she was able to find files "on each of the men," but there was no documentation of any of the events I described. How very convenient. She further stated that she had no personal knowledge of either man and was having a hard time finding anyone who did—because of the many years that had elapsed.

Of course, one of the ironies of this whole process has been that it took so many years to bring this information forward *because* the Salvation Army told me to "go away tell no one" and I did just that. My obedience to their command protected them until I was finally able to advocate for myself—going outside their command for silence—first with Dr. Evans and then by contacting the Salvation Army itself.

When a month had elapsed with no further word after the phone conversation, I wrote to Ms. Bradley on September 2, 2010. A copy of that letter follows.

Bunny (Umbaugh) Stevens
3700 N. Highway 101 - #29
Depoe Bay, OR 97341
(541) 764-0803
September 2, 2010

Charleen Bradley, Major
Assistant Secretary for Personnel
The Salvation Army
180 East Ocean Boulevard
Long Beach, CA 90802-4709

Dear Major Bradley:

During our extensive phone conversation on August 2, 2010, I detailed for you the circumstances surrounding my sexual victimization by two Salvation Army officers. I answered all your questions candidly, truthfully and with as much historic substance as possible.

I appreciated the time you spent listening. As stated then and affirmed again as of this writing, this has been very difficult for me. As I requested then, I am asking that the Salvation Army reimburse me for actual out-of-pocket expenses incurred by me for physical and psychological treatment because of damage done by Captain John Hart and Major Lincoln Upton, both of whom were my superior officers when I was pursuing my calling to serve God as a Salvation Army officer. The amount stated was $300,000. This is a very modest sum when compared to judgments against other organizations for like offences. (I am enclosing two more articles which refer to such settlements.) There are so many things that cannot be reimbursed—my idealism, my virginity, my spiritual calling, my relationship with my own mother. I am not pursuing revenge. I am asking for fairness and integrity—two things that were sorely lacking when the Salvation Army's total concern was protecting its own name rather than helping the innocent victim of heinous crimes perpetrated by ordained ministers *in God's name.*

At the end of our conversation, you said to me, "You will hear from us. I promise you that." Since it has now been a month, I am following-up. I trusted your word. I hope I was not wrong to do so. Please let me hear from you.

Yours very truly,

Bunny Stevens

cc: Commissioner Israel L. Gather, National Commander, The Salvation Army

Dear Major Bradley:

During our extensive phone conversation on August 2, 2010, I detailed for you the circumstances surrounding my sexual victimization by two Salvation Army officers. I answered all your questions candidly, truthfully and with as such historic substance as possible.

I appreciated the time you spent listening. As stated then and affirmed again as of this writing, this has been very difficult for me. As I requested then, I am asking that the Salvation Army reimburse me for actual out-of-pocket expenses incurred by me for physical and psychological treatment because of damage done by Captain John Hart and Major Lincoln Upton, both of whom were my superior officers when I was pursuing my calling to serve God as a Salvation Army officer. The amount stated was $300,000. This is a very modest sum when compared to judgments against other organizations for like offences. (I am enclosing two more articles which refer to such settlements.) There are so many things that cannot be reimbursed—my idealism, my virginity, my spiritual calling, my relationship with my own mother. I am not pursuing revenge. I am asking for fairness and integrity—two things that were sorely lacking when the Salvation Army's total concern was protecting its own name rather than helping the innocent victim of heinous crimes perpetrated by ordained ministers *in God's name*.

At the end of our conversation, you said to me, "You will hear from us. I promise you that." Since it has now been a month, I am following-up. I trusted your word. I hope I was not wrong to do so. Please let me hear from you.

Yours very truly,

Bunny Stevens

cc: Commissioner Israel L. Gather, National Commander, The Salvation Army

And then, in a letter dated September 15, 2010, I received my response from Ms. Bradley, officially representing the Salvation Army of 2010. In that letter—which follows this page—Ms. Bradley cites lack of "corroboration information."

I remember taking that letter out of my mailbox, reading it in the rain on my way back to my cottage, and feeling bereft. I was being dismissed again. I once again felt the sting of repudiation—in spite of Ms. Bradley's lip service, "Please understand that I am not saying that the things you described did not happen …"

For a few weeks I tried to put the whole thing behind me. I had done what I could, hadn't I? At least this time I had told the details they were unwilling to hear in 1963: I was raped by one of their officers. When I reported this event, I was summarily dismissed, cast out. I was subsequently raped by another of their officers.

I tried to convince myself this had to be enough.

THE SALVATION ARMY
USA Western Territorial Headquarters
180 East Ocean Boulevard
Long Beach, CA 90802-4709

THQ Personnel

WILLIAM BOOTH
Founder

SHAW CLIFTON
General

JAMES M. KNAGGS
Territorial Commander

PRIVATE and CONFIDENTIAL

September 15, 2010

Bunny Umbaugh Stevens
3700 N. Highway 101 #29
Depoe Bay, OR 97341

Dear Bunny,

I apologize for not reconnecting with you earlier, but I have been doing my best trying to find information concerning the various events you described in your letters and in our recent telephone conversation. As you can appreciate, this has not been an easy task given the passage of time. Many of the people who might have been able to shed light on the matter are no longer alive, including both John Hart and Lincoln Upton, and others have either lost touch with the Army or did not have any memory of the things you described. Also, I was not able to find any records that mention either directly or indirectly any of the incidents that you described. I was able to piece together enough information to know of your relationship to the Army, your time at Officer Training College, and your connection to the people and places you described. However, as I mentioned, I was not able to uncover any information about incidents of sexual abuse you discussed and, without that type of corroboration information, I am afraid that I am not in a position to recommend to the Army making the kind of payment you are seeking.

Please understand that I am not saying that the things you described did not happen or that you did not suffer. It is simply that, under the circumstances, I do not believe that I can recommend to leadership that we pay the sums you are seeking. Having said that, I remain hopeful that reconciliation and closure might be possible in some other way, and we certainly welcome any desire on your part to explore that with the Army. Please also know that you are welcome to contact me to share with me anything else that you might wish to discuss about this or any other subject.

Sincerely,

Charleen A Bradley

Charleen Bradley, Major
Assistant Secretary for Personnel for Officer Development

CB:fsh

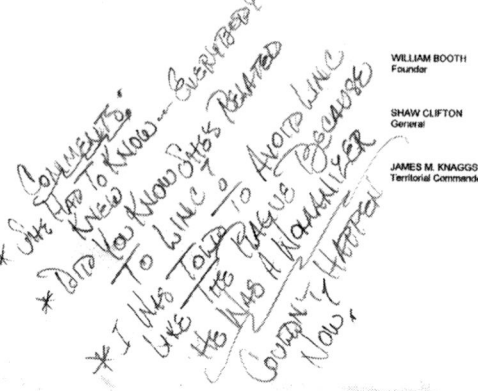

Fax: (562) 491-8460
Phone: (562) 491-8430

EMail: charleen.bradley@usw.salvationarmy.org

Dear Bunny,

I apologize for not reconnecting with you earlier, but I have been doing my best trying to find information concerning the various events you described in your letters and in our recent telephone conversation. As you can appreciate, this has not been an easy task given the passage of time. Many of the people who might have been able to shed light on the matter are no longer alive, including both John Hart and Lincoln Upton, and others have either lost touch with the Army or did not have any memory of the things you described. Also, I was not able to find any records that mention either directly or indirectly any of the incidents that you described. I was able to piece together enough information to know of your relationship to the Army, your time at Officer Training College, and your connection to the people and places you described. However, as I mentioned, I was not able to uncover any information about incidents of sexual abuse you discussed, and, without that type of corroboration information, I am afraid that I am not in a position to recommend to the Army making the kind of payment you are seeking.

Please understand that I am not saying that the things you described did not happen or that you did not suffer. It is simply that, under the circumstances, I do not believe that I can recommend to leadership that we pay the sums you are seeking. Having said that, I remain hopeful that reconciliation and closure might be possible in some other way, and we certainly welcome any desire on your part to explore that with the Army. Please also know that you are welcome to contact me to share with me anything else that you might wish to discuss about this or any other subject.

Sincerely,

Charleen Bradley, Major

Assistant Secretary for Personnel for Officer Development

CB:fsh

And then one Sunday in worship, the text was from the Gospel of Luke. It talked about a woman who sought justice from a judge who just did not care about doing what was right. He sent her away over and over. She kept coming back. Finally, he gave her justice just to get rid of her. I sat in church that morning thinking, "I'm that woman."

I knew what I could do. I could contact someone who knew. Someone who was one of the best friends I ever had. The young man who offered to marry me in spite of the fact I was carrying my corps officer's child.

I had no idea if Rich was still alive. I knew that 10 years previously he had still been an officer in the Salvation Army. The friends who introduced us had remained in contact with Rich but had lost touch after he retired. Was he still alive? And how could I find him? Would he remember? And, most important, would he be willing to tell what he remembered?

I wrote to Ms. Bradley on October 18, 2010. A copy of that letter follows this page.

Bunny (Umbaugh) Stevens
3700 N. Highway 101 - #29
Depoe Bay, OR 97341
(541) 764-0803
October 18, 2010

Charlene Bradley, Major
Assistant Secretary for Personnel
The Salvation Army
180 East Ocean Boulevard
Long Beach, CA 90802-4709

Dear Major Bradley:

    This will confirm my receipt of your letter dated September 15, 2010. In that letter you state that--because of no corroborating evidence--"...I do not believe that I can recommend to leadership that we pay the sums you are seeking." Of course, Major Bradley, the reason that there is no corroborating evidence to the factual occurrences of clergy sexual abuse I enumerated to you is that the Salvation Army has purged such information from the files you possess on each of the men named. This seems inordinately convenient and self-serving for the Salvation Army.

    You further state that, "I remain hopeful that reconciliation and closure might be possible in some other way." I am currently in communication with the Oprah Wilfrey organization regarding publication of my book <u>Unholy Union</u>. As you know, this book is a memoir of the abuse perpetrated on me by ordained officers of the Salvation Army. Publication would certainly be a form of "closure." I am also conducting a search of my own for persons who can provide corroboration for the facts of my story.

    I must say that when I first received your letter of September 15th, I was very discouraged and felt again the sting of repudiation by the organization which housed and harbored the perpetrators of which I spoke. Then I rediscovered the parable Jesus used in the first eight verses of the 18th chapter of the Gospel of Luke to recommend persistence in a just cause. Jesus talks about a widow who seeks justice. The problem is that the person from whom she seeks justice is himself unjust--caring not for God or man. He will not be an instrument of justice because he just does not care. She eventually receives justice from him, not because he cares, but because she just won't give up and go away. I will not go away either. According to Jesus, some things are worth fighting for. Justice is one of those things.

                      Yours very truly,

                        Bunny Stevens

Cc: Commissioner Israel L. Gaither, National Commander, the Salvation Army

Dear Major Bradley:

This will confirm my receipt of your letter dated September 15, 2010. In that letter you state that—because of no corroborating evidence—". . .I do not believe that I can recommend to leadership that we pay the sums you are seeking." Of course, Major Bradley, the reason that there is no corroborating evidence to the factual occurrences of clergy sexual abuse I enumerated to you is that the Salvation Army has purged such information from the files you possess on each of the men named. This seems inordinately convenient and self-serving for the Salvation Army.

You further state that, "I remain hopeful that reconciliation and closure might be possible in some other way." I am currently in communication with the Oprah Wilfrey organization regarding publication of my book <u>Unholy Union</u>. As you know, this book is a memoir of the abuse perpetrated on me by ordained officers of the Salvation Army. Publication would certainly be a form of "closure." I am also conducting a search of my own for persons who can provide corroboration for the facts of my story.

I must say that when I first received your letter of September 15th, I was very discouraged and felt again the sting of repudiation by the organization which housed and harbored the perpetrators of which I spoke. Then I rediscovered the parable Jesus used in the first eight verses of the 18th chapter of the Gospel of Luke to recommend persistence in a just cause. Jesus talks about a widow who seeks justice. The problem is that the person from whom she seeks justice is himself unjust--caring not for God or man. He will not be an instrument of justice because he just does not care. She eventually receives justice from him, not because he cares, but because she just won't give up and go away. I will not go away either. According to Jesus, some things are worth fighting for. Justice is one of those things.

Yours very truly,

Bunny Stevens

Cc: Commissioner Israel L. Gaither, National Commander, the Salvation Army

In my newfound zeal to educate the Salvation Army about the abuses visited on me, I wrote to the Salvation Army's own International Social Justice Commission and to the Salvation Army's international commander, General Shaw Clifton.

Copies of those two letters and General Clifton's response follow this page.

Bunny (Umbaugh) Stevens
3700 N. Highway 101 - #29
Depoe Bay, OR 97341
(541) 764-0803
October 18, 2010

The Salvation Army
International Social Justice Commission
221 East 52nd Street
New York, NY 10022

Dear Sirs/Madams:

    I am looking for social justice. I am looking for social justice from the Salvation Army. I was the victim of clergy sexual abuse perpetrated on me by two ordained officers of the Salvation Army. I am enclosing copies of all correspondence I have sent to the Salvation Army's Western Territory Headquarters in my quest for justice.

    I have been rebuffed because the Salvation Army could find no corroborating information--occasioned, conveniently for the Salvation Army, by the fact that the files on the two officers involved still exist but all reference to the charges brought by me and others have been purged.

    Is there justice? For me? For someone so heinously assaulted, repudiated and discarded by the very organization with an "International Social Justice Commission" on which you serve? The incidents I enumerated are historical facts. Please read Luck 18:1-8 which is about a woman seeking justice. Again I ask, is there justice?

                  Yours very truly,

                  Bunny Stevens

enclosures

Dear Sirs/Madams:

I am looking for social justice. I am looking for social justice from the Salvation Army. I was the victim of clergy sexual abuse perpetrated on me by two ordained officers of the Salvation Army. I am enclosing copies of all correspondence I have sent to the Salvation Army's Western Territory Headquarters in my quest for justice.

I have been rebuffed because the Salvation Army could find no corroborating information—occasioned, conveniently for the Salvation Army, by the fact that the files on the two officers involved still exist but all reference to the charges brought by me and others have been purged.

Is there justice? For me? For someone so heinously assaulted, repudiated and discarded by the very organization with an "International Social Justice Commission" on which you serve? The incidents I enumerated are historical facts. Please read Luck 18:1-8 which is about a woman seeking justice. Again I ask, is there justice?

Yours very truly,

Bunny Stevens

enclosures

Bunny (Umbaugh) Stevens
3700 N. Highway 101 - #29
Depoe Bay, OR 97341
(541) 764-0803
October 18, 2010

General Shaw Clifton
Commissioner Helen Clifton
The Salvation Army
International Headquarters
101 Queen Victoria Street
London, England

Re: <u>Unholy Union</u> - A Memoir of Sexual Abuse

Dear General Clifton and Commissioner Clifton:

  I am enclosing herewith all correspondence I have sent to the Salvation Army's Western Territory Headquarters in the United States of America. As you will see, this correspondence relates to my experience of clergy sexual abuse perpetrated on me by two ordained officers of the Salvation Army. I have been rebuffed by the Western Territory Headquarters because they could find no "corroborating evidence" in their files. I was told that files still exist on both men but they have been purged of all information pertaining to the charges of sexual abuse which were duly filed with the Women's Chief Side Officer at the School for Officers Training when I found that I was pregnant with my Corp Officer's child.

  As you will note from my letter of this date to Charlene Bradley, Major, I am likening my quest for justice to the parable of Jesus recorded in the first eight verses of the 18th chapter of the Gospel of Luke. The widow in the parable persists in her search for justice even though the unjust judge—who does not care about God or his fellowman—rebuffs her over-and-over again. The unjust judge finally gives her justice, not because he cares, but because he just wants her to go away. Jesus endorsed this approach of persistence. I will persist in my search for justice. I read on your website that you, General Clifton, have a background in ethics. I read that you, Commissioner Clifton, have experience with women's issues. Will you also rebuff me?

           Yours very truly,

           Bunny Stevens

Enclosures: Correspondence
      First Chapter of <u>Unholy Union</u>

Re: <u>Unholy Union</u> - A Memoir of Sexual Abuse

Dear General Clifton and Commissioner Clifton:

I am enclosing herewith all correspondence I have sent to the Salvation Army's Western Territory Headquarters in the United States of America. As you will see, this correspondence relates to my experience of clergy sexual abuse perpetrated on me by two ordained officers of the Salvation Army. I have been rebuffed by the Western Territory Headquarters because they could find no "corroborating evidence" in their files. I was told that files still exist on both men but they have been purged of all information pertaining to the charges of sexual abuse which were duly filed with the Women's Chief Side Officer at the School for Officers Training when I found that I was pregnant with my Corp Officer's child.

As you will note from my letter of this date to Charlene Bradley, Major, I am likening my quest for justice to the parable of Jesus recorded in the first eight verses of the 18th chapter of the Gospel of Luke. The widow in the parable persists in her search for justice even though the unjust judge—who does not care about God or his fellowman—rebuffs her over-and-over again. The unjust judge finally gives her justice, not because he cares, but because he just wants her to go away. Jesus endorsed this approach of persistence. I will persist in my search for justice. I read on your website that you, General Clifton, have a background in ethics. I read that you, Commissioner Clifton, have experience with women's issues. Will you also rebuff me?

Yours very truly,

Bunny Steven

Enclosures: Correspondence

First Chapter of <u>Unholy Union</u>

The Salvation Army
International Headquarters

101 QUEEN VICTORIA STREET
LONDON EC4P 4EP
Telephone: [44] (20) 7332 8001
Fax: [44] (20) 7332 8010

A Christian church and registered charity

OFFICE OF
THE GENERAL

1 November 2010

Ms Bunny (Umbaugh) Stevens
3700 N Highway 101 - #29
Depoe Bay
OR 97341
UNITED STATES OF AMERICA

Dear Ms Stevens,

Correspondence concerning sexual abuse

I write to thank you for your letter of 18 October 2010 and the correspondence attached thereto.

I am sure you will most readily understand that I am in no position to comment on the matters which you raise.

However, I take most seriously any allegation of sexual wrongdoing on the part of Salvation Army personnel and will therefore be asking for a full report to be sent to my office from territorial headquarters for the USA Western Territory based in California.

I seek your understanding and patience while these internal communications are pursued.

Meanwhile I pray for you to know the abiding presence of God the Holy Spirit in all things.

Yours in Christ,

Shaw Clifton

Shaw Clifton
GENERAL

Copies: Commissioner Barry Swanson, Chief of the Staff, IHQ
           Commissioner Larry Bosh, IS – Americas & Caribbean, IHQ
           Commissioner William Roberts, NC USA NHQ
           Commissioner James Knaggs, TC, USA Western

WILLIAM BOOTH
Founder
SHAW CLIFTON
General

Dear Ms Stevens,

Correspondence concerning sexual abuse

I write to thank you for your letter of 18 October 2010 and the correspondence attached thereto.

I am sure you will most readily understand that I am in no position to comment on the matters which you raise.

However, I take most seriously any allegation of sexual wrongdoing on the part of Salvation Army personnel and will therefore be asking for a full report to be sent to my office from territorial headquarters for the USA Western Territory based in California.

I seek your understanding and patience while these internal communications are pursued.

Meanwhile I pray for you to know the abiding presence of God the Holy Spirit in all things.

Yours in Christ,

Shaw Clifton
GENERAL

Copies:

Commissioner Barry Swanson, Chief of the Staff, IHQ

Commissioner Larry Bosh, IS - Americas & Caribbean, IHQ

Commissioner William Roberts, NC, USA NHQ

Commissioner James Knaggs, TC, USA Western

And then I contacted Rich.

When I was wondering how I might locate him, I talked to my older son Douglas. While we were on the phone discussing it, Douglas said to me, "Mom, I just Googled 'Richard Love in the Salvation Army,' and it took me to a web page for the Red Shield Youth Club in Denver, Colorado. He's the administrator, and his email address is right there."

Isn't modern technology great?

I sent Rich a short message. You will find a copy on the following page.

And you will find Rich's response. Good friends are not so hard to find if you know how to Google!

Business Administrator - Red Shield
Cell 623 824 2080

From: BunnyStevens@aol.com
To: richard.love@usw.salvationarmy.org
Date: 11/03/2010 04:33 PM
Subject: Are You The Good Friend I Remember?

From: BunnyStevens@aol.com
To: richard.love@usw.salvationarmy.org
Sent: 11/3/2010 3:04:46 P.M. Pacific Daylight Time
Subj: (no subject)

I had a good friend once. His name was Rich Love. He lived in San Jose, California. I lived in Salinas, California. We both entered training school in San Francisco in 1963. Could you just possibly be that friend?
Bunny (Umbaugh) Stevens

From: BunnyStevens@aol.com
To: richard.love@usw.salvationarmy.org
Date: 11/03/2010 04:33 PM

Subject: Are You The Good Friend I Remember?

From: BunnyStevens@aol.com
To: richard.love@usw.salvationarmy.org
Sent: 11/3/2010 3:04:46 P.M. Pacific Daylight Time

Subj: (no subject)

I had a good friend once. His name was Rich Love. He lived in San Jose, California. I lived in Salinas, California. We both entered training school in San Francisco in 1963. Could you just possibly be that friend?

Bunny (Umbaugh) Stevens

Subj: Re: Are You The Good Friend I Remember?
Date: 11/4/2010 6:17:03 A.M. Pacific Daylight Time
From: richard.love@usw.salvationarmy.org
To: BunnyStevens@aol.com

Hello Bunny. Yup, I just might possibly be that friend from a lifetime ago.

How are you? Still living in Salinas?

I have thought of you over the years. In fact, whenever anyone asks about why I am a Christian and more particularly why I am in The Salvation Army,
I of course tell them the story and mention that I (also) had a good friend who introduced me to the Army where I found the Lord.

I don't think I ever thanked you for that...too much going on at the time.

My, where did the time go? Reminds me of that old song, "Those were the days my friend, we thought they would never end". But of course they did...
and life goes on.

We retired as the Divisional Commander in San Francisco (seemed only fitting) and whenever I would visit Salinas, especially when Majors Duke and
Pam Markham were the Corps Officers they would tell me about a nice lady from the Nazarene Church who volunteered at the Corps. I thought it must be you...how many Bunny's are there in Salinas.

We retired (2004) in the Phoenix area...and soon found positions out of the Army. I was Associate Pastor in a large Congregational Church in Sun City, Arizona and Bettie became the CEO of a non-profit agency working with Homeless Families

We did that for four years or so....then decided it was time for a change. The Divisional Commander in Denver is an old friend, he was the Songster Leader when we were the Corps Officers at Seattle Temple, and he asked us to help for a few months. So here we are in Denver. Bettie is the Divisional Director of Development and I am the Business Administrator at the Red Shield Corps Community Center...which is a large operation..gym, youth programs, Boxing, Basketball and Football teams, etc.

We will be here probably until next August then probably retire again...but who knows...we've always been very active and fortunately are in good health.
Our permanent home is in Goodyear, Arizona.

We have three daughters, April Lentz, Allison Storey and Amy Love. Amy came along about 9 years later..she is engaged to a great guy and plan on getting married soon.They all live in the Bay Area. Two Grandsons...Nathan and Joshua (Allison).

Well...here I am boring you with way too much information.

It was good to hear from you...hope you are well and that life has been good to you.

Rich

Blessings,
Lt. Colonel Rich Love
The Salvation Army

Tuesday, November 09, 2010 AOL: BunnyStevens

Subj: Re: Are You The Good Friend I Remember?

Date: 11/4/2010 6:17:03 A.M. Pacific Daylight Time

From: richard.love@usw.salvationarmy.org

To: BunnyStevens@aol.com

Hello Bunny. Yup, I just might possibly be that friend from a lifetime ago.

How are you? Still living in Salinas?

I have thought of you over the years. In fact, whenever anyone asks about why I am a Christian and more particularly why I am in The Salvation Army, I of course tell them the story and mention that I (also) had a good friend who introduced me to the Army where I found the Lord.

I don't think I ever thanked you for that...too much going on at the time.

My, where did the time go? Reminds me of that old song, "Those were the days my friend, we thought they would never end". But of course they did...and life goes on.

We retired as the Divisional Commander in San Francisco (seemed only fitting) and whenever I would visit Salinas, especially when Majors Duke and Pam Markham were the Corps Officers they would tell me about a nice lady from the Nazarene Church who volunteered at the Corps. I thought it must be you... how many Bunny's are there in Salinas.

We retired (2004) in the Phoenix area...and soon found positions out of the Army. I was Associate Pastor in a large Congregational Church in Sun City, Arizona and Bettie became the CEO of a non-profit agency working with Homeless Families

We did that for four years or so....then decided it was time for a change. The Divisional Commander in Denver is an old friend, he was the Songster Leader when we were the Corps Officers at Seattle Temple, and he asked us to help for a few months. So here we are in Denver. Bettie is the Divisional Director of Development and I am the Business Administrator at the Red Shield Corps Community Center...which is a large operation..gym, youth programs, Boxing, Basketball and Football teams, etc.

We will be here probably until next August then probably retire again...but who knows…we've always been very active and fortunately are in good health. Our permanent home is in Goodyear, Arizona.

We have three daughters, April Lentz, Allison Storey and Amy Love. Amy came along about 9 years later.. she is engaged to a great guy and plan on getting married soon. They all live in the Bay Area. Two Grandsons...Nathan and Joshua (Allison).

Well...here I am boring you with way too much information.

It was good to hear from you...hope you are well and that life has been good to you.

Rich

Blessings,

Lt. Colonel Rich Love

The Salvation Army

I subsequently called Rich. When we talked on the phone, it was a huge affirmation of the nobility of the human spirit. Rich was delighted to reconnect. I had thought of him often over the years, but of course, did not make any effort to contact him because the Salvation Army told me not to. And, personally, I did not want Rich to be tainted by any interaction with me. That was the legacy the Salvation Army had left: the feeling of my own baseness that could and would contaminate good people. The amazing thing was Rich remembered me warmly. He did not feel tainted. He remembered me as the one who led him to the Lord. It doesn't get much better than that—at least according to one rabble-rousing, itinerant preacher named Jesus …

Rich immediately offered to write a letter to Ms. Bradley affirming what he knew about the relationship with Captain John Hart.

It was so easy to find him. And he was more than willing to tell the truth. This begs the question: Why couldn't Ms. Bradley or anyone else in the organization find "corroboration information?"

What I learned through further investigation on the internet was:

Ms. Bradley is *related* to Lincoln Upton

"She had to know, Bunny; everyone knew about Lincoln Upton." Quoted from a Salvation Army officer.

"I was told to avoid Major Upton like the plague. He was a known womanizer." Quoted from a Salvation Army officer.

"I think Charlene (Ms. Bradley) is very aware of Linc's sexual proclivity. The whole territory knew." Quoted from a Salvation Army officer.

Isn't it funny that sometimes the truth will come out in spite of all efforts at self-serving denial? In spite of all the years of suppression? In spite of the casting aside of the inconvenient victim? Sometimes, the truth will out.

A copy of my letter of November 9, 2010 to Ms. Bradly and a copy of Rich's letter of November 8, 2010, documenting in detail the episode at training school, follow this page.

Bunny (Umbaugh) Stevens
3700 N. Highway 101 - #29
Depoe Bay, OR 97341
(541) 764-0803
November 9, 2010

Charlene Bradley, Major
Assistant Secretary for Personnel
The Salvation Army
180 East Ocean Boulevard
Long Beach, CA 90802-4709

Dear Ms. Bradley:

    If you have not already received a letter from Lt. Colonel Richard Love, you should receive the same shortly. Rich advised me that he mailed a letter to you on November 8. He provided me with a copy of that letter.

    In your last letter to me, you stated, "Many of the people who might have been able to shed light on the matter are no longer alive. . . and others have either lost touch with the Army or did not have any memory of the things you described." You mentioned a lack of "corroboration information." In my response to you of October 18, I told you, "I am . . .conducting a search of my own for persons who can provide corroboration for the facts of my story." I was speaking of Rich. He knew everything. The search was not that difficult in this computer age. Once I had located him at the Red Shield Center in Denver, I was very nervous about actually contacting Rich—I had no idea what to expect. Would he also "have no memory?" To my immense relief, Rich was kind, compassionate and welcoming. In his first email to me he said, "I have thought of you over the years. In fact, whenever anyone asks about why I am a Christian and more particularly why I am in the Salvation Army, I of course tell them the story and mention that I had a good friend who introduced me to the Army where I found the Lord." He's talking about me. That's who and what I was—a person who led others to the Army and to the Lord.

    Lt. Colonel Richard Love is my corroboration, Ms. Bradley. He is alive, he has not lost touch with the Army, and he does have very clear memories of the things I described. As Rich states in his letter, I have had no contact with him since I was sent out of training. I did not want him to be tainted by any contact with me. I was gratified by the depth of his memories with clearly stated details including names of all involved at the training school. The fact that he was more than willing to share these with you is, in and of itself, a huge victory for truth and transparency. He is the same good friend I remember. I will be interested in hearing from you when you have had an opportunity to read and understand what your comrade has to say about me and the events we have been discussing over these past several months.

                        Yours very truly,

                          Bunny Stevens

cc: Commissioner Israel L. Gaither, National Commander, The Salvation Army

Dear Ms. Bradley:

If you have not already received a letter from Lt. Colonel Richard Love, you should receive the same shortly. Rich advised me that he mailed a letter to you on November 8. He provided me with a copy of that letter.

In your last letter to me, you stated, "Many of the people who might have been able to shed light on the matter are no longer alive. . . and others have either lost touch with the Army or did not have any memory of the things you described." You mentioned a lack of "corroboration information." In my response to you of October 18, I told you, "I am ... conducting a search of my own for persons who can provide corroboration for the facts of my story." I was speaking of Rich. He knew everything. The search was not that difficult in this computer age. Once I had located him at the Red Shield Center in Denver, I was very nervous, about actually contacting Rich—I had no idea what to expect. Would he also "have no memory?" To my immense relief, Rich was kind, compassionate and welcoming. In his first email to me he said, "I have thought of you over the years. In fact, whenever anyone asks about why I am a Christian and more particularly why I am in the Salvation Army, I of course tell them the story and mention that I had a good friend who introduced me to the Army where I found the Lord." He's talking about me. That's who and what I was--a person who led others to the Army and to the Lord.

Lt. Colonel Richard Love is my corroboration, Ms. Bradley. He is alive, he has not lost touch with the Army, and he does have very clear memories of the things I described. As Rich states in his letter, I have had no contact with him since I was sent out of training. I did not want him to be tainted by any contact with me. I was gratified by the depth of his memories with clearly stated details including names of all involved at the training school. The fact that he was more than willing to share these with you is, in and of Itself, a huge victory for truth and transparency. He is the same good friend

I remember. I will be interested in hearing from you when you have had an opportunity to read and understand what your comrade has to say about me and the events we have been discussing over these past several months.

Yours very truly,

Bunny Stevens

cc: Commissioner Israel L. Gaither, National Commander, The Salvation Army

November 8, 2010

Major Charleen Bradley
Assistant Secretary for Personnel

Dear Major Bradley,

Re: Bunny (Umbaugh) Stevens

I was contacted last week by Bunny Umbaugh Stevens who shared her situation with me and the fact that there is no corroboration to her story. This is the first time I have any contact with Bunny since 1963. I am writing this because I was involved in the first part of what Bunny has apparently shared with you.

Bunny and I were engaged in 1962 and in fact the story begins when she went to see the then Corps Officer of the Salinas Corps, A/Captain John Hart, to arrange for our wedding. In that conversation, Captain Hart prayed with Bunny and she re-committed her life to Christ. She had been raised in the Army but had fallen away for several years.

Bunny then began attending the Salinas Corps. I met the Army for the first time, attending the Salinas Corps with Bunny. It was all wonderfully strange. Captain Hart was very charismatic with a commanding platform presence. I still remember the eagerness I had to learn all about the Army. It was fascinating.

I was living in San Jose at the time and it was not always convenient to attend the Corps in Salinas. I introduced myself to the Corps Officer in San Jose, Major Merv Morelock, and started attending the San Jose Corps on those Sundays when I was not able to drive to Salinas.

In subsequent months several things happened. First I was converted in a Sunday Morning Service in San Jose and almost immediately sensed a call to Officership. The other development was that the relationship between Bunny and me deteriorated and we broke off the engagement. I still felt the same but it was obvious to me that Bunny had changed.

We remained friends and I would occasionally attend the Salinas Corps with her. It was during this time I sensed that something was going on between her and Captain Hart. It was not anything I could definitely pinpoint, but it was obvious in the ways that he acted around her that caused me concern.

Eventually both Bunny and I entered the School for Officers' Training in San Francisco in September of 1963 as part of the Proclaimers of The Faith Session.

During the first several weeks of Training Captain Hart came to the School on several Saturdays, ostensibly to see both of us, but he spent almost all the time with Bunny. Bunny acted very uncomfortable around him and again I was aware that something was wrong but really had no clue as to what.

Not long into the Training Session and I do not actually remember when it was, Bunny confessed to me that she thought she was pregnant. When I asked who the father was, she said it was Captain John Hart.

Because I still had strong feelings for Bunny I suggested to her that we needed to inform the Principal, the then Lt. Colonel Harry Larson, that I was the father. We knew we would need to leave the School, but it would be less of a shock to everyone.

We went to see the Assistant Principal, Major Gene Rice, and told him the story. We were interviewed by other Officers on Staff and, If my memory serves me right, by the Personnel Secretary, Lt Colonel C. Emil Nelson.

That evening we were preparing to pack our belongings to leave the next morning.

However, Bunny approached me the next morning and told me that her conscience would not allow her to proceed with our plan. I tried to talk her out of it, but she confessed to the Officers at the School that it was not me, but rather that Captain Hart that was the father.

At some point in all of this, she told me that it was a false pregnancy, no doubt brought on by a heavy sense of guilt. I discovered only recently in my conversation with Bunny that she had a miscarriage and that she indeed had been pregnant.

I was questioned again by Major Rice, and I recanted my culpability with the pregnancy story.

At that point, my story ends. Bunny left the School quite secretly without allowing any of the Session allowed to say good bye. I thought at the time this was very strange, but since an Officer was involved, that maybe this was the standard procedure.

I had always been under the impression that Bunny eventually returned to Salinas, met a nice guy, got married and had a family and lived happily ever after.

It was only recently when Bunny contacted me that I heard 'the rest of the story'.

While I cannot prove that Captain Hart had sexual relations with Bunny because obviously I was not there when it happened, there was no doubt in my mind at the time, nor is there now, that Captain Hart took advantage of her.

An obvious question might well be how do I remember events that happened nearly 48 years ago with such clarity.

The answer is that those were defining, life changing days for me. I was engaged to be married, I met the Army for the first time, I was converted and felt a sense of calling; the engagement was off; I entered the School for Officers' Training; my previous fiancé told me she was pregnant; the marriage seemed to be on again, and then abruptly was off again.

For all of these reasons those days are etched into my memory.

I am sharing this now with no ulterior motive other than to state for the record that I believe that what Bunny has shared is true. I can attest to my involvement.

While the easy recourse is to say that this all happened long ago and some of the parties involved are deceased and therefore her story cannot be verified, it is obvious there has been a life time of dealing with the consequences for Bunny.

I expect had this happened today with our increased sensitivity to sexual impropriety it would be handled differently.

I hope this retelling of my part of the story will in some way be helpful both to Bunny and to the Army in finally putting this sad episode to rest

Sincerely,

Richard Love, Lt. Colonel
Denver, Colorado

Dear Major Bradley,

Re: Bunny (Umbaugh) Stevens

I was contacted last week by Bunny Umbaugh Stevens who shared her situation with me and the fact that there is no corroboration to her story. This is the first time I have any contact with Bunny since 1963. I am writing this because I was involved in the first part of what Bunny has apparently shared with you.

Bunny and I were engaged in 1962 and in fact the story begins when she went to see the then Corps Officer of the Salinas Corps, A/Captain John Hart, to arrange for our wedding. In that conversation, Captain Hart prayed with Bunny and she re-committed her life to Christ. She had been raised in the Army but had fallen away for several years.

Bunny then began attending the Salinas Corps. I met the Army for the first time, attending the Salinas Corps with Bunny. It was all wonderfully strange. Captain Hart was very charismatic with a commanding platform presence. I still remember the eagerness I had to learn all about the Army. It was fascinating.

I was living in San Jose at the time and it was not always convenient to attend the Corps in Salinas. I introduced myself to the Corps Officer in San Jose, Major Merv Morelock, and started attending the San Jose Corps on those Sundays when I was not able to drive to Salinas.

In subsequent months several things happened. First I was converted in a Sunday Morning Service in San Jose and almost immediately sensed a call to Officership. The other development was that the relationship between Bunny and me deteriorated and we broke off the engagement. I still felt the same but it was obvious to me that Bunny had changed.

We remained friends and I would occasionally attend the Salinas Corps with her. It was during this time I sensed that something was going on between her and Captain Hart. It was not anything I could definitely pinpoint, but it was obvious in the ways that he acted around her that caused me concern.

Eventually both Bunny end I entered the School for Officers' Training in San Francisco in September of 1963 as part of the Proclaimers of The Faith Session.

During the first several weeks of Training Captain Hart came to the School on several Saturdays, ostensibly to see both of us, but he spent almost all the time with Bunny. Bunny acted very uncomfortable around him and again I was aware that something was wrong but really had no clue as to what.

Not long into the Training Session and I do not actually remember when it was, Bunny confessed to me that she thought she was pregnant. When I asked who the father was, she said it was Captain John Hart.

Because I still had strong feelings for Bunny I suggested to her that we needed to inform the Principal, the then Lt. Colonel Harry Larson, that I was the father. We knew we would need to leave the School, but it would be less of a shock to everyone.

We went to see the Assistant Principal, Major Gene Rice, and told him the story. We were interviewed by other Officers on Staff and, if my memory serves me right, by the Personnel Secretary, Lt Colonel C. Emil Nelson.

That evening we were preparing to pack our belongings to leave the next morning.

However, Bunny approached me the next morning and told me that her conscience would not allow her to proceed with our plan. I tried to talk her out of it, but she confessed to the Officers at the School that it was not me, but rather that Captain Hart that was the father.

At some point in all of this, she told me that it was a false pregnancy, no doubt brought on by a heavy sense of guilt. I discovered only recently in my conversation with Bunny that she had a miscarriage and that she indeed had been pregnant.

I was questioned again by Major Rice, and I recanted my culpability with the pregnancy story.

At that point, my story ends. Bunny left the School quite secretly without allowing any of the Session allowed to say good bye. I thought at the time this was very strange, but since an Officer was involved, that maybe this was the standard procedure.

I had always been under the impression that Bunny eventually returned to Salinas, met a nice guy, got married and had a family and lived happily ever after.

It was only recently when Bunny contacted me that I heard 'the rest of the story'.

While I cannot prove that Captain Hart had sexual relations with Bunny because obviously I was not there when it happened, there was no doubt in my mind at the time, nor is there now, that Captain Hart took advantage of her.

An obvious question might well be how do I remember events that happened nearly 48 years ago with such clarity.

The answer is that those were defining, life changing days for me. I was engaged to be married, I met the Army for the first time, I was converted and felt a sense of calling; the engagement was off; I entered the School for Officers' Training; my previous fiancé told me she was pregnant; the marriage seemed to be on again, and then abruptly was off again.

For all of these reasons those days are etched into my memory.

I am sharing this now with no ulterior motive other than to state for the record that I believe that what Bunny has shared is true. I can attest to my involvement.

While the easy recourse is to say that this all happened long ago and some of the parties involved are deceased and therefore her story cannot be verified, it is obvious there has been a life time of dealing with the consequences for Bunny.

I expect had this happened today with our increased sensitivity to sexual impropriety it would be handled differently.

I hope this retelling of my part of the story will in some way be helpful both to Bunny and to the Army in finally putting this sad episode to rest

Sincerely,

Richard Love, Lt.

Colonel Denver, Colorado

Rich sent me a copy of Ms. Bradley's response to his letter. She is guarded and cautious and seems to still minimize. By this time, of course, I was not surprised. It's interesting the scripture she uses at the bottom of her letterhead, "… Be strong and courageous; do not be afraid or lose heart!"

Rich continued to caution me to not get my hopes up. He told me the Salvation Army's legal department would not give in lightly or without a struggle. I tried to remember this, but each step of the way, the Salvation Army's refusal to allow a place for my story was painful.

A copy of Ms. Bradley's letter to Rich follows this page.

----- Forwarded by Richard Love/RO/USW/SArmy on 11/16/2010 08:51 AM -----

From:	Charleen Bradley/USW/SArmy
To:	Richard Love/RO/USW/SArmy@USW
Cc:	Dave Hudson/USW/SArmy@USW, Howard Yamaguchi/USW/SArmy@USW
Date:	11/12/2010 04:41 PM
Subject:	Letter Received

Rich,

Thank you very much for your open and candid letter that I received today. This continues to be a very challenging situation and as you said one that has certainly weighed heavily on Bunny's heart for many years. Unfortunately there literally is no paper trail and we have tried to find something that would indicate the events she describes. As I have told her we are not saying that what she has revealed did not happen it just is very difficult to trace and find a trail that would bring complete clarity and disclosure.

Your reflections certainly validate that something indeed took place and it was very traumatic. Where we go from here it is difficult to say. With the receipt of your letter we will continue in dialog with the legal department, Chief Secretary and the TC.

I did relay to her what we are doing these days to prevent this type of behavior and how we are doing everything possible to protect the vulnerable people that come under the care of The Salvation Army. You are correct that this would have been handled very differently today.

Once again thank you for your willingness to share your knowledge about a portion of her story. It is possible that we might be in contact with you again in the future.

Blessings!Link

Charleen Bradley, Major
Assistant Secretary for Personnel for Officer Development
Western Territory

"...Be strong and courageous; do not be afraid or lose heart!   I Chronicles 12:13

Subject: Letter Received

Rich,

Thank you very much for your open and candid letter that I received today. This continues to be a very challenging situation and as you said one that has certainly weighed heavily on Bunny's heart for many years. Unfortunately there literally is no paper trail and we have tried to find something that would indicate the events she describes. As I have told her we are not saying that what she has revealed did not happen it just is very difficult to trace and find a trail that would bring complete clarity and disclosure.

Your reflections certainly validate that something indeed took place and it was very traumatic. Where we go from here it is difficult to say. With the receipt of your letter we will continue in dialog with the legal department, Chief Secretary and the TC.

I did relay to her what we are doing these days to prevent this type of behavior and how we are doing everything possible to protect the vulnerable people that come under the care of The Salvation Army. You are correct that this would have been handled very differently today.

Once again thank you for your willingness to share your knowledge about a portion of her story. It is possible that we might be in contact with you again in the future.

Blessings!

Charleen Bradley, Major

Assistant Secretary for Personnel for Officer Development

Western Territory

"...Be strong and courageous; do not be afraid or lose heart! I Chronicles 12:13

On November 18, 2010, I returned home to find a message from Ms. Bradley in my voicemail. She requested that I call her as soon as possible to set up a time when she and the Salvation Army's legal counsel could meet with me.

When I spoke with her, she requested that I meet her and Mr. Yamaguchi in Portland. It being the middle of December with roads here in Oregon prone to black ice, I declined to travel. She did some investigating and said she did not want to travel the roads from Portland to Depoe Bay either. Could we arrange a conference call?

The conference call took place. It lasted approximately 90 minutes. I recounted to Mr. Yamaguchi much of what this book describes about sexual liaisons initiated first by Captain John Hart and then by Major Lincoln Upton. I also recounted my knowledge of what happened to Jan Black, and I stated that I had been able to obtain further information about that period of time in the Salvation Army from others I contacted on the internet. I mused on how easy it had been to find information, in spite of the fact that the Salvation Army had protested that there "was no trail" because of the length of time that had ensued. Jesus, Himself, said something about having eyes to see and ears to hear. Sometimes, you only have to *want* to see and know. Sometimes, the truth has been there all the time.

I recorded the conversation—asking their permission first—so that I would have a record of all that transpired. I did not trust them to be interested in what was best for me. I had finally learned to advocate for myself.

I waited. I had no idea what—if anything—to expect, and Rich remained skeptical that the Salvation Army would offer anything. Wouldn't that be admitting that they were, in fact, responsible?

I received a phone call from Ms. Bradley stating that "the council" had met to discuss "my case" and she had been asked to contact me personally to convey the territory commander's deep regret for my suffering. No "alleged." No "situations you describe."

Just his regret for my suffering. I told her that words are great, but I had asked for reimbursement of my psychiatric expenses. She then stated that she was holding a letter that she would mail immediately asking that I obtain legal counsel so they can "discuss how best to resolve my concerns." She further stated that the Salvation Army would pay for my attorney.

I received the letter from the Salvation Army's general counsel a few days later. A copy of that letter follows this page.

THE SALVATION ARMY
USA Western Territorial Headquarters
180 East Ocean Boulevard, 9th Floor
Long Beach, CA 90802-4709

WILLIAM BOOTH
Founder

SHAW CLIFTON
General

MICHAEL J. WOODRUFF
General Counsel

PHILIP SWYERS
Territorial Commander

December 14, 2010

Mrs. Bunny Stevens
3700 N. Highway 101 - #29
Depoe Bay, Oregon 97341

Dear Mrs. Stevens:

I am the corporate secretary and general counsel for The Salvation Army at its Territorial Headquarters in Long Beach. I am writing on behalf of the board of directors to follow up on your recent conversation with Major Charleen Bradley and Mr. Howard Yamaguchi. We understand that you described to them your suffering sexual abuse from separate incidents involving Salvation Army officers, namely, Richard Hart and Lincoln Upton, both now deceased. You indicated that these incidents occurred many years ago when you were a young adult living in different states. Major Bradley has verified that both of these individuals were known to and associated with The Salvation Army in the Western Territory during the reported time period. In her investigation to respond to your claim, she states that she could find neither a record, document, letter, notice of concern, nor report on file, historic or current, from anyone, other than yourself, about either of these individuals abusing others.

At the Board of Directors meeting this past Thursday, we heard from Major Bradley and Mr. Yamaguchi about your concerns and your request for reimbursement for counseling fees. On behalf of the Board, I want to assure you that we deeply regret your suffering. We apologize for the past misdeeds and for the insensitivity at the time to victims who could not then come forward without risking further emotional suffering. As Major Bradley may have told you, The Salvation Army, Western Territory, has implemented policies and procedures to help protect vulnerable persons, particularly children and seniors, who participate in Army programs. Fortunately, the record of preventing harm is now very good. But we cannot undo the past. You can understand how difficult it is now for us to respond to a new claim on historic incidents when the perpetrators are deceased, the parties were adults at the time, and the claimant is the sole source of information about the abuse. However, none of these circumstances take away from the pain you must feel and for that we are truly sorry.

Telephone: (562) 491-8755
Facsimile: (562) 491-8855

www.salvationarmyusawest.org
EMail: Michael.Woodruff@usw.salvationarmy.org

Mrs. Bunny Stevens
December 14, 2010
Page 2 of 2

While we understand that you want a response to your request to be reimbursement for costs of professional counseling, we are under a professional ethical obligation to speak to your counsel, as Major Bradley mentioned that you told her that you recently sought the advice of legal counsel. We must ask you to share this letter with your attorney and ask him/her to contact me so that we might discuss how best to resolve your concerns. To minimize the financial burden on you, The Salvation Army is willing to directly pay your counsel the hourly rate charged for any reasonable and necessary legal services rendered to you for consultation with you or communication with us in this matter.

We look forward to hearing from your counsel to discuss this matter further.

Very truly yours,

Michael J. Woodruff

Michael J. Woodruff

Dear Mrs. Stevens:

I am the corporate secretary and general counsel for The Salvation Army at its Territorial Headquarters in Long Beach. I am writing on behalf of the board of directors to follow up on your recent conversation with Major Charleen Bradley and Mr. Howard Yamaguchi. We understand that you described to them your suffering sexual abuse from separate incidents involving Salvation Army officers, namely, ~~Richard~~ [John] Hart and Lincoln Upton, both now deceased. You indicated that these incidents occurred many years ago when you were a young adult living in different states. Major Bradley has verified that both of these individuals were known to and associated with The Salvation Army in the Western Territory during the reported time period. In her investigation to respond to your claim, she states that she could find neither a record, document, letter, notice of concern, nor report on file, historic or current, from anyone, other than yourself, about either of these individuals abusing others.

At the Board of Directors meeting this past Thursday, we heard from Major Bradley and Mr. Yamaguchi about your concerns and your request for reimbursement for counseling fees. On behalf of the Board, I want to assure you that we deeply regret your suffering. We apologize for the past misdeeds and for the insensitivity at the time to victims who could not then come forward without risking further emotional suffering. As Major Bradley may have told you, The Salvation Army, Western Territory, has implemented policies and procedures to help protect vulnerable persons, particularly children and seniors, who participate in Army programs. Fortunately, the record of preventing harm is now very good. But we cannot undo the past. You can understand how difficult it is now for us to respond to a new claim on historic incidents when the perpetrators are deceased, the parties were adults at the time, and the claimant is the sole source of information about the abuse. However, none of these circumstances take away from the pain you must feel and for that we are truly sorry.

Mrs. Bunny Stevens
December 14, 2010
Page 2 of 2

While we understand that you want a response to your request to be reimbursement for costs of professional counseling, we are under a professional ethical obligation to speak to your counsel, as Major Bradley mentioned that you told her that you recently sought the advice of legal counsel. We must ask you to share this letter with your attorney and ask him/her to contact me so that we might discuss how best to resolve your concerns. To minimize the financial burden on you, The Salvation Army is willing to directly pay your counsel the hourly rate charged for any reasonable and necessary legal services rendered to you for consultation with you or communication with us in this matter.

We look forward to hearing from your counsel to discuss this matter further.

Very truly yours,

Michael J. Woodruff

I have done as they asked. I have obtained an attorney. And so, as of this writing, the last chapter remains to be written. My attorney will contact the Salvation Army.

I can only wonder why they changed their minds after the letter from Rich—which Ms. Bradley initially minimized—the conference call in which I relayed some of the information that is freely available on the internet, and my stated intent to publish this book about the ghastly morass of abuse I endured.

On the face of it, it seems they "got religion" only when their backs were against the wall. I obtained the corroboration. I went on the internet. I have contacted the Oprah organization requesting an opportunity to tell my story. I have written a book. Are they finally willing to talk because they want to silence me again? What about all the other victims? I'm sure they are out there.

Having written all this, I am sure of one thing: *I'm the one who made it*. I have lived a life of joy and abundance—continually offering the glass of water, the bite to eat. I have seen up close and personal during the past year that the Salvation Army is a group I am thankful to be *outside of*. For years I believed what they told me I was, and I struggled to overcome that stigma. I know now that *I'm the one who made it*. **Not them**. If and when they offer me reimbursement for my psychiatric out-of-pocket, it will only be because they have determined that they *have to* to protect themselves. There is no goodness in that. There is only the self-serving, overdue attention precipitated by fear of disclosure. Again, *I'm the one who made it*. To me they have not changed much—in spite of their protestations to the contrary.

I do believe that justice sometimes has a dollar sign. Sometimes there is no other way to punish the type of institutionalized betrayal that has been documented in recent years within the Catholic Church and the Boy Scouts of America. What I have been able to state over the past year is that it happened in other places too. I know. It happened to me. In the Salvation Army.

The Last Chapter

"Every problem implies a question:
Are you ready to embody what you say you believe?"

The Gift of Change by Marianne Williamson

When I completed *Unholy Union*, I knew the last chapter remained to be written. By the Salvation Army.

As suggested in their letter of December 14, 2010, I engaged an attorney. My attorney wrote to the Salvation Army on July 15, 2011.

There was no response.

My attorney wrote to the Salvation Army again on September 15, 2011.

There was no response.

That is now two and one half years ago.

The last line of Mr. Woodruff's letter states, "We look forward to hearing from your counsel to discuss this matter further."

Really? Their two and one half years of silence puts a lie to that statement.

And so there were commands to remain silent, to tell no one.

I finally broke my silence.

Only to be confronted with theirs.

Photos

Cherrill, Bunny, and Lei Lani in front of the house on F Street in Modesto on Easter Sunday in 1944.

Bunny with brothers Buzz and Pete on California Avenue in Modesto in 1947.

(Salinas, Calif.) Corps Cadets pose with Lt.-Colonel and Mrs. R. Martin and Sr.- Captain and Mrs. Irby, after a meeting with these leaders.

Bunny (center front) flanked by best friend twins Sharon (on her right) Karen (on her left) at the Salinas Corps in 1957. Her beloved Corps Officers, Captain and Mrs. Irby, are in rear. Photo from *The Young Soldier*, Aug. 10, 1957.

Adjutant Frances Beard, whose grave is being decorated, was Bunny's maternal aunt who died while serving the Salvation Army in Hawaii. Photo from *The Young Soldier*, Aug. 10, 1957.

Bunny's beloved English teacher, Mr. McLennan, at Salinas High School in 1959.

Bunny and Rich Love in Salinas in 1961.

Bunny (far left) with a group of Sunday school campers at Arroyo Seco Camp in 1962.

Bunny and a divisional headquarters co-worker in a dramatic tableau at a Salvation Army Advisory Board banquet in Phoenix in 1964.

"And now here is my secret, a very simple secret:
It is only with the heart that one can see rightly; what is essential is invisible to the eye."

The Little Prince by Antoine de Saint-Exupery

Author Bio

Throughout her varied professional life, Bunny Stevens has been a legal secretary, an insurance department manager, owner and operator of a busy automotive repair shop, newspaper columnist, photographer, and director of Christian education and middle school ministries at a large Presbyterian Church. She has participated in life's more poignant moments as a minister in the Universal Life Church. She's found great joy in some of life's lighter moments—especially as "Leafy" the mascot for the Salinas Packers semi-pro baseball team during the summer she was 64 years old! She looks upon her continuing participation in the lives of her two grown sons as the most precious thing of which she has ever been a part. Now living in a tiny cottage in an enchanted forest on the Oregon Coast, Bunny participates in the daily activities that make her new home special—giving back by volunteering as chef to the homeless outreach program, visiting (with her dog Buddy) at the assisted living facility in her area, and running half-marathons. She is happy.

How to Order

UNHOLY UNION:
A Memoir of Clergy Sexual Abuse Within the Salvation Army

by Bunny Stevens

Paperback | 978-0-9911201-0-9

Also available as Kindle & ePub
Kindle 978-0-9911201-1-6 | ePub 978-0-9911201-2-3

Available through popular online and retail outlets such as:

- Amazon.com
- BarnesAndNobel.com
- Powells.com

Wholesale distribution through Ingram and Baker & Taylor.

More Information

Scan the QR code or visit the website for more book details, scheduled events. contact the author, links to the book trailer, and more.

www.UnholyUnionBook.com

CPSIA information can be obtained at www.ICGtesting.com
Printed in the USA
BVOW08s1046020314

346336BV00003B/18/P